CHINESE POST OFFICE
Despatched by Aeroplane
TIENTSIN TO PEKING

K. u. K. FLIEGERREGIMENT
FLIEGERKOMPANIE No 14

Schweizerische Flugpost
8. VI. 13.
Poste aérienne suisse

ANGELES, CAL
JAN 21
2.00 P.M.
1912
AVIATION STATION

Aviation Field

BAYER:SCHER KURIER-FLIEGER-DIENST

CARRIED BY
DAILY MAIL
WATERPLANE.
PROMOTED BY
THE GRAHAME WHITE AVIATION Co. Ld.

FIRST
EUROPE PAN-AMERICA
GRAF ZEPPELIN
U.S. AIR MAIL
ROUND FLIGHT

POSTE AERIENNE AU MAROC
DU "PETIT JOURNAL"
البريد الهوائى الأقصى
بالمغرب
LE 13 September 19
19 11
جريده البتى
جورنال

NED. IND. POST.-TELEGRAAF-EN TELEFOONDIENST.
WELTEVREDEN
27.4.20.11-12v
VLIEGPOST

EFORDRET pr
AVIATIONEN
FLYVEPOST
R-SAND —KR-A—
19=21=JUNI 1920

由中國創設航空報班開始發次班遣等之一班

Donald B. Holmes

edited and designed by
Ladislav Svatos

Clarkson N. Potter, Inc./Publishers
DISTRIBUTED BY CROWN PUBLISHERS, INC., NEW YORK

AIR MAIL

an illustrated history   1793 - 1981

Text of *Success by perseverance*
An incredible aerial journey
The flying schoolgirl
The fabulous career of LZ-127
Chaos, then consolidation
Pacific and Atlantic services
is based on preliminary research and writing
by Frank H. Schaufler

This is a
Graphicon Book
prepared and produced
by Graphicon Visual Communications, Ltd.

Copy editors:
Evie Righter
Ellen Coffey

Index:
Maro Riofrancos

Inquiries should be addressed
to Clarkson N. Potter, Inc.,
One Park Avenue, New York, New York 10016

Published simultaneously in Canada
by General Publishing Company Limited

Library of Congress Cataloging in Publication Data

Holmes, Donald B.
Air mail, an illustrated history 1793-1981
Includes index.
1. air mail service—History. I. Title
HE6238.H63   1981   383′.144′09   81-5942
ISBN 0-517-541467   AACR2

10   9   8   7   6   5   4   3   2   1

First edition

Printed in Japan

*Due to insufficient space, p. 215 shall be considered
a part of this copyright page.*

Contents

Growth under government *83*

Contracts and private carriers *135*

Acknowledgments

The circle of people to whom I am indebted for their energy, encouragement, example and practical assistance is wide…

Three "pioneers" have been present to me through correspondence. *E. Hamilton Lee*, air mail and airline pilot, has lived more of this history than I could ever report here. *Edith Dodd Culver*, wife of military and mail pilot H. Paul Culver, not only witnessed significant air mail events in 1918 but chose to love those events into a writing that I treasure. *Erik Hildeshiem*, an Early Bird of Aviation, has been a very special kind of inspiration, having flown early in his life in his native Denmark and having joined the aero-philatelic ranks before I was born. The generous sharing of these three prepared the way for this book in ways that I am still coming to appreciate.

My thanks go to *Louis S. Casey*, recently retired from the National Air & Space Museum, and to *Carl H. Scheele* of the Smithsonian Institution, who served as textual consultants and made many helpful suggestions. Curator Casey's short course in aviation fundamentals—when to say "engine" and when to say "motor" hopefully bore some fruit.

I am grateful for the welcome and assistance that Ladislav Svatos and I received from *Phil Edwards* of National Air and Space Museum's Library, *Jane Kennedy*, General Manager, Library Division of the United States Postal Service in Washington, *Ray Norby*, Curator of the National Philatelic Collections, Smithsonian Institution, and *Paul White* of the National Archives.

Whether the moment involved a request for use of rare material, a photograph, a fact or an opinion, various forms of help were constantly forthcoming and enthusiastically conveyed by fellow members of the American Air Mail Society. Due a full measure of appreciation are *Philip Silver, Thomas J. O'Sullivan, Ernst M. Cohn, Roland F. Kohl*, Major *Richard K. Malott* of Canada and *Albert A. Le Shane, Jr.* Without the researches and writings of these gentlemen and their colleagues—especially *Dr. Max Kronstein*—much of the air mail story would still be lost to us.

As noted elsewhere, *Frank H. Schaufler* did much of the research for particular chapters and his extensive knowledge of early aircraft was immensely helpful. Also, *Judith Schiff*, Research Archivist, Yale University Library, *Merrill Stickler* of Hammondsport's Glenn H. Curtiss Museum of Local History, Ann Whyte, staff historian of Pan American World Airways and *Angus McClure* of TWA all made inputs at various stages and helped make research hours enjoyable.

My gratitude and that of the Editor goes to *Jane West* and *Michael Fragnito, Carolyn Hart, Pamela Pollack* and *Teresa Nicholas* of Clarkson N. Potter, Inc., whose unfailing sense of teamwork helped bridge some difficult waters. *Carl Apollonio* of Crown Publishers provided vision and trust that gave this project wings whenever the need was there.

Finally, a word of thanks where words alone fail. To *Ladislav Svatos*—a friend who made this story his own and whose esthetic and value judgments have never failed to delight me. And to *Nan*—who invested herself in this work in such a way that impossible tasks became possible, that wounds were healed and that energies were allowed to flow. Such is the labor of a love.

D.B.H.

EDITOR'S NOTE: Many heartfelt thanks to *Sam Gigliotti* and *John Federici* of J&J Typesetters, *Carl Moreus* and *Nancy Parks*, and to *Evie Righter* and *Ellen Coffey*. Without their excellent and patient cooperation this book never would have become a reality.

Preface

Initially, as this book began to unfold, I saw it as narrow, modest in scope and somewhat specialized. But, such was not the case. The story of air mail pushed itself outward from the start and would not remain boxed in. It seemed to have a veritable life of its own, choosing its course and always insisting upon an attachment to a broader scope and message than I had envisioned for it.

Rather than a fragment of United States history, *Air Mail* became an international story; rather than a series of unrelated vignettes about spectacular pioneer mail flights, it turned into a survey of an enterprise leading right up to the present day; rather than a mere tale of aero-venturing, it emerged as an integral phase of the much greater process of man establishing the myriad of interconnections that are taken for granted today. *Air Mail* could have remained only an aviation nostalgia piece or a text for the specialist; it elected to do neither. Rather it evoked an awareness in me of a signficant historical thread that has often been overlooked by all except a very few.

The purpose of *Air Mail* was initially two-fold. The historical intent was to blend aviation and air post histories to demonstrate the profound effect they had on each other, pointing particularly to the vital role that the air mail "subsidy" played in the development of commercial aviation in the United States. The second purpose of *Air Mail* has been to demonstrate the challenges, rewards and contributions of a form of stamp collecting—aerophilately—that is becoming increasingly popular and readily available to anyone with an interest in gathering and researching the artifacts of air mail history.

Thanks, however, to unexpected insights, synchronistic meetings and the always helpful advice of many people, the purposes addressed by this book have been enhanced. *Air Mail* deals perhaps less with technical, specialized information than with the larger matter of what it has meant for the world's future when air mail services have permitted millions upon millions of written communications to speed across oceans and land masses helping to link people together in a world-wide community.

Air Mail does not presume to be a definitive report. The full story is too vast to be encompassed in one volume. Moreover, it is an on-going story that is still being written daily as the airplane and other aerial vehicles extend their range and reach out to new corners of this glorious universe. As much of the story of air mail as we have now, however, clearly centers on the courage, resourcefulness and determination of the comparatively few men and women who helped bring the system into being. At one level, *Air Mail* is solely intended as a tribute to them.

Donald B. Holmes

To my Beloved Brother Pilots and Pals...

I go west, but with a cheerful heart. I hope what small sacrifice I have made may be useful to the cause.

When we fly we are fools, they say. When we are dead we weren't half-bad fellows. But everyone in this wonderful aviation service is doing the world far more good than the public can appreciate. We risk our necks; we give our lives; we perfect a service for the benefit of the world at large. They, mind you, are the ones who call us fools.

But stick to it, boys. I'm still very much with you all. See you all again.

Leonard Brooke Hyde-Pearson offered these words for all of the air mail pioneers in a letter "to be opened only after my death." This aviator, who willingly accepted the challenge of the early air mail, was one of three who died in 1924. Hyde-Pearson's DeHavilland went down in the Alleghenies of Pennsylvania after a treacherous fog enveloped the plane while en route to Bellefonte.

Leonard Brooke Hyde-Pearson

Prologue

Clues from antiquity point to the existence of postal services of various kinds for thousands of years, and one could well argue that the administrative excellence of an ancient state or empire could be gauged by the sophistication and efficiency of its postal system. Wherever and whenever cultural patterns became complex, the need for reliable communications caused mankind to devise a postal technology to facilitate a flow of letters in support of the cultural form.

To the Persians goes credit for perfecting a postal service that became a model for the entire ancient world. Combining a knack for careful administration, inherited from their Assyrian predecessors, and a desire for efficient care and usage of their spreading network of roads leading to sources of and outlets for goods and materials, the Persians established a courier system that effectively served their imperial and trading needs and inspired the Romans, centuries later, to incorporate its best features. The Greek historian Herodotus related details of Persian postal methods, declaring, "Nothing mortal travels so fast as these Persian messengers . . . these men [dispatch riders on horseback] will not be hindered from accomplishing at their best speed the distance which they have to go, either by snow, or rain, or heat or by darkness of night."

Inevitably, over the many centuries, the spread of education, construction of post roads, increased use of ocean-going vessels, and a mushrooming of commercial contacts combined to produce a significantly expanded volume of mail. With this increase arose the twofold need to find ways to handle the mail safely and to convey it to its destinations. "Royal" monopolies usually controlled the mails, having learned early on the revenue benefits that operation of the posts could obtain. They also allowed smaller, less threatening courier services to carry on in remote areas. For the most part, however, entrenched powers always resisted institutionalization of any form of postal competition that might deny them such a convenient means of taxation. This struggle between government and private interests over supervision of the mails has occurred again and again in history; recently we have seen the struggle revived.

In Europe in the fifteenth and sixteenth centuries, a centralized system of posts, known as the Thurn and Taxis system, gained sanction from the Holy Roman Empire and maintained exclusive courier rights throughout much of Europe. Unlike most other early postal systems, however, this one was open to broad public use, offering to carry letters and parcels anywhere in continental Europe for a specified fee. Where other messenger systems existed, it was always with the blessing and permission of this central authority. The Thurn and Taxis posts began as a courier service but passed through succeeding phases when couriers no longer traveled on horseback but in post wagons and later in one-, two- and four-horse stagecoaches that also transported travelers. The remnants of the Thurn and Taxis posts, including its network of hostels, were purchased by the Prussian government in 1867.

In Great Britain, the tension between government postal prerogatives and private rights to operate courier services involved the question of foreign mail. Royal proclamations of 1591 and 1609 established government postriders as the only legal carriers of foreign mail and granted the government full right of censorship of all such mail in times of national emergency. Eventually, competing carriers of domestic or internal mails were forcibly put down as increased volume made a centralized operation of all posts too profitable a venture for the Exchequer to ignore.

With a network of postal roads completed by 1741 and postal coaches introduced on those roads by 1784, Great Britain approached an historic moment when her postal reforms would have far-reaching implications for every postal service in the world. Initiated through the proposals of an ingenious educator named Rowland Hill, the reforms received royal assent on August 17, 1839, and carried several provisions that still guide contemporary postal practices, including mail slots (or boxes) in the home. The major articles of Hill's reform package were: a startling reduction in postal rates; a uniform domestic rate based on the weight of a letter rather than on the number of sheets that it contained (1 penny for letters of one half ounce or less, 2 pence for letters between a half ounce and one ounce in weight, and 2 pence for each additional ounce or fraction thereof); and a method for prepayment of postal fees either through use of prestamped, government-issue letter sheets and envelopes or by use of small adhesive paper slips that could be affixed to one's own personal stationery.

Rowland Hill and his supporters expected prestamped envelopes to be popularly received. However, it was the small adhesives that got the strongest nod of approval from the British public; postage stamps were here to stay. Previously, letters were hand-stamped upon arrrival at a post office and postage was then collected from the addressee.

These first postage stamps issued by any government for regular postal use were sold in 1840 for either one or two pennies. The one-penny stamp was printed in black on a whitish paper, and it featured a portrait of Queen Victoria taken from Wyon's city medal that was struck to commemorate her visit to the Guildhall in 1837—the year of her accession to the throne—and has been traditionally called the "Penny Black." The two-pence denomination was printed in blue but had the same design scheme. Hill had described his postage stamps as a "bit of paper

just large enough to bear a stamp [meaning the impression of postage value as used on the newly issued prestamped envelopes], and covered at the back with a glutinous wash which by applying a little moisture, might be attached to the letter."

After penny postage was introduced in Great Britain, letter mail handled soared to about 72 million pieces the first year. Only a few years later the British Postal Service was processing letters at a rate of 208 million per year.

At the time of Sir Rowland Hill's death in 1879 Gladstone wrote of him "His great plan ran like wild-fire through the civilized world, and never, perhaps, was a local invention...and improvement applied in the lifetime of its author for the advantage of such multitudes of his fellow creatures."

Postal procedures in the British colonies in North America had been well established by the colonists before they were taken over and carefully controlled by the Postmaster General of England. Postal practices in the United States, therefore, were eventually modeled upon those of the mother country. Deputy postmasters general were appointed in all English colonies after 1710, and these officials were directed by and held accountable to London.

Generally speaking, mail service was not to be depended upon through the entire Revolutionary period. Until the crown posts were finally evicted on Christmas Day of 1775, with the closing of the New York City Post Office, the service was openly resisted by the colonial peoples, who saw the postal rates as another taxing device. And even when the mail did move with postriders, it was often intercepted by fervent "Sons of Liberty" who attacked and robbed the inland riders.

By the time the British postal apparatus was dismantled, the Continental Congress had taken action to deal with the question of a replacement service, naming Benjamin Franklin as the first Postmaster General on July 26, 1775, at a yearly salary of $1,000. The new service, however, was preoccupied with maintaining lines of communication between the armies and Congress, and transport of mail over all established routes was entirely contingent upon the constantly changing military situation. Censorship, a sanctioned practice of the young colonial postal service, posed another threat to many who would have otherwise used the service.

In 1789, with the war over and George Washington about to be inaugurated as president, there were only seventy-five United States post offices in existence, partially connected by 2,000 miles of post roads. After the turn of the century, postal affairs in the United States changed markedly. The prevailing themes were growth and greater complexity, and the catalysts for change were westward expansion, speedier communications over new and improved north-south highways, and eventually, the advent of railroads.

Mail contracts for steamboat services appear in post office records after 1813, and Congress declared all railroads to be "postal roads" in 1834. An "Eastern" Pony Express was inaugurated in 1836, predecessor of the more famous "Western" Pony Express of the 1860 era. By 1845 in the United States, 14,183 post offices were operating and postal revenues had risen from $38,000 in 1790 to almost $4,300,000, an amount just slightly below the cost required to maintain the full service.

A private collection and delivery organization, City Dispatch Post in New York, following Rowland Hill's lead in England, issued in 1842 the first adhesive postage stamp in the United States. This stamp was, to be sure, of private authorization, but it presaged the future direction of United States postal practice and was a clear indicator of Hill's spreading influence on this side of the Atlantic.

United States Postmaster General Amos Kendall, who ended his term of office in 1840, did indeed take careful note of England's postal reforms of 1839 and 1840 and, in fact, sent an observer there to study them at close hand. Perhaps Kendall's immediate successor was too intimidated by a possible loss of revenues. In any case he failed to initiate any comparable reforms in the United States. However, on March 3, 1845, a new Postmaster General by the name of Cave Johnson was able to get a new Congress to enact some far-reaching revisions.

Effective July 1, 1845, a simplified scale of reduced rates went into effect, and postage charges were, for the first time, based on weight rather than the number of sheets. Distance zones, too, became two in number, a reduction from the previous five. The charge for a half-ounce letter was set at 5 cents if transported within a 300-mile radius of its starting point, or 10 cents for over 300 miles. The prepayment of postage remained optional, and frequently charges continued to be paid by the addressee.

The authorization for the first general issue of United States postage stamps was approved in Congress on March 3, 1847. The act called for the production of a five- and a ten-cent stamp. Printed on a lightweight bluish paper and without perforations, the five-cent stamp featured an oval portrait of Benjamin Franklin, printed with brown ink. The ten-cent stamp was printed with black ink and depicted the head of Washington after a portrait by Gilbert Stuart. When new postage rates and new stamps were introduced in 1851, the first United States issue of 1847 became invalid. Approximately 3.7 million five-cent Franklins of the 1847 issue had been sent to postmasters, as were 891,000 copies of the ten-cent denomination.

The following dates mark significant milestones in the evolution of postal practices in the United States: April 1, 1855—the date when prepayment of domestic postage was made compulsory; January 1, 1856—the date when prepayment of postage *by use of postage stamps* for domestic letters became law; and, 1857—the year when United States postage stamps were first perforated for convenient separation.

After the Montgolfier brothers, Joseph and Etienne, had successfully lauched an unmanned hot-air balloon from the tiny marketplace at Annonay, France, on June 5, 1783, further significant advances transpired within a few months. A hydrogen-filled balloon, developed by Dr. J. A. C. Charles, went aloft at Champ de Mars in Paris on August 27. Then, recorded on September 18, was the flight of a sheep, a cock, and a duck, all crowded into the same small basket-cage. This flight directed by the Montgolfiers was made in the presence of King Louis XVI and his royal court.

Finally, in a Montgolfier balloon on November 21, 1783, before half a million people in the garden of the Château de La Muette in Paris, Pilatre de Rozier, a young scientist, and his friend, the Marquis d'Arlandes, became mankind's first aerial travelers. They drifted through the air for five miles.

A new era had dawned. Man finally was able to fly.

1793 United States

An accidental beginning

A festive air prevailed when an excited crowd gathered in a Philadelphia prison yard near State House Row. Several cannons were fired at regular intervals as if to mark a dramatic countdown. Dignitaries were present—Alexander Hamilton, Martha Washington, John Jay, and Betsy Ross Claypoole. All were assembled to observe the first balloon ascension in the Western Hemisphere.

Preliminary ceremonies on that Wednesday morning, January 9, saw President Washington step forward to present the aeronaut, forty-year-old Frenchman Jean-Pierre Blanchard, with a handwritten letter (later referred to by many as a "passport"). It was to be carried on Blanchard's person to guarantee safe passage wherever he might land at the conclusion of his historic journey. It was deemed necessary for him to have such credentials because he spoke very little English. Although the letter itself has never been found, Blanchard kept a journal, which preserved the content of General Washington's brief letter.

Blanchard's flight lasted about 45 minutes and took him, an assortment of scientific instruments, some biscuits and wine, and his little black dog across the Delaware River into New Jersey. He landed safely near Woodbury at 10:56 A.M., to the astonishment of several area farmers.

The Frenchman was escorted by the citizens of New Jersey back to Philadelphia where he promptly informed the President "of the happy effects of the passport he had been pleased to grant me. I had the honor," Blanchard's journal reads, "to offer him my colours, which he politely accepted, and thereby acquired a fresh claim to my gratitude."

1

On currents of air

Letters sent by Jupiter

The events in Lafayette, Indiana, centered around an energetic fifty-one-year-old "student" of aeronautics from Lancaster, Pennsylvania, named John Wise. On July 1, Wise and three eager companions had taken off before a large crowd in St. Louis in a mammoth balloon called *Atlantic* that was filled with 65,000 cubic feet of gas. The four were attempting to enter the upper air currents above St. Louis and ride them all the way to New York City.

Instead of reaching their goal, Wise and company experienced a hair-raising encounter with a storm over Lake Ontario and barely escaped to a rough landing in trees near Henderson, New York, at 2:35 P.M. on July 2. Their gambit, however, set a distance record for balloons that held for more than forty years. In just under 20 hours of flight, the *Atlantic* had carried its passengers more than 850 miles at an average speed of 46 mph.

Because the *Atlantic* had been observed along its evening course in northern Indiana, a public appearance of its pilot there held promise of becoming a spectacular attraction. An enterprising committee of businessmen from Lafayette moved into action. Their idea was to invite Wise to try another flight from their city, which possessed a large gasworks where a balloon could be inflated. Lafayette also boasted a fine geographic position for a shot at New York City, assuming the flow of air overhead cooperated as it almost had on the St. Louis–Henderson venture. Around July 20, the committee, headed by Joseph Danziger, received a favorable response to their invitation. In accepting, Wise indicated that a flight could take place sometime in August. An $800 honorarium was offered and, no doubt, carried some weight in the balloonist's decision.

From a young age Wise had been enthralled by accounts of European ballooning, and at age twenty-seven he abruptly left his cabinetmaking craft to devote himself fully to it. Before he made his final flight over Lake Michigan at age seventy-one—a flight from which he never returned—Wise had made 446 free ascensions and became known as "the father of ballooning in America."

Wise arrived in Lafayette on August 1, and announced from the steps of the Tippecanoe County courthouse that Tuesday, August 16, would be ascension day, "rain or shine." While Wise and his son Charles busied themselves with preparations for the flight and made themselves available for a continuous round of interviews and personal appearances, the general populace prepared their city for the biggest day in its history. Midst all the furor and excitement it is a wonder that anyone saw the small notice that Lafayette Postmaster Thomas Wood inserted in the *Evening Courier* the afternoon before the scheduled lift-off. The six-line item simply announced that "Professor" Wise would be taking mail with him on his flight. Patrons were admonished to have their balloon mail in the post office before noon the next day if they wished to send letters, properly stamped and marked "via Balloon," to the seaboard. In such fashion the stage was set for the world's first official flight of regular mail.

Small as it was, the mail announcement elicited a fair response; 123 letters and 23 circulars were collected in a mail pouch for Wise, who was designated an official carrier by the Lafayette postmaster.

Early on the morning of August 16, Charles Collier, superintendent of the gasworks, began to inflate Wise's balloon *Jupiter*. As the process went on, a small group had separated itself from the throng at Courthouse Square to watch the expanding balloon. It took about three hours to fill the great bag with some 20,000 cubic feet of gas. Meanwhile, trains arrived, pouring out hoards of excited children, wagons with families from the country clogged the streets, and bands were heard in the background. The weather was hot but clear. Parasols dotted the crowd, colorful and frilly shields against a brilliant sun.

Then a problem beset the undertaking. A tiny valve that had seemed to pose only a minor problem during the day turned out to be a major problem for Wise and everyone present. To the aeronaut's dismay, he suddenly realized in the midst of the ceremonies that *Jupiter* was deflating. "Finding that gas was escaping fast," he reported later, "and feeling desirous of getting the balloon out of this dense mass of people, I requested my son to sail out of town. He ascended several thousand feet in half an hour and landed on the outskirts of town. From this point we had the balloon towed back to the gasworks. Here I had the top of her hauled down and discovered that one of the India rubber springs had snapped and flew in under the valve clapper, causing the leaking."

It was announced that the voyage and experiments would be made the next day at two o'clock. By nightfall many of the spectators had gone home, deeply disappointed. Others dallied on street corners and porches; some sought the solace of the taverns.

By noon the next day, *Jupiter* was again prepared for flight. America's foremost aeronaut was also prepared for ascent 233, having again secured his provisions and "parachute," technical instruments, and some chemically treated paper for ozone testing supplied by a Dr. Wetherill. Also aboard was the United States mail bag, brass-locked and addressed to the Post Office in New York, New York. This time *Jupiter* was not hauled to Courthouse Square but to an open area at the gasworks, and there, at 2 P.M. on August 17, 1859, the flight began.

Unfortunately for Wise, his ascension at Lafayette took place on an afternoon when the air was extremely calm, and he remained fixed in space over the city for nearly an hour. With such

Our officers kept us back, for we were not numerous enough to charge upon the enemy. This was, moreover, most prudent, for this murderous fire—so fatal to the white coats—did us but little harm. Our conical balls penetrated their dense masses, while those of our Austrians whistled past our ears and respected our persons. It was the first time I had faced fire, nor was I the only one. Well, I am satisfied with myself. True, I dodged the first balls, but Henry IV., they say, did the same at the beginning of every battle. It is, in fact, a physical effect, independent of the will.

But, this tribute paid, if you could only feel how each shot electrifies you. It is like a whip on a racer's legs. The balls whistle past you, turn up the earth around you, kill one, wound another, and you hardly notice them. You grow intoxicated; the smell of the powder mounts to the brain.— The eye becomes bloodshot, and its look is fixed on the enemy. There is something of all the passions in that terrible passion excited in a soldier by the sight of blood and the tumult of battle.

Everybody who has tried it, testifies to the peculiar intoxication that is produced by being in a battle. There is an infatu- ating influence about the smell of powder, the shrill whistle of a bullet, and the sight of human blood, that instantly transforms men from cowards to heroes—from women sometimes to monsters. None can tell of the nature and mystery of that influence, but those who have been in the fray them- selves

Effect of "Moral Suasion" on Gam- blers.

A man from Louisville, who had lost nearly two thousand dollars at a gambling hell in Memphis, a night or two since, dis- covered late in the evening that his com- panions were not, like the Austrians, doing everything on the "square," drew a formid- able looking Deringer, and threatened the lives of all in the room if their ill gotten gains were not immediately returned.— This "moral suasion" had the desired effect, and the "golden fleece" was at once dis- gorged.

DAUGHTERS OF MALTA.—The lady editor of the Rockford (Ill.) Standard says: "The Daughters of Malta are becoming as dis- tinguished, and seems to be quite as be- nevolent in their designs, as the Sons of Malta. Their object is said to be to relieve widowers, destitute bachelors, dandies, Hot- tentots, and orphan male children. By the time the Sons obtain control of the Island of Cuba, the Daughters confidently expect to subjugate "the Isle of Man."

There was an interesting suit a De- troit the other day, for the recovery of a patent extension hooped skirt, the property of Mary Sadle, which had been feloniously appropriated by Catherine Kinkel. The ar- ticle in dispute was carried into court by a small boy, who had ingeniously placed his head where Mary's waist ought to have been, and looked like a monkey escaping from his cage. The hoops were restored.

From some cause or other, weddings are very bad for the eyes. The moment the knot is tied the bride's maid and two aunts and a mother rush into the "hall bed- room" and have "a good cry" for hours to- gether. Why a poor fellow's promise to pay "a young woman's board bill" should operate thus on the "finer feeling of our na- ture," puzzles us to divine.

In the late whirlwind at Gloucester, Mass., a negro man who kept the ferry, was blown away, and has not yet been found — When last seen he was going through the air, mixed up with the flying rubbish, and creaming at the top of his lung. He has evidently "gone where the good niggers go."

An up country California paper, mentions mosquitoes so large that they can stand on their hinds legs and drink out of a pint cup.

---

those interested.

the City Attorney, reported ...ce in regard to butchers oc- ...rket space without license, ...and void.

he City Attorney was in- ...w up an ordinance that ...grounds of complaint, and ...mplaint could be made to

...n made complaint to the ...ond of water accumulated ...Ferry and Leonard streets ...of the improvement of Fer

...ported that the only way to ...evil complained of, was to ...rom Leonard street to the ...construct an underground

...f Mr. Barford, the Street ...was instructed to fill said ...rel of the Ferry street gut-

...poke at length on the sub- ...pposed to filling the ditch. ...gated the matter fully, and ...only way was to pave the ...ide the surplus water be- ...reet, the alley, and Brown

...of the Valley Road, urged ...action. He thought that ...d of the ravine to the level ...and cutting a channel ...e the best plan. ...ithdrew his motion.

...opposed to cutting through ...improvement. The proper ...ion, was to make a culvert ...oad, at the head of Ferry ...er culvert, and dig a chan- ...ide of the railroad to con- ...w culvert.

...Mr. Ball, the City Engineer ...have said nuisance abated ...t or otherwise.

...lled up the matter suggest- ...months since, in regard to ...grade of all streets in the

...e that he should introduce ...e subject at the next meet- ...l.

...e salaries of the city offi- ...rs of the Council were al-

...Mr. Ball, Mr. Jacob Pyke ...th were appointed a com- ...tend the work now being ...reet. ...djourned to meet in two

For the Courier.
...logical Question.

...w makes Joseph the son of ...atthan; Matthan of Eleazar, ...that Joseph was the son ...Matthat, Matthat of Levi, ...kc. Why don't the Evan- ...hey are enunciating the

...found the foregoing on ...r day, and having looked ...little, I see it has some ...attention of Christians ...ore learned in Theology ...answer the interrogation?
S.

A Sell.

...rrible affair,—the murder ...sealing up of his remains ...What Dean?' asked a half ...once. Why Sar-dean, of ...ngent reply. "No levity."

...t know that Dryden was in ...lips, "from a remark he ..." said he, "may be made ...f happiness!"

still air and a great portion of his sand ballast released during his ascent, he must surely have surmised early in the flight that *Jupiter* would not carry him to the seaboard this time. Yet, for a while, he persisted in trying.

At nearly three miles of altitude, he found himself sailing due east. However, a check of his sand ballast indicated only about fifty pounds remaining. "Knowing that this would not suffice for a whole night's sail, as the air upon the setting of the sun would alone require nearly all of it to compensate for condensation of the gas, I concluded to make a landing," he reported. He landed the *Jupiter* in the vicinity of Crawfordsville, Indiana—but not before he decided upon a novel way to deliver the mail.

> In order to make my arrival [at Crawfordsville] more interesting, I concluded to send my letter mail ahead. Having with me a muslin sheet nine feet square, I attached to each of its corners strings of about five yards length. They were tied together at their lowest extremity, and to this end was attached the mail bag and then I dropped it overboard. It made an admirable parachute. We kept near together all the way down as I could regulate the descent of the balloon to the descent of the parachute. Both of the aerial machines landed within 50 feet of each other on a public road six miles south of Crawfordsville.

The world's first officially flown mail had returned to earth about 4½ hours and some 30 miles from its takeoff point. During this flight, Wise kept a detailed record of barometric and temperature readings and was responsible for the first recorded detection of the presence of ozone in the upper air. He also demonstrated extreme faithfulness in carrying out his duties as a sworn mail carrier. He chased his mail chute down to the ground and saw that the bag was placed in care of a Colonel Reed, postal agent for the New Albany and Salem Railroad at Crawfordsville. Reed, in turn, placed the mail on the next train for New York.

8   Before departing Crawfordsville, Wise made a number of public statements in which he looked ahead, sharing his visions of a great transcontinental aerial highway. He attributed his failure to reach the seaboard to faulty winds and the quality of the gas.

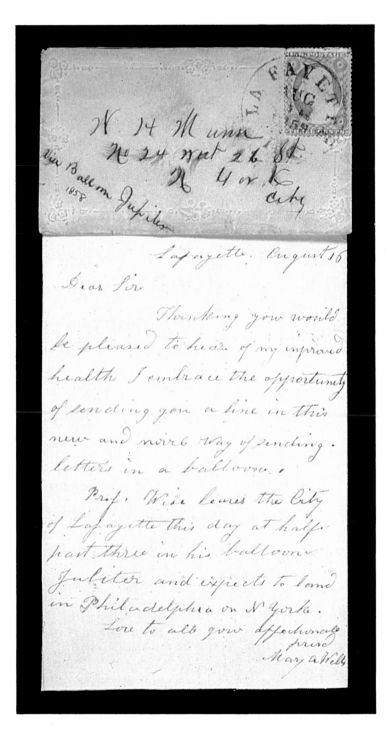

Manuscript marking "via Balloon Jupiter" identifies this only known piece of the first officially flown U.S. mail, which reached New York City by train August 20, 1859. A vertical 7¢ U.S. airmail marks the centennial of Wise's flight.

1870-1871 France

The amazing Ballon Poste

Due to their encirclement during the Franco-Prussian War and an interruption of contacts with the rest of their country, Parisians were forced to devise a way of establishing communications beyond the German lines. Written communications carried out of the besieged city in manned balloons seemed to offer the best solution. Displaying a remarkable blend of ingenuity and determination, the people of Paris put together their Ballon Poste, and this makeshift operation became the world's first semi-regular air mail service.

Early on the morning of September 23, 1870, the French released their first balloon, a large cotton bag filled with coal gas. The balloon had been given the name *Le Neptune* and was piloted by a balloonist of some experience, Jules Duruof. The prevailing winds that day carried the *Neptune* in a safe westerly direction, and after a flight of 3¾ hours it landed near Evreux in friendly territory. Duruof had his mail taken at once to the post office in a small town called Craconville where it was processed and sent on its way. Approximately 275 pounds of mail were on board on its 75-mile journey.

Pleased with this success, the French then launched three more manned balloons plus one unmanned balloon in the following order during the first week of the new air mail service:

launch date	name of balloon	landing place	time of landing
Sept. 25	*La Ville de Florence*	Vernouillet	2:30 P.M.
Sept. 29	*Etats-Unis* (United States)	Magnanville	1:30 P.M.
Sept. 30	*Celeste*	Dreux	11:50 A.M.
Sept. 30	Unnamed, unmanned	near Ville d'Avray	1:15 P.M.

There was a delay in any further launching until October 7, which gave the French time to assess their airlift. The first four balloons had been highly successful; they had carried large quantities of mail—over 900 pounds in the four flights alone—to "safe" territory. In addition, they had transported at least one passenger and several pigeons out of Paris. The homing pigeons, sent out primarily for governmental purposes, enabled written communications of an official nature to be carried back into Paris strapped to them. The fifth balloon, and first of three unnamed balloons, was an unmanned paper one, successfully brought down by the vigilant Prussians who were, by this time, well aware of the balloon post strategy. The bulk of this mail was lost to the enemy, though a few pieces eventually found their way back to the Secteur Central, the main post office, in Paris.

Felix Nadar, founder of the Société d'Aviation of France and an organizer of the Ballon Poste, was busy at this time arranging for production lines to build the balloons that would be needed to maintain the postal service. Spacious railroad sheds, abandoned when the siege halted all rail traffic in and out of Paris, were pressed into service as factories. A few of the railway yards adjacent to the factories also served as departure points. There were eight or nine such spots around the city. Since the balloons were being released in an urban area with towers and buildings, the chief criterion for the takeoff sites involved their location in open space, as free as possible from obstructions.

These concerns became critical early in November when the lift-offs were shifted to nighttime hours for security reasons. Daylight hours greatly increased the chances for balloons to be shot down. But if the nighttime hours improved the balloon's chances of getting past the enemy, they increased the hazard posed by tall structures. Among the sites chosen for departures were the railroad stations Gare du Nord, Gare de l'Est and Gare d'Orléans, LaVillette gasworks, and the Tuilleries.

While balloon production went forward speedily, the recruiting of pilots continued, but less frantically. A French society of balloonists had volunteered its members for the mail service, providing a reservoir of experienced pilots from which to draw. These civilian pilots offered their services enthusiastically in the full knowledge that once out of the city they would most likely be kept away from Paris and their families until the war ended.

Regulations governing the service were printed and made their appearance in Paris before the *Armand Barbes* resumed balloon flights on October 7. The regulations stipulated that letter weight was not to exceed four grams (one-seventh of an ounce), that regular French postage stamps were to be used for franking, and that an officially issued postal card was now available for use at half the letter rate. Decrees of September 26 and 27 both specified that the *"par ballon monte"* legend would be required on the address portion of all folded letters. Not everyone who made use of the balloon post observed the regulations; *par ballon monte* is often missing from letters that were flown.

With the resumption of flights, the world's first air mail service continued with 16 flights being made in October, 14 in November, 18 in December and 14 more in January before the final flight of *Le General Cambronne* on January 28, 1871. Over the 128 days that the postal service existed, 67 flights were made, with 2 departures being recorded on 12 of those days. Of the 67 flights, 55 (or possibly 56) involved mail carries. Between 2 and 3 million letters were flown, a figure that demonstrates the magnitude of this pioneer air mail system.

Five of the 67 flights, including the first of the unmanned ones on September 30, fell into enemy hands. Two balloons were lost at sea, though most of the mail aboard one of these was recovered off the southern coast of England; neither pilot survived. Five of the errant flights wound up in Belgium, three landed in Holland, and two rode eastbound winds that propelled them straight into Germany and captivity. The longest flight of the Ballon Poste took its pilot and passenger some 800 miles into Norway.

A special type of mail that deserves further comment in any account of the Paris balloon post is the pigeon mail. As mentioned, the French balloons transported a number of caged carrier pigeons to outlying areas so that the birds could be sent back with a limited number of official communications. Shortly after the siege of Paris, an inventor-photographer there thought of a way to allow the general populace in the unoccupied areas of France to make use of the pigeon post.

If letters intended for Paris were collected, photographed, reduced to a small size that could not be read, and then transferred to a collodion film, they could be sent to Paris in great numbers via the pigeons. Upon arrival, the filmed letters would be projected on a screen, several at a time, for a battery of secretaries to copy by hand. The letters would then be turned over to mail carriers for delivery. The plan turned out to be entirely feasible and on November 12, 1870, two balloons—the *Niepce* and the *Daguerre*—sailed from Paris with a team of experts and a mandate from the Postmaster General "to establish in province a service of photomicroscopical dispatches to be sent to Paris by traveling pigeons."

The mission was accomplished even though the *Daguerre* was downed by enemy fire and several of the *Niepce's* pigeons were overcome by cold on the ride to Vitry-le-François, where the balloon landed. It was found that each piece of collodion film could accommodate about 2,500 individual letters. Literally thousands of letters were delivered by means of this primitive system of microfilming. To be sure, the returning pigeons became fair game for Prussian sharpshooters in the environs of Paris. However, most of the birds did get through, and the Ballon Poste became, to some modest extent, a two-way system of communication.

A small seven-line notice appeared in the *London Times* of Monday, November 28, 1870. The next day, the same event was unobtrusively reported in eleven lines in *The New York Times*. Medals commemorating it were struck in Christiania (Oslo) shortly after it happened, and there, even ballads were composed about it. More than thirty years later, men were still talking about the event as a modest stone monument was erected to mark the place where it happened. Such was the influence of a landing in the snow-covered hills of central Norway by two French balloonists, couriers of the famed Paris Ballon Poste.

It began one evening. The balloon that rose from the Gare du Nord in Paris at 11:45 P.M. on November 24, 1870, was called *La*

The launching of the second balloon of the famed "Ballon Poste." Ville de Florence *departs Paris on September 25, 1870, rising from* Place la Glaciere *with homing pigeons aboard.*

Ville d'Orléans. Aboard were two men, several pigeons, and a heavy load of mail. Their intended destination: Tours, where one courier would attempt to deliver an urgent *pli confie*, (personally carried letter), from General Louis Jules Trochu, governor of Paris and commander-in-chief of its defense, to the leader of the French resistance, Léon Gambetta.

Piloting was a thirty-year-old volunteer from Paris named Paul-Valéry Rolier. His passenger, with the Gambetta letter on his person, was Léon Bezier, a self-described "volunteer guerrilla" engaged in service to his country. Both men had anticipated an easy flight: the weather was clear and the breeze, at least at ground level, favorable.

No. 64, 1870.

OPEN LETTERS for PARIS.

Transmission of by Carrier Pigeons.

THE Director-General of the French Post Office has informed this Department that a special Despatch, by means of Carrier Pigeons, of correspondence addressed to Paris has been established at Tours, and that such Despatch may be made use of for brief letters, or notes, originating in the United Kingdom, and forwarded by post to Tours.

Persons desirous of availing themselves of this mode of transmission must observe the following conditions:—

Every letter must be posted open, that is, without any cover or envelope, and without any seal, and it must be registered.

No letter must consist of more than twenty words, including the address and the signature of the sender; but the name of the addressee, the place of his abode, and the name of the sender—although composed of more than one word—will each be counted as one word only.

No figures must be used; the number of the house of the addressee must be given in words.

Combined words joined together by hyphens or apostrophes will be counted according to the number of words making up the combined word.

The letters must be written entirely in French, in clear, intelligible language. They must relate solely to private affairs, and no political allusion or reference to the War will be permitted.

The charge for these letters is five-pence for every word, and this charge must be prepaid, in addition to the postage of sixpence for a single registered letter addressed to France.

The Director-General of the French Post Office, in notifying this arrangement, has stated that his office cannot guarantee the safe delivery of this correspondence, and will not be in any way responsible for it.

By Command of the Postmaster-General.

GENERAL POST OFFICE,
16th November, 1870.

Printed for Her Majesty's Stationery Office, by W. P. Garrett, Prujean Square, Old Bailey, London, E.C.

When Prudent Rene Patrice Dagron and four assistants departed Paris on November 12, 1870 in the balloon Niepce, their mission was to inaugurate the microfilm/pigeon service announced in this leaflet.

Civilian volunteer balloonist Paul-Valéry Rolier, pilot of La Ville d'Orléans, survived the longest flight of the war, landing in snow near the Lifjeld region of Norway on November 25.

When the ascent slowed at about 6,000 feet, Rolier and Bezier were suddenly confronted with a fresh wind from the south. Their balloon began to move in a northerly direction with increasing speed. The current carried them toward the French coast, which they reached just as a dense fog moved in. From that moment on and until daylight hours later, the two men were completely at the mercy of the elements. Unable to obtain any ground sightings whatever, they could not calculate or estimate either their speed or course. When daylight came, Rolier released one of his pigeons with a message of distress indicating his total ignorance of their position.

In fact, *La Ville d'Orléans* had flown a course almost due north

and was about to make landfall at the southernmost tip of the Norwegian coast. The balloon had been allowed to descend once the fog cleared, and the sight of water and a few ships informed Rolier and Bezier for the first time that they were over water. Just as they caught sight of land through the mist, they cut away a mail sack in order to lighten their load and attain some altitude for an expected landfall. The time was approximately 11 A.M. on the morning of November 25. They had been airborne for almost twelve hours.

After three hours of drift in a northward direction, Rolier spotted a bit of terrain that seemed to offer a favorable landing opportunity. Releasing some of the gas from the large bag, he

11

brought the balloon down and to the end, or so he thought, of its long and dangerous journey. As it turned out, it was indeed journey's end for Rolier and Bezier, but not for the balloon, its cargo, or pigeons. As the two men dropped from the basket to terra firma, a gust of wind wrenched the grounding ropes from their grasp and pushed the balloon forward through the air on a new course.

A Paris balloon-post collection would include stamps and specimens of the actual mail. A French semi-postal issue of 1955 (left) and an air mail issue of 1971 both commemorate the remarkably successful aerial postal service of 1870–71. The airmail depicts a mail balloon rising near the Gare d'Austerlitz railroad station. Below: A possible relic of the renowned Ville d'Orléans flight, the cover having been cancelled at the Rue d'Enghien post office, Paris, on November 23, 1870.

The unmanned balloon landed many miles away near Sandum farm in Krödsherred, Norway. A letter sent later from Krödsherred to Christiania described the final landing *La Ville d'Orléans* would ever make.

It was equally amazing to observe it from close up, which clearly showed that it was not a thing of witchcraft as we first had been slightly tempted to believe; but a French postal balloon, sent out from the besieged Paris with letters and newspapers. It is equally clear that it came confusingly far away from its real destination. Be that as it may, here it lies for the time being, still half filled with gas, slightly billowing and as if panting after its long and difficult trip.

Rolier and Bezier believed that they had landed in Iceland. They spent their first freezing night in a dilapidated hut minus its roof, using hay and branches to provide some protection against the intense cold. The next morning they came upon a second hut and were subsequently discovered there by two woodsmen, Harald and Klas Strand. This fortuitous meeting, somewhat hampered by a language barrier, started their gradual, triumphant return to France.

Rolier, who was referred to as "the naval officer" by his Norwegian hosts, soon learned that he and Bezier had come down near Lifjeld in the county of Telemark in south-central Norway, approximately one hundred miles directly north of the coastal town of Mandal. He also eventually found out that all the mail, including the sack dropped into the North Sea near Mandal, had been recovered.

Great excitement spread throughout Norway as news of the French balloon became known. Norwegian newspapers, which began by announcing the wildest of speculations about the mysterious visitor from the sky, ended up reporting the tiniest fragment of information.

Column after column aired the story in a seemingly endless rehearsal of the latest findings. As a result of this publicity, Rolier and Bezier were treated like heroes.

Most of the letters carried on *La Ville d'Orléans* were placed safely in the hands of the French postal service and processed within France. Today, they are prized additions in any aero history or French postal history collection. But what of the vehicle that bore these letters? Perhaps one clue to the destiny of *La Ville d'Orléans* is contained in an article on ballooning that appeared in *Morgenbladet,* a Christiania newspaper, in 1895. The extract reads:

The remarkable balloon was given to Christiania University, where it still is. Unfortunately, it has been put in the cellar where it lies full of dust and dirt, concealed from the view of all uninitiated.

Balloon postage—five cents, please

Another episode in the history of air mail concerns a comparatively obscure mail-carrying balloon flight that took place in Tennessee. Only in recent years has the full story of the balloon *Buffalo* been made known and a small scattering of her postal artifacts gradually been brought to light.

In an aeronautical sense there was nothing earthshaking about Samuel Archer King's 169th ascension. The professional balloonist rose from Nashville in the *Buffalo,* a balloon made in and named after the city in New York State whose citizens underwrote her construction, with one associate and five passengers and flew 26 miles to Gallatin. He departed Nashville at 5 P.M. June 18 and required a little over 2 hours to complete the initial stage of his journey, which was concluded with a second hop the next day. In terms of ballooning, the flight was nothing special. In a philatelic sense, however, there is ample reason to remember it and to celebrate its unique place in postal history.

For the first time, mail was carried through the air bearing an adhesive postage stamp or label that had been specifically printed for mail being transported through the air. Because the stamp's vignette features an illustration of King's balloon, it has always been known as the *Buffalo* Balloon Stamp. Privately produced and never sanctioned by anyone in the United States postal service, it is, therefore, unofficial in nature.

A Nashville *Daily American* article of June 15, 1877, announced that the stamps were available to use on letters that anyone wished to send on the *Buffalo.* The article read in part:

> We have received a stamp thus termed from Wheeler Bro., No. 20 North Cherry Street designed by Jno. B. Lillard, and engraved by Mr. J. H. Snively of this city. It is 1⅛ by 1⅜ inch, has the words "Balloon Postage" "five cents" in straight lines at the top and bottom, and is printed in blue, with a good picture of the *Buffalo* in the centre.

The *Daily American* reporter, who planned to make the flight with King, also allowed how he would take a supply of the stamps with him to put on all the letters that he intended to "drop from the clouds." An extract from John F. B. Lillard's correspondence of 1894 reports that 300 of the 5-cent *Buffalo* Balloon Stamps were printed in June of 1877 from a single die and that 23 were used.

King died in 1914 at eighty-six. He had made 458 balloon flights in his lifetime, the first being at the Fairmount Water Works in his home city of Philadelphia. An innovator, he developed, in 1858, the technique of using the drag rope to slow a balloon's motion and he also took the first aerial photographs from a balloon in the United States. In a book that he had published in 1879 about his memorable balloon voyages, he touched very briefly upon the Nashville–Gallatin flight but made no mention of the mail he carried or the special stamp that pictured his balloon. It seems obvious that his interest lay more with his aeronautical than his postal accomplishments. Even the newspaper accounts of the day mentioned ballast and what the passengers had for dessert, but not a word about the attractive blue adhesive that many have called the world's earliest air mail stamp.

Printed in tête-bêche blocks of 20, Buffalo Balloon stamps took letters only as far as S.A. King could fly his balloon. Upon landing, "Buffalo" mail was given to the P.O. at Gallatin, Tennessee, and franked again with U.S. postage for transport to destinations. Thus, these privately produced balloon adhesives, of which only 23 were reportedly used in 1877, were semi-official in nature. This cover's unique date-stamp–cachet proves that King's flight was still remembered exactly 100 years later.

Elements of a postal cover

An envelope, or *cover*, enfolds, protects and directs a letter to its destination. A veritable data bank, a cover is the best means of encountering and preserving postal, and frequently cultural, history and may have a more fascinating story to tell than the written communication contained within. The diverse markings and adhesives affixed to an envelope explain to the trained eye much about the origin of the piece of mail as well as about its passage within one or more postal systems.

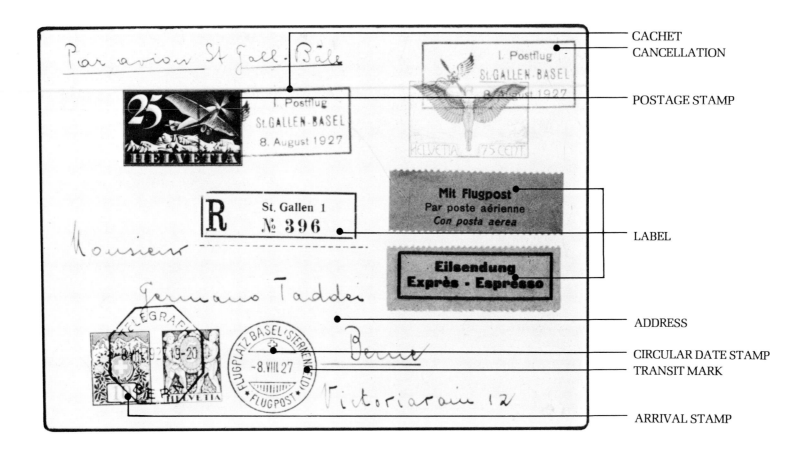

CACHET
CANCELLATION
POSTAGE STAMP
LABEL
ADDRESS
CIRCULAR DATE STAMP
TRANSIT MARK
ARRIVAL STAMP

Air mail glossary

ADDRESS: the stated destination of a cover. Confirms the correctness of the prepaid postage used.

ADHESIVE: normally, a synonym for postage stamp. To be distinguished from printed postage valuations found on postal cards and other forms of official postal stationery.

AIRMAIL: an adhesive specially issued to pay an air mail rate. Most governments do not limit their use exclusively to air mail.

ARRIVAL STAMP: a postal marking, usually a circular date stamp, applied to indicate arrival at a transit point or at destination. Generally found on the reverse side of a cover as a backstamp. Key confirmation that a cover traveled on a particular flight.

CACHET: a special inscription or design applied to a cover for informational, commemorative or decorative reasons. Two rectangular cachet-date stamps cancel the airmails on Swiss first flight cover on opposite page.

CANCELLATION: postal marking applied to a stamp to make it unusable for further prepayment of postage. Applied by machine or by use of a hand stamping device.

CIRCULAR DATE STAMP: often used in combination with a canceller, the c.d.s. indicates when and where a cover enters a postal system. This Swiss cover has rectangular, octagonal and circular date stamps all used for different purposes.

CORNER CARD: the return address portion of a cover. Corner cards are generally printed, hand-written or typed.

COVER: an envelope that has carried a letter through a mail system and still bears its stamp(s), label(s) and/or postal marking(s).

DEFINITIVE: a postage stamp issued for "permanent" use on ordinary mail.

HANDSTAMP: to be distinguished from a postal marking applied by machine. Size, location and decorative considerations often determine whether or not a handstamp is to be used.

LABEL: any gummed adhesive on a cover that is not a postage stamp. The Swiss cover (opposite) displays labels for Air Mail ("Flugpost"), Special Delivery ("Eilsendung") and for the St. Gallen registry number (#396).

OVERPRINT: any word, inscription or design printed on the face of a postage stamp.

PERFORATONS: small holes punched out between stamps to facilitate their separation from each other.

POSTAGE STAMP: the small adhesive that almost always prepays an established fee for transporting a letter from a sender to a receiver. A mint stamp is one that has not yet been used for postal purposes. Postage due adhesives (lower left corner of the Swiss cover shown opposite) are a form of postage stamp applied at the post office of destination to make up for insufficient postage applied earlier.

PROVISIONAL: a postage stamp issued for temporary use.

SEMI-OFFICIAL STAMPS: those stamps issued under other than government auspices, but to which some degree of official recognition is accorded.

SEMI-POSTAL STAMPS: issued stamps displaying two values, one value indicating an authorized postage fee and the other value representing a surcharge, returns from which are directed to a government cause, charity or officially sponsored activity.

TRANSIT MARK: a postal marking, usually in the form of a date stamp, applied in the postal system at some point of handling or redispatch between the starting place and the final destination.

Air mail on schedule

The Paris Ballon Poste was hardly the first utilization of pigeons to carry messages between distant or inaccessible locations. Recorded history is replete with instances where these swift, trained birds were enlisted by men to speed their communications over barriers of distance, topography, and military threat.

The first service of flown mail on a regular schedule (the Ballon Poste had been a semi-regular one) involved a pigeon-mail service in the United States. Operated by two brothers from Los Angeles by the name of Zahn, a homing pigeon service providing daily contact between Santa Catalina Island and the city of Los Angeles was established in 1894. With the advent of wireless telegraphy still a few years away, and, given the prohibitive cost of laying a forty-eight-mile cable between the two points, the Zahns saw the commercial possibilities of operating their service for the benefit of the island's summer populace.

In addition to brief private messages transmitted and delivered at the sender's risk, the Zahn service also occasionally summoned doctors in time of emergency. An exchange of news between the island and the *Los Angeles Times* also developed, as can be seen in this chatty column printed in the *Times* called "From Catalina":

> Avalon (Catalina Island) August 26—(Special to The Times by Homing-pigeon "Clara W" of the Catalina Carrier-pigeon Service: time 1:01.) This morning's steamer bore away a large number of over-Sunday visitors, among them Dr. J. H. Utley and E. P. Bryan, who was accompanied by his wife and daughters, who have been spending some time here...Mrs. J. W. Campbell went over to attend the tin wedding celebration of Mr. and Mrs. S. P. Mulford and will remain until Thursday.

Charges for a message ranged between fifty cents and one dollar and hardly supported the enterprise, which ceased after three full summers of dependable operation.

A similar pigeon service was organized in New Zealand in 1897 and obtained greater notoriety than the Santa Catalina one. Known as the Original Great Barrier Pigeongram Service, it was instituted to make up for the lack of communication between Auckland and Great Barrier Island, located in the Pacific Ocean some sixty-five miles northeast of Auckland. The service began full operation in the fall of 1898, and within a year a rival organization had also begun calling itself the Great Barrier Pigeongram Agency. Both firms competed for business over the same general route.

Messages sent by the Great Barrier Island Pigeongram companies were written on flimsy, tissue-like forms and sealed with their own privately issued stamps. Because of their rarity, both the stamps and flown messages are extremely valuable. It is the use of adhesive stamps that distinguishes the Great Barrier

On January 12, 1957, France issued this 15-franc commemorative honoring the homing pigeon, the winged messenger that had played a vital role in her history and that of the world.

Island pigeon services and causes them to be well remembered by philatelists today.

Toward the end of the nineteenth century, it seemed that balloons had given way to pigeons as carriers of the air mail. Soon, however, it appeared that the pigeons would be superseded by rigid airships.

Posters announcing the first daily "air mail" service between Los Angeles and Santa Catalina Island were distributed on the mainland, and at key locations around the island, in 1894. Various hazards encountered by the pigeons prompted the Zahns to offer a money-back guarantee for messages that failed to arrive, and to dispatch three birds bearing identical message sets to help ensure delivery. New Zealand's Great Barrier Pigeon Post advanced the art by introducing pigeon post stamps in 1898.

Success by perseverance

Hugo Eckener, a young economics professor, was at work on a manuscript when his housekeeper entered his studio to announce an unexpected visitor. "It is Graf Zeppelin, Herr Doktor!" Puzzled as to why the old man, popularly referred to as the Crazy Count, would come to see him, Eckener prepared to meet him in the drawing room.

Eckener had seen Count Ferdinand von Zeppelin several years before on July 2, 1900. At that time, Eckener had been asked by the editor of *Der Frankfurter Zeitung* to prepare an article on Zeppelin's airship projects. Not particularly interested in doing a story about a man many regarded as an old crank, Eckener nevertheless joined hundreds of others—townspeople, tourists, scientists, fellow journalists—on the crowded shores of Lake Constance (Bodensee) near Friedrichshafen to witness the maiden flight of Zeppelin's first airship.

As the small steamer *Buckhorn* began to tow the dirigible barge from its lakeside hangar, cheers could be heard along the shore. Finally, the full 425 feet of the huge cigar-shaped craft had cleared the hangar, and the *Buckhorn* turned into the breeze. Suspended from the bulging fabric bag of the airship were two gondolas joined by a catwalk from which hung a weight that could be moved forward or aft to alter the balance and thereby the pitch of the craft when airborne. In the gondolas were five busy men, including the Count.

After the pair of four-cylinder Daimler engines were started and the tow ropes were cast off, the *Luftschiff Zeppelin No. 1 (LZ-1)* rose majestically to approximately 1,300 feet and moved slowly but steadily over the lake. Suddenly, her movable weight's sliding lever broke, causing the craft to pitch forward, nose down toward the water. Almost immediately the hull was punctured by a stake protruding from the surface of the lake. Her flight was abruptly over. That evening the *Buckhorn* towed the remains of Count von Zeppelin's dirigible back to the hangar.

In the July 4 edition of *Der Frankfurter Zeitung*, Eckener mused about the disappointment:

> The entire countryside was invited to attend a performance, to which, as soon became apparent, not even the overture could be played successfully.

Eckener concluded his article by suggesting that LZ-1's debut was "much ado about little."

A few years later on January 17, 1906 Zeppelin's second airship was tested. Again Eckener was on hand to cover the story. This time, after rudder cables jammed and engines flooded, and following an out-of-control drift, the LZ-2 was finally brought to a ground landing on a dairy farm near Kisslegg, a railway junction. Then a windstorm impaled the craft on some trees. When Eckener prepared his report on LZ-2's fate, he seemed prepared to take Count von Zeppelin's work a shade more seriously than

he had in 1900 and ventured several suggestions about airship design, stress factors, and aerodynamics. It was this article that brought Zeppelin into Eckener's drawing room a few week's after it appeared in print.

Wasting little time with formalities, Von Zeppelin flourished a copy of the newspaper and asked the professor upon what basis he could make such remarks. It turned out that in addition to having his doctorate in economics, Eckener was also an amateur engineer. Further, he was a sailor and, being brought up in Flensburg, knew something about wind pressure. The two men had a brief discussion about airship theory, engines, and the fact that there were no carburetors yet designed for aeronautical purposes. When von Zeppelin took his leave, Eckener remained confused about the visit. Of one thing he was sure: Count von Zeppelin was not so crazy after all.

Three days later Eckener received and accepted a dinner invitation from von Zeppelin. This informal meeting at the *Deutsches Haus* in Friedrichshafen was the beginning of a close association that was to link the names of Zeppelin and Eckener together. With his plans to court military support as well as to create an airship for passenger, mail, and freight service, von Zeppelin's aim was to recruit the power of Eckener's pen—not as an adversary this time, but as a useful ally.

On October 9, 1906, *Luftschiff Zeppelin 3* (LZ-3) made its maiden flight, and the results were greatly encouraging. The ship stayed aloft for over 2 hours and flew a distance of 60 miles before returning to its hangar. LZ-3 steered easily; it had overcome 25 mph headwinds. Overnight, everyone, including Kaiser Wilhelm II, sought to identify with the new Zeppelin rage. So popular was the design that any rigid airship from this point on would be generically referred to as a "Zeppelin," regardless of the manufacturer. The Reichstag now willingly granted him financial aid for a fourth ship, and the army proposed to order it provided the ship could remain airborne for twenty-four hours and transverse a specified route in that time. Later, the LZ-3 met these specifications and became the first rigid airship of the Prussian Army.

By mid-year 1908, LZ-4 was ready for a 24-hour duration trial. The largest airship ever built, 446 feet long, 42 feet wide and containing a total of 519,000 cubic feet of flammable hydrogen, the LZ-4 had two 104 hp Daimler engines that propelled it at 40 mph as it left Friedrichshafen at 7:00 A.M. on July 1, 1908, on a 12-hour test flight along the Rhine and Aar valleys and over the Alps into Switzerland. The *Schweizerfahrt*, as this flight was known, flew over crowds in Manzell, Luzern, and Zurich. Church bells pealed in greeting. In the evening, LZ-4 returned to its floating hangar on Lake Constance.

Attendant upon the airship's popularity, and about the time of

Contemporary postcard showing LZ-4 in flight over Luzern commemorated the famous Schweizerfahrt.

Luftschiff „Zeppelin" über Luzern.

this first Swiss flight, small postage-stamp-sized labels, known as vignettes, began to appear throughout Germany. Usually, the vignette design would picture an airship in flight or a portrait of von Zeppelin. Vignettes frequently had values inscribed on them, but these were not postal values, nor did the vignettes possess any franking value for mail at this time. Essentially, vignettes were printed for commemorative or commercial purposes or to help raise money in a nationwide collection intended to underwrite further airship development in Germany.

The earliest flight commemorated by a vignette was, in fact, the Swiss flight of July 1, 1908, but this vignette (3 × 2⅛ inches in size) appears to have been part of an historical series published a few years after the flight. The vignette, in this instance, depicts the LZ-4 in flight over Lake Constance. Another known vignette that carried a picture of von Zeppelin seems to have been printed about the time of the first Swiss flight. In both cases, the vignettes are quite rare and, though not of postal usage, represent interesting documentation of early airship development.

Some of the vignettes from the national collections period (1900–1909) contain inscriptions that reflect an intense German interest in Count von Zeppelin's work and flights. One reads: "Men will talk about the Zeppelin as long as the mountains stand on their ground." Another, around a framed portrait of Zeppelin, was inscribed: "Good Air—Happy Ascent—Success by Perseverance."

On August 4, 1908, the LZ-4 was entirely devoured by flames, without loss of life, during her duration trials near the village of Echterdingen. With trembling hands and a broken heart, Count von Zeppelin turned away from the wreckage. Every flag in Friedrichshafen flew at half-mast that evening.

The next morning, however, a dejected Ludwig Marx, Zeppelin's chief engineer, was chided for being depressed by an immaculately dressed and apparently jovial von Zeppelin. Confused, Marx was escorted into a room where he was shown a table piled with telegrams and money. What seemed the end of the Zeppelin dream had suddenly become another stage of growth as public contributions from the German people poured in. Von Zeppelin would fly again in even greater splendor, thanks to what has been referred to ever since as "the miracle of Echterdingen." Like the legendary Phoenix, the Zeppelin company continued to revitalize itself and prosper in the face of incredible setbacks.

Dr. Hugo Eckener was again summoned to Friedrichshafen where he met thirty-five-year-old Alfred Colsman, scion of the family-owned firm that supplied aluminum to von Zeppelin. Prior to the Echterdingen disaster, Colsman had offered to assist in a reorganization of the Zeppelin company. Because of the Count's rising popularity, money was continuously being contributed for further development of the rigid dirigible as a transportation entity. It was decided that a trust organization called the Zeppelin Stiftung (Foundation) would be incorporated to act as parent company for the Luftschiffbau Zeppelin. Eckener was offered a leading position as public relations director, economic advisor, and legal counsel of the new organization.

Thus, in 1908, a solvent Zeppelin company was in operation. This company had an early boost when LZ-3 (subsequently known as Z-1) was delivered to an army unit at Metz. LZ-5 was

19

then being built for the army and LZ-6 was on the drawing board. The proposed LZ-7 and LZ-8 designs were being adapted for transportation service.

The following year, von Zeppelin, Eckener, and Colsman outlined their plans for an airline using dirigibles. This announcement roughly coincided with a mammoth international aviation exhibition, planned at Frankfurt, the German center of aeronautical activities, for the period of July 10 to October 10, 1909. Von Zeppelin was a member of the international Honor Committee for the exhibition, along with the great Swedish explorer Roald Amundsen, French aeronaut Comte de la Vaulx, and F. C. Bishop of the Aero Club of America. During the exhibition, which involved balloons and airplanes as well as airships, von Zeppelin and Eckener invited all the German mayors to discuss with them the proposed airline and to bid for the privilege of a connection at their city. With a sense of the dramatic, von Zeppelin chose to land his LZ-5 at the exhibition on his way to make delivery of the ship to the German army at Cologne.

As part of the impressive series of events at the Frankfurt exhibit, the German postal administration provided a special aviation postal cancellation, the second of its kind in Germany. They also produced cacheted postal cards with the regular 5-pfennig postage stamp imprinted in the upper right-hand corner. The cards were not intended as flown souvenirs, but as mailing pieces to publicize the event. Blue and yellow gummed labels in the colors and style of the cacheted postal cards were also used to promote the three-month convention.

At Frankfurt-am-Main the Deutsche Luftschiffahrts Aktien Gesellschaft, known more commonly by its acronym DELAG, was founded in November 1909 to build air terminals in Frankfurt, Berlin, Hamburg, Potsdam, and Dresden. Thus, the world's first passenger-mail transport airline service was established between German cities. Contrary to popular belief, these prewar flights of DELAG did not run on a regular schedule, due to the comparative slowness of the craft and its inability to fly in inclement weather.

DELAG began mail and passenger service on June 22, 1910, with LZ-7, an airship appropriately christened *Deutschland*. She was able to carry 20 passengers and 1,000 pounds of mail. At the helm of the first commercial lighter-than-air flight in the world was von Zeppelin. He flew the maiden voyage from Friedrichshafen to Dusseldorf in 9 hours, covering over 300 miles. "Zeppelin dirigibles" would become household words throughout Germany and as well known by name as the transatlantic ocean liners of the same era.

In August of 1909, Dr. Hugo Eckener had become an airship commander, which came about mainly as a result of Alfred Colsman's realization that after von Zeppelin's retirement—and

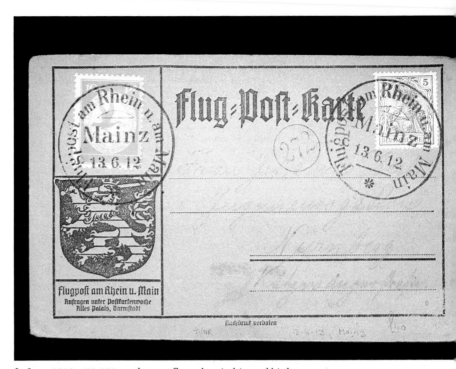

In June 1912, 460,000 cards were flown by airship and biplane between Rhine/Main River cities in support of an infant-care center. Taken aboard the Schwaben (LZ-10) at Mainz, this card displays appropriate cancels, and a 10-pfennig airmail sold for the occasion. Below: A recent German semi-postal pictures the LZ-1.

20

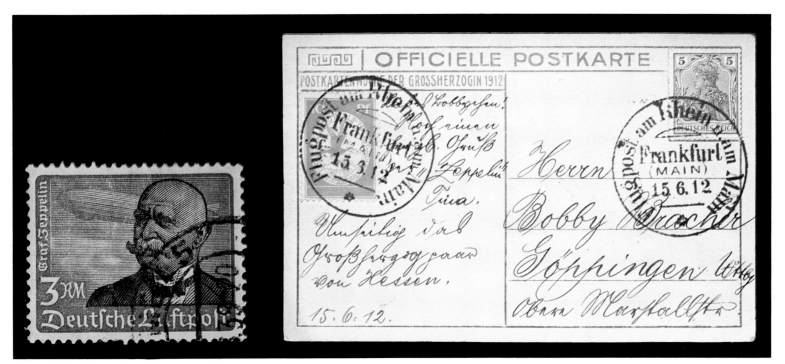

Another variety of Rhine/Main postcard cancelled at Frankfurt (on the Main River) on June 15, 1912. Germany's first postal tribute to her "Conqueror of the air" von Zeppelin was this 3-mark airmail issued in 1934.

he was then well on—someone with aerial experience as well as administrative ability would be needed at the helm of the Luftschiffbau. Eckener was not only a yachtsman who understood navigation, wind currents, and weight distribution, but also an engineer with the judgment necessary to make precise and effective decisions in the air. The fact that he had knowledge about economic and promotional factors along with a quick mind for assimilating technical details made it clear that he was the man to be groomed as von Zeppelin's successor.

The tenth Zeppelin, called the *Schwaben*, was piloted by Eckener on its inaugural flight in 1911. The *Schwaben* carried 3,622 passengers in the eleven months she operated, totaling 230 flights. With a cruising speed of 47 mph, she was the first of the DELAG line to fly against adverse weather conditions. She became DELAG's "Lucky" ship until she was damaged in a violent gale in Dusseldorf and caught fire. Fortunately, Captain Dorr, her commander, was able to unload the passengers before the storm struck. LZ-11, the *Viktoria Luise*, sister ship of the *Schwaben*, entered service in 1912. The *Hansa* (LZ-13) and *Sachsen* (LZ-17) were added to the fleet in 1913. Over 37,250 passengers were carried on 1,600 DELAG flights. The ships were aloft 3,200 hours and flew over 100,000 miles entirely without injury to any traveler.

Once DELAG was in full operation, much mail was processed aboard the airships and received special "on board" cancellations that named the airship and the date on which the dispatches were handled. Since the Zeppelin fleet also resorted to the practice of dropping mail in certain locations where they did not land, some Zeppelin mail, prized by philatelists, has both the on-board cancellation of the airship that carried it and the local postal mark of the city or village where it was dropped. Passengers who flew aboard the DELAG vessels were encouraged to send specially printed postcards to friends and family, and these were processed en route and often delivered into the postal service at the flight's destination.

When war broke out in August 1914, all German passenger-carrying flights abruptly ended. The three remaining Zeppelins —*Hansa, Viktoria Luise* and *Sachsen*—were taken over by the army and navy and used extensively as training ships before they were finally declared obsolete. The Zeppelin designs between 1914 and 1918 continued to grow in size, range, and durability. They were able to reach a ceiling of 25,000 feet, when necessary, but due to their limited speed and their vulnerability to weather conditions, the task of carrying mail was eventually turned over to the speedier and more versatile heavier-than-air craft—the airplane.

The Wrights' well-kept secret On August 8, about thirty persons were assembled at the Hunandiéres racetrack near Le Mans. On the fringe of the gathering were two wide-eyed youngsters, who had pedalled their bicycles to the track to observe some unusual happenings. What had attracted them was the rumor that an American inventor was there to assemble, and perhaps attempt to ascend in, a flying machine. When the boys reached their destination, the American—a man named Wright—had completed a series of adjustments on his strange-looking craft and had received help in setting it on its "catapult" rail.

One of the boys, Henri Delgove, later recalled that many of the spectators were "official people," likely members of the Aero-Club de France. "But," he reported, "brats like us were not permitted on the course, so my friend and I climbed a fence just behind the grandstand and waited to see what would happen." What did happen not only startled the youthful pair but all of the adult witnesses as well. For after the balky engine was finally made to run smoothly and after a heavy weight was dropped from the wooden tower beside the rail, the machine darted forward on the rail and quickly rose from the ground.

The Wright *Flyer* sailed forward in a straight path, then began a graceful but unexpected swing to the left. Upon reaching a safe altitude, Wilbur Wright completed one full circle followed by a second. At one point the plane made a wide sweep of the field, passing behind the grandstand. To everyone's relief the plane appeared again under perfect control. Soon Wilbur landed near his takeoff point, only to become engulfed by a laughing, jubilant, and nearly hysterical group of Frenchmen.

Entirely caught up in the wild excitement, the young boys dashed forward toward the American, then suddenly turned and rushed for their bikes. Racing down the road toward Le Mans, they called out to everyone in sight: "Il vole! Il vole!" Thus did two enthralled messengers spread the word for which all the world awaited. "He flies! Monsieur Wright flies!"

In spite of the marvelous and significant strides in manned heavier-than-air flight made in France by men like Alberto Santos-Dumont, Louis Blériot, the Farman brothers Henri and Maurice, and Léon Delagrange, the French were nonetheless electrified by Wilbur Wright's performance at Le Mans. When the American again flew from the same field two days later, after having declined to "break the Sabbath," the tiny crowd of 30 had exploded to over 4,000. This time a figure-eight inspired the spectators to ecstasy. Speaking for all of France's pioneer aviators, René Gasnier was heard to say, "We are as children compared with the Wrights."

The initial flights made by Wilbur in France and simultaneous demonstrations in the United States by Orville were the first

2

Man spreads his wings

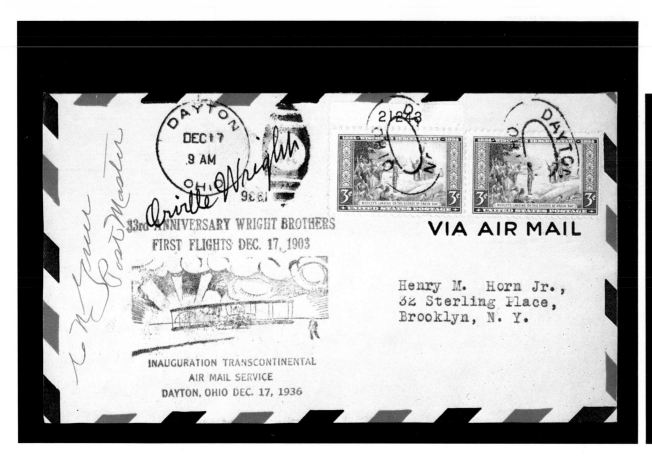

public confirmations of all that the brothers claimed to have accomplished at Kill Devil Hill near Kitty Hawk in 1903. Free, controlled and sustained powered flight had been achieved almost five years before the world received proof of it. Having at last taken "the wraps" off their airplane, the Wrights became headline news the world over. Wilbur modestly advised his sister Katherine in a letter from Europe to "tell Bubbo [Orville] that his flights have revolutionized the world's beliefs regarding the practicability of flight. Even such conservative papers as the London *Times* devote leading editorials to his work and accept human flight as a thing to be regarded as a normal feature of the world's future life."

This sudden rise of the Wrights to the pinnacle of world attention in 1908 through their invention and refinement of a practical flying machine was hardly a matter of chance. On the contrary, these two inventors had followed a well-defined and careful plan. Sons of Methodist Bishop Milton Wright of Dayton, Ohio, they simply drove themselves to become the most knowledgeable and thorough aeronautical technicians the world had yet known.

24   Wilbur and Orville had first been drawn to aviation through the work of others, notably that of the great German glider enthusiast Otto Lilienthal, one of history's first true pilots, and the Parisian-born American engineer Octave Chanute. With Chanute's help the brothers obtained and ingested every book, article, and treatise they could get their hands on that related to flight. They spent hours observing birds. Out of this expanding familiarity with the problems and theoretical considerations associated with flight grew a firm conviction that a practical flying machine was indeed within their grasp. Far from discouraging them in the least, the tragic deaths in glider crashes of Lilienthal in 1896 and his British disciple, Percy Pilcher, in 1899, only served to reinforce the brothers' unyielding determination to press on with their self-appointed task.

The Wrights continued their study of available aeronautical literature. Where gaps appeared in the science, as in the case of screw-propeller theory, they undertook their own experiments in their bicycle shop in Dayton, and wrote the book themselves. When automotive manufacturers declined their invitations to supply a light-weight engine to power their airplane, they went ahead and produced their own four-cylinder horizontal engine, built in accordance with the best existing automotive principles. Most importantly, Wilbur and Orville isolated and then described the various problems associated with controlled flight with a greater clarity than had ever before been achieved. Once the problems were identified, the way was prepared for experimentation: first with kite models, then in 1900 with man-carrying gliders, and finally with their powered aircraft in 1903.

Opposite: This first-flight cover signed by Orville Wright celebrates the 33rd anniversary of his epic flight at Kill Devil Hill, as well as TWA's inclusion of Dayton on its transcontinental route in 1936. Beside the cover, a pair of U.S. 31¢ (overseas air mail rate) stamps which initiated in 1978 a series honoring U.S. aviation pioneers. Above: Three of many issues relating to the Wrights. The 20¢ U.S. parcel-post stamp of 1912 is the world's first authorized postage stamp to feature an aircraft in its design. The U.S. 2¢ commemorative came out in 1928 on the occasion of an international aviation conference, and the Latvian semi-postal of 1932 sought to help raise money for wounded Latvian aviators.

Orville would state in later years that the development and ordering of a body of reliable information leading up to their successful assembly of the first practical flying machine remained unquestionably the achievement that gave the brothers their greatest satisfaction. Most people, however, would eventually remember Orville's brief 12-second flight of slightly more than 100 feet into the face of a 25 mph wind at Kill Devil Hill near Kitty Hawk, North Carolina. It was approximately 10:30 of a Thursday morning, December 17, 1903, when he accomplished what no man before him had. He had made a free—untethered— flight that was powered, controlled, and sustained. As the brothers finished their work on that memorable morning, Wilbur achieved in their first *Flyer* an astonishing flight of 852 feet.

In the years that immediately followed upon their little publicized success at Kill Devil Hill, a skeptical world paid the brothers very little attention. Too many crackpots and charlatans had claimed mastery of flight only to disappoint. Even the Wrights' home paper, the Dayton *Journal*, hopelessly confused the initial reports emanating from the outer banks of North Carolina and failed to investigate further those events.

Undaunted by the lack of attention, the brothers continued their work in relative privacy. For more than a year they furthered their aeronautical experimentation, virtually undetected on some rented acres several miles east of Dayton. Called Huffman Farm near Simms Station, the pasture was a ninety-acre prairie of soft grass completely encircled by forty- and fifty-foot trees. There was little road traffic and the area was sparsely populated. The only distracting factor was a turn-around point for the electrified interurban trolley near the northwest corner of the pasture. Wilbur and Orville dealt with this intrusion simply by learning the trolley schedule and limiting their flying to periods between the arrival of trolleys.

One hundred five flight attempts were made at Huffman prairie in 1904 in their improved aircraft, *Flyer II*, and another fifty flights the following year. As a measure of their progress, before the Wright brothers imposed a two and one-half year moratorium on their flying while they attempted to interest various governments in their machine, Wilbur, on October 5, 1905, made thirty circles of the hidden field in a period of 39 minutes and was forced to descend only when his fuel supply ran out. The Huffman prairie years were far more than a period when the inventors tinkered with and improved their airplane; they were also most surely the years in which Orville and Wilbur assiduously taught themselves to fly.

Through the years airmen have wondered about the reasons for the Wright brothers' success when countless others before them had failed. Aviation historian Robert B. Johnston suggests that a key factor was that the brothers had each other. By work-

A Wright aeronautical student, and later a member of their exhibition flying team, Phil O. Parmalee pioneered aerial express in 1910, flying a bolt of silk from Dayton, Ohio, to Columbus, Ohio on November 7th. Before crashing to his death in a Wright biplane, Parmalee also piloted an early U.S. mail flight at Sacramento, California on March 2, 1912.

ing smoothly together they obtained a synergistic multiplication of individual inputs, and they were able to argue technical questions without friction because of the profound respect they had for each other. Further, as each brother took his turn in the air, a totally demanding task, he always had a competent observer on the ground to help him analyze the experience. Johnston referred to this "remote type of dual control" as perhaps the very factor that gave the Wrights an edge in the dawning years of the air age.

This ability to be open to the contributions of others, a sign of innate humility, certainly served Wilbur well at Le Mans. Taking stock of what French airmen had to offer about inherent stability of an aircraft, the Wrights moved the elevators from the front to the rear of their newer models and eventually attached wheels to the landing skids. The brothers' Model B became known as the *Headless Wright* and was the winged vehicle for many pioneer mail flights.

Postal recognition seemed grudgingly offered to Wilbur and Orville Wright, considering the magnitude of their contribution. To be sure, their plane appeared on the twenty-cent value of the parcel post series of stamps issued by the United States Post Office in 1912 and 1913, but this stamp was one of a series depicting methods of transporting mail and was not a special tribute to the brothers from Dayton. It was not until December 1928, as the twenty-fifth anniversary of Orville's momentous "first flight" approached, that the United States Post Office department officially called attention to the fact that the first practical flying machine had been invented by Americans. In addition to issuing a two-cent red commemorative stamp that pictured the Wright *Flyer* in flight between the Washington Monument and the Capitol in Washington, D.C., the department also authorized a special flight of mail from Kitty Hawk to celebrate the anniversary. Most of the more than 27,000 pieces of mail carried by famed pilot Dick Merrill sported an officially authorized cachet that had been prepared for the occasion. Spain was the first foreign nation to picture the Wright *Flyer*. The stamp, issued as part of an aviation series that came out in 1930, ironically saluted not the Wright Brothers, but the Brazilian pioneer flier Santos-Dumont, who had flown publicly in France even before Wilbur took to the skies near Le Mans.

1909

A vessel monoplane from Calais Just short of a year after Wilbur Wright's breathtaking exhibition at Le Mans, on July 25, Louis Blériot, a stocky Frenchman with brooding eyes and a generous moustache, flew an aircraft of his own design across the English Channel, thus linking Great Britain and continental Europe for the first time by airplane. The flight was 23½ miles from Calais to Dover. In crossing the Channel, Blériot vanquished a seemingly timeless symbol of Britain's impregnability. "There are no islands anymore!" Awareness of this fact accompanied the surge of emotion over the trip itself.

Preceding Blériot's 1909 flight, French aviation had a rich and varied history. As the originators of manned balloon travel, the French still remained the world's chief proponents of ballooning. They also evinced a keen interest in dirigibles, being constantly aware of and intrigued by von Zeppelin's work.

Thanks to a timely visit to Paris in 1903 by Franco-American glider expert Octave Chanute, French attention was more forcefully directed to prospects for heavier-than-air, power-driven machines. Chanute did author a series of articles on gliders for French magazines. More importantly, though, he spoke to members of the Aero-Club de France, recounting the lessons he had learned in association with the Wright brothers at Kitty Hawk. His enthusiasm helped mightily to convince the French that mankind was on the verge of successfully attaining mechanical flight. Responding to Chanute, a few Frenchmen of wealth, who were governed by patriotic inclinations, contributed fresh motivation for French aeronautical technology to take the great leap forward.

The first confirmed flight of a heavier-than-air machine in Europe occurred on October 23, 1906, and was made by Alberto Santos-Dumont, the thirty-three-year-old son of a wealthy Brazilian coffee grower. He was awarded 3000 francs put forward by Ernest Archdeacon. The memorable flight, made at the Bagatelle cavalry grounds in Paris, covered almost 50 meters (164 feet) and was carefully measured by officials of the Aero-Club de France and the more recently formed Fédération Aéronautique Internationale. There were two unique aspects of the boxy-looking flying machine constructed by Santos-Dumont for his trail-blazing effort; he flew his model XIV *bis* standing up and he flew this plane in a tail-forward position. The XIV *bis* was powered by a 50 hp Antoinette 8-cylinder water-cooled engine.

The next major step in European aviation came less than fifteen months later when one of France's most distinguished pioneer fliers won a substantial prize of 50,000 francs at Issy-les-Moulineaux, on the Left Bank in Paris. Flying a Voisin biplane, Henri Farman dramatically proved French progress in flight by navigating, at an altitude of approximately 10 meters, a closed-circuit course of one kilometer, and thereby gaining the Arch-deacon de la Meurthe prize. The Farman flight took place on January 13, 1908, only a few months before Alexander Graham Bell's Aerial Experiment Association achieved the first *public* flight in the United States. Farman's was a controlled flight that provided immense satisfaction to the many Europeans who persisted in asking, and rightfully so, whether the Wright brothers had flown at all. Not until August, at Le Mans, would Wilbur finally silence all skeptics.

Farman provided yet another entry for the French record book on October 30, 1908. Flying a biplane of his own design, he made a spectacular cross-country excursion from Bovy near Chalons, where he maintained a workshop, to Reims, a distance of 27 kilometers. This venture was the first cross-country flight in Europe and is commemorated today by a marble monument placed at the spot in Reims where Farman landed.

Most of the French pioneer aviators—the Voisin brothers (Charles and Gabriel), Henri and Maurice Farman, Ferdinand Ferber, Léon Delagrange and others—sided with the Wrights in believing that biplanes offered the best possibility for powered flight and claiming that single-surface machines would sacrifice too much lift to be effective. A Romanian living in Paris, Trajan Vuia, however, had a different view. His own self-made craft was fashioned in the style of a monoplane. Driven by a quite primitive-in-structure 25 hp motor that ran on carbonic acid gas, the tiny plane was credited with some short leaps into the air at Montesson in 1906. Vuia's monoplane was the first in the world of its kind.

When Louis Blériot, a wealthy manufacturer of acetylene headlamps, turned his attention to aeronautics in the early 1900s, he established contact with Gabriel Voisin and had Voisin's factory incorporate some of his ideas in their machine. These efforts by Blériot were conspicuous failures, and his inventive mind quickly swung away from the biplane configuration to an investigation of monoplanes. No doubt Vuia's limited success at Montesson had impressed him.

As others before him had done, Blériot centered his flying activities at Issy-les-Moulineaux and began to build a series of experimental machines that he numbered consecutively. Like everyone else at the time, he was wrapped up in basic questions of design and mechanics. Propellers, for example, involved questions of material, shape, number, and size; were they to be tractor or pusher types? Were rudders and other control elements to be placed up front, as they had been on the Santos-Dumont model XIV *bis*, or to the rear as a "tail assembly"? The talented Blériot achieved several patentable breakthroughs in the methods of control that he devised. But his actual progress in the air was embarrassingly slow. Model after model of his production series either was wrecked or proved ineffective from the

27

start. Having reached the limit of his projected expenditures for research, Blériot had to make a decision. Fortunately for him and the world, his creative decision bore unexpected fruit.

With a string of costly crack-ups behind him, Blériot decided to consolidate his gains, make use of all that he had learned, and build one final monoplane with which he could go after some of the cash prizes then being dangled before the eyes of enterprising, and often daring, aviators. One prize that seemed within reach to him was the 500 pounds offered in October 1908 by Lord Northcliffe's London *Daily Mail* for the first heavier-than-air craft flight across the English Channel.

The trip, which had been undertaken successfully by balloonists on thirty-five occasions since Jean-Pierre Blanchard and an American from Boston, Dr. Jeffries, had led the way in 1785, went without any takers in the year 1908. As a result, the newspaper renewed the offer in 1909, increasing the prize to 1,000 pounds and requesting notice of at least forty-eight hours in advance of any attempt to capture the prize.

Several pilots were determined to try the Channel crossing after the weather improved in the late spring of 1909, but no one actually did until a Frenchman of English descent by the name of Hubert Latham had a go at the prize on July 19. Latham had actually traversed the Channel as a passenger in a balloon with his cousin.

Latham had only been piloting airplanes since February. In that month the well-to-do sportsman had been introduced by a mutual friend to Léon Levavasseur, engineer and boatbuilder turned aircraft designer. Levavasseur asked Latham to become his chief pilot. Being attracted to the Antoinette monoplane, a design of Levavasseur's, Latham was quick to accept the offer, seeing in aviation the challenge of an untried sport.

Unfortunately for Latham, the engine of his impressive machine failed when he was seven miles out from the French coast, and he had to ditch his Antoinette in the Channel. After twenty minutes in the water, he was rescued by the French destroyer escort *Harpon* and returned to his base at Sangatte, near Calais. He quickly ordered another plane to be rushed to him from the Antoinette factory at Puteaux, having learned that a former associate of Levavasseur's, Louis Blériot, was now officially in the wings waiting for a try at the Channel.

Early in July, Blériot had won several minor prizes with the eleventh and twelfth models of his monoplane. His left foot was burned twice by an uninsulated exhaust pipe. Nevertheless, he had made one flight in July that covered 42 kilometers, and this convinced him that he was ready to take his Blériot Model XI on the quest for glory. He arrived on crutches at the Hôtel Terminus overlooking the harbor at Calais on July 21. His takeoff field was being prepared at Les Baraques, a village nearby.

28

Many nations, like San Marino and the Malagasy Republic, have pictured the Blériot monoplane on their postage stamps, as did his native France on her 1934 airmail issue.

Opposite: *This cover, the 76th in a Smithsonian Institution series, pays tribute to airman Blériot on the 70th anniversary of his Channel flight. Below: Latvia depicted a 1909 Blériot XI in a climbing attitude in its 1932 aviation set, while Monaco overprinted a silhouetted Blériot monoplane on a 1925 postal issue in 1933 to create its first air mail stamp.*

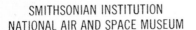

SMITHSONIAN INSTITUTION
NATIONAL AIR AND SPACE MUSEUM

Milestones of Flight Commemorative Series

Number 76

70th ANNIVERSARY
First Crossing of the English Channel
by an Airplane
Blériot XI Piloted by Louis Blériot
July 25, 1909, Calais, France

MILESTONES OF FLIGHT
Smithsonian Institution
Nat. Air & Space Museum
Washington, D. C. 20560

Blériot's Model XI, prototype of undoubtedly the most famous monoplane of the pioneer era, was powered by a 3-cylinder fan-type radial engine of 25 hp produced by Alessandro Anzani, a manufacturer of lightweight engines for motorcycles. Blériot had selected for his Channel flight a 6.6 foot propeller made of laminated walnut.

Due to a delay caused by unfavorable wind conditions, Latham had sufficient time to ready his replacement plane at Sangatte, thus assuring that a two-man race would ensue. While the pilots nervously waited for a turn in the weather, newspapers on both sides of the Channel played an editorial guessing game, wondering who would leave first. Excitement was at a fever pitch.

Suddenly in the dark of night on the 25th, Blériot was awakened at 2:30 A.M. by his associate, Alfred Leblanc, and advised that the wind had settled. It was calm; the stars were shining brightly. Pulling on his dark blue overalls, he decided to go ahead with his flight.

After a small dog was killed running into his whirling propeller, and after he had completed a short test flight to confirm the smooth operation of his craft, Blériot departed.

The London *Daily Mail* edition of July 25, 1909, offered this personally dictated account of the aviator's experience under a dateline of Dover, Sunday, July 25:

At 4:30 we could see all round. Daylight had come…My thoughts were only upon the flight, and my determination to accomplish it this morning. 4:35! *Tout est pret!* Leblanc gives the signal and in an instant I am in the air, my engine making

29

Several nations, including the United States, Switzerland, Great Britain, South Africa, Australia, and Bolivia, employed Blériot-type airplanes to transport their first aerial mail. Type XI had a takeoff weight of 661 pounds and flew at 47 mph.

1,200 revolutions—almost its highest speed—in order that I may get quickly over the telegraph wires along the edge of the cliff. As soon as I am over the cliff I reduce my speed. There is now no need to force my engine.

I begin my flight, steady and sure, towards the coast of England. I have no apprehensions, no sensations, *pas du tout*. The *Escopette* [a torpedo destroyer escort] has seen me. She is driving ahead at full speed. She makes perhaps 42 kilometres [about 26 miles] an hour. What matters? I am making at least 68 kilometres [42½ miles]. Rapidly I overtake her, travelling at a height of 80 metres [about 250 feet]. The moment is supreme, yet I surprise myself by feeling no exultation. Below me is the sea, the surface disturbed by the wind, which is now freshening. The motion of the waves beneath me is not pleasant. I drive on. Ten minutes have gone. I have passed the destroyer, and I turn my head to see whether I am proceeding in the right direction. I am amazed. There is nothing to be seen, neither the torpedo-destroyer, nor France, nor England. I am alone. I can see nothing at all—*rien du tout!* For ten minutes I am lost...

And then, twenty minutes after I have left the French coast, I see the green cliffs of Dover, the Castle, and away to the west the spot where I had intended to land. What can I do? It is evident that the wind has taken me out of my course. I am almost at St. Margaret's Bay and going in the direction of the Goodwin Sands.

Once more I turn my aeroplane, and describing a half-circle, I enter the opening and find myself again over dry land. Avoiding the red buildings on my right, I attempt a landing; but the wind catches me and whirls me round two or three times. At once I stop my motor, and instantly my machine falls straight upon the land from a height of 20 metres [65 feet]. In two or three seconds I am safe upon your shore. Soldiers in khaki run up, and a policeman. Two of my compatriots are on the spot. They kiss my cheeks. The conclusion of my flight overwhelms me.

Both in England, and later in Paris, Blériot was praised and acclaimed by millions. The press printed tribute after tribute to the modest, soft-spoken Frenchman, sensing the full implications of his victory over the Channel. In no clearer terms had the dawn of international air travel been announced and the essential character of the twentieth century been predicted than by this single flight from Calais to Dover.

In amusing contrast to all the laudatory comments made to their guest by the grateful English were these routine words of the customs men who approached Louis Blériot following his breakfast in Dover on the morning of July 25.

> I certify that I have examined Louis Blériot, master of a vessel "Monoplane," lately arrived from Calais, and that it appears by the verbal answers of the said master to the questions put to him that there has not been on board during the voyage any infectious disease demanding detention of the vessel, and that she is free to proceed.

And proceed Blériot Model XI did from the grassy field beside Dover Castle to a salon at Selfridge's department store in London, where thousands filed past her over a three-day period to view the tiny craft whose exploits had had such far-reaching effect.

On the evening of July 27, Hubert Latham made another attempt to cross the Channel, but failed again when his Antoinette VII went into the water just a few miles short of his goal. Had Latham succeeded on this flight, he would have been the first man to fly a letter across from France to England, for he carried a communication addressed to Lord Northcliffe from Walter Windham, an Englishman who had observed the preparations of both Blériot and Latham at Calais. The letter was recovered on the 27th, but it was too water-soaked to offer for delivery, according to its writer.

PRICE LIST of
BLERIOT XI MONOPLANES
(CROSS CHANNEL TYPE)

Assembled machine, Less power plant; for 50-100 H. P. motor,	**$1,000**
Assembled machine, Less power plant; for 25-50 H. P. motor,	**$850**
Not assembled machine, Less power plant; but all parts shaped and cut to size, accompanied with working drawings for assembling,	**$600**

SPECIFICATIONS

FOR 25-50 H. P. MOTOR	FOR 50-100 H. P. MOTOR
SPREAD OF WINGS, 28 FEET 9 INCHES	SPREAD OF WINGS, 34 FEET
LENGTH OVER ALL, 24 FEET 10 INCHES	LENGTH OVER ALL, 27 FEET
CHORD MAIN PLANES, 6 FEET 8 INCHES	CHORD MAIN PLANES, 7 FEET
SUPPORTING SURFACE, ABOUT 160 SQUARE FEET	SUPPORTING SURFACE, ABOUT 200 SQUARE FEET
SEATING CAPACITY, 1 PERSON	SEATING CAPACITY, TWO PERSONS

ALIGHTING GEAR AND CONTROL, GENUINE BLERIOT	IMPORTED MUSIC WIRE AND ROEBLING EXTRA
COVERING: NAIAD PREPARED CLOTH	FLEXIBLE CABLE USED THROUGHOUT
CASTINGS and FITTINGS of ALUMINUM and STEEL	SHELBY SEAMLESS STEEL TUBING USED

ONLY HIGHEST QUALITY OF MATERIAL AND WORKMANSHIP USED THROUGHOUT

ALL ASSEMBLED MACHINES GUARANTEED TO FLY

PRICES OF PARTS

Main planes, assembled, uncovered, $125; covered, $200 | Vertical rudder, assembled, uncovered, $20, covered, $28
Stabiliser and elevating planes   " $50;   " $72 | Fusilage and Chassis Assembled   -   -   - $200

Control, $125. STEERING WHEEL, SEAT, FOOT YOKE, DEVICE, OPERATING, WARPING OF MAIN PLANES, ELEVATING PLANES AND VERTICAL RUDDER.

Alighting Gear, $200. 3 WHEELS, TIRES, CASTINGS, ETC., ALL BRAZED AND ASSEMBLED

Aluminum lever, operating elevating planes	$5		Aluminum brackets, holding stabiliser to fusilage, pair,	$6.
Aluminum knees chassis, set (4)	$3.		Aluminum device, changing angle of incidence of stabiliser,	$10.
Steel tubes, connecting main spars of fusilage, (4)	$3.		Aluminum sheeting, cutting edge, main planes, shaped, each,	$6.
Aluminum hinges, vertical rudder, pair	$5.		Steel cable adjusters, on spars, main planes, set (16)	$8.
Steel U bolts	each 15 cts.; $10. per 100		Turnbuckles, Size No. 1, per 100, $25; No. 2, per 100,	$35.

WORKMANSHIP GUARANTEED

LET US KNOW YOUR WANTS

AMERICAN AEROPLANE SUPPLY HOUSE

GARDEN CITY, L. I. N. Y.   P. O. BOX 100   TEL., 213 GARDEN CITY

Hudson, Fulton, and Glenn H. Curtiss

When early aviation developments in the United States are considered, only one name deserves to rank with the name of Wright—Glenn Hammond Curtiss. Like Blériot, Glenn Curtiss made early and spectacular flights that inspired Americans and seemed to herald a new era in the nation's, and even the world's, affairs. Before Curtiss passed away in 1930, he had at least five hundred inventions to his credit, mostly in the field of aviation, and his company produced many of the airplanes that would later fly the mail.

Curtiss was ever true to his two ruling passions: speed and engines. His fascination for speed was initially exercised on a bicycle over the rolling hills of upstate New York; by the time he reached his teens, he was the champion racer in his corner of the world. While still under twenty, he opened a cycle shop in his hometown, much as Bishop Wright's sons had done in Dayton. As his business prospered and the demand for Curtiss-built bicycles grew, the youthful entrepreneur opened two other outlets, in Bath and Corning, and then turned his attention to motorcycles and engine-powered racing. So intensively were his energies applied to the pursuit of speed that Curtiss, using one of his own machines, raced to a world's record for motorcycles, at 136.3 mph in Ormond Beach, Florida, in 1907, a record that stood for seven years.

With this triumph the Curtiss reputation for the development and manufacture of lightweight engines became established, eliciting wide-ranging contact with firms and individuals who had problems or needs relating to power sources.

Enlisting the Curtiss know-how about this time was a group of men under the leadership of the Scottish-born inventor Alexander Graham Bell. Bell had assembled at his home near Baddeck, Nova Scotia, a group of three talented young fellows to discuss theories about systems of aerial locomotion. While Bell himself was specifically interested in the possibility of using gigantic tetrahedral kites for flying, his associates were more closely involved with the question of manned, heavier-than-air flight. At the suggestion of Mrs. Mabel Bell, a lady of insight and financial means, the group in September 1907 formalized its structure and adopted the name of the Aerial Experiment Association (A.E.A.). Under the chairmanship of Dr. Bell, the association also stated its aim—to build a practical airplane able to carry a man and be driven through the air under its own power. Glenn Curtiss became the association's director of experiments, the members having realized that an expert on engines would be a prime need of any effective developmental team.

The associates in the A.E.A., in addition to Dr. Bell and Curtiss, were two recent mechanical engineering graduates from Toronto University, F. W. "Casey" Baldwin and John A. D.

32

Glenn Curtiss memorabilia includes this 1930 cover carried on a Curtiss Condor that retraced the Hudson River flight of 1910. Curtiss died in a Buffalo hospital at the age of 52, shortly after the re-enactment flight.

Opposite: Thomas Scott Baldwin, seeking to utilize Glenn Curtiss's genius with light-weight engines, brought his powered balloons to Hammondsport c. 1905. Curtiss gains his first experience of flight in a Baldwin balloon. Later, his attention turned to the airplane, in which craft speed and maneuverability were greatly enhanced. His intensity registers clearly as he handles the controls of the June Bug.

A smiling Curtiss prepares, with friends and dignitaries, to retrace in a Condor his 1910 route from Albany to New York City.

"Doug" McCurdy. The fifth member was Lieutenant Thomas Selfridge, on detached duty from the United States Army.

After the A.E.A. had reached a temporary resting point in their work with kites, they decided to move operations to a part of the Curtiss plant in Hammondsport, New York, where further experimentation in service of their goal could be supported by those facilities and where the climate was more suited to flight trials of heavier-than-air craft. Here, after a number of test programs with a glider were completed, the group was prepared to try their collective hand at building a motor-powered flying machine. The basic scheme of the organization permitted each man in turn to constellate his own design ideas, with the advice of the others available to him, and to carry those ideas forward to the point of actual construction of a workable machine.

The first A.E.A. prototype produced was a pusher plane, having its propeller located behind the wing. It was, for the most part, the creation of Selfridge, and it was called the *Red Wing*. On a cold day in March of 1908, the *Red Wing* was flown by Baldwin for a distance of 318 feet, 11 inches, over the solid ice-covered surface of Keuka Lake, near Hammondsport, finally coming down in a lurch because it lacked any stabilizing control. Since the Wright brothers' flights at Kitty Hawk and Dayton had been secretive and unpublicized, the *Red Wing's* brief sortie of 20 seconds' duration could fairly be called the first public flight in America.

Baldwin's own design was tried next. On May 22, 1908, the *White Wing*, piloted by Curtiss and equipped with rubber tires for a land takeoff, flew over a thousand feet and landed safely in a plowed field near the takeoff point. This result was cause for great elation among the A.E.A. members and came after many failures caused by hard landings. Much had been learned from the failures, and changes in structural detail had led to Curtiss' encouraging trial of May 22.

A key change in control was suggested by Alexander Graham Bell as the group eagerly began work on a new machine under the leadership of Curtiss. This airplane, also a pusher type, was to be called the *June Bug* and incorporated for the first time a pair of adjustable lateral surfaces at each wing tip that were activated by a system utilizing a shoulder harness and the body (shoulder) movements of the pilot. This system of rudders (or ailerons) later became the focus of a prolonged patent infringement suit brought against Curtiss by the Wrights; Orville and Wilbur claimed the A.E.A. control system copied their own exclusive wing-warping method of control.

The initial salvo of the law suit, however, did not occur until after Curtiss and his *June Bug* had scored a major breakthrough in the annals of early aviation history in the United States. So successful were the *June Bug's* early test flights that A.E.A.

33

members decided to enter the plane in the first stage of an annual competition sponsored by *Scientific American* magazine. A silver trophy was to be presented for one year for the first public flight in the United States that equalled or exceeded a straight-line distance of one kilometer [⅝ of a mile].

Early on the morning of July 4, 1908, with members of the New York and Washington, D.C. sections of the Aero Club of America in attendance, it appeared that unfavorable weather would allow the assembled crowd to celebrate a dampened Independence Day but not a successful try for the coveted trophy. However, by late afternoon, conditions had improved, and in the calm twilight hours Glenn Curtiss took *June Bug* aloft. Traveling just under a mile, in the first officially observed and measured flight in the United States, Curtiss became the *Scientific American's* first winner. He had traveled a distance of 5,090 feet at an average speed of 39 mph. One residual benefit of his fine performance came three years later when his *June Bug* flight was considered sufficient reason to present him with the first pilot's license issued in the United States.

The A.E.A. during its short life, produced another plane based on a design worked out by Doug McCurdy. Known as the *Silver Dart*, the plane eventually made aviation history when it became the first heavier-than-air machine to fly in Canada. This flight covered ¾ of a mile, and it was accomplished near the Bell home at Baddeck, Nova Scotia, with McCurdy at the controls.

When the Aerial Experiment Association disbanded in March of 1909, having achieved its stated purpose, the group was short one member. Lieutenant Selfridge had become the first aviation fatality in history. His death occurred while flying as a passenger with Orville Wright during a demonstration for the army at Fort Myer, Virginia. Their plane's right propeller sliced through a wire and splintered, causing the plane to plunge to the ground from an altitude of 75 feet. Wright was seriously injured in the crash.

McCurdy and Baldwin returned to Canada to form a short-lived aircraft manufacturing company but later joined Glenn Curtiss in the United States, with McCurdy becoming one of the first to take a flying boat into the air in 1910. Alexander Graham Bell returned to his kite experiments and died in 1922.

Curtiss, now fully immersed in his aviation activities, continued to explore new frontiers. The year 1909 proved a watershed period for the former bicycle mechanic from Hammondsport. On June 16, he won the second leg of the *Scientific American* trophy by flying the first plane entirely of his own design—the *Golden Flier*—a distance of 24.7 miles around a triangular course on Long Island, New York, before an enthralled crowd of officials and spectators. He thus established an American distance record. In August, competing against the best pilots

in Europe and the sole entrant from the United States, he won the Gordon Bennett Cup speed event in his Reims racer at the first international aviation tournament at Reims. An average speed of 46.5 mph brought him the precious victory.

It was shortly after Curtiss returned home from France, with the genuinely enthusiastic plaudits of Reims still ringing in his ears, that he learned of the New York World's extension of its munificent offer of $10,000 to the first individual to make the Fulton Flight between Albany and New York City. This prize, undoubtedly sanctioned by World publisher Joseph Pulitzer would now be valid until October 10, 1910. Early in 1910, Curtiss decided to try for the prize and quietly instructed his chief mechanics, Henry "Henny" Kleckler and Damon Merrill, to start work on a new plane specifically for this effort. A primary motive for Curtiss related to his knowledge that if he won this test, he would undoubtedly win the third leg of the Scientific American trophy, thereby qualifying for permanent possession of the prestigious award. It seemed unlikely that anyone would exceed the distance, approximately 150 miles, required by a Hudson River flight, and whoever achieved it would automatically establish a new cross-country record for the Western Hemisphere.

Curtiss and his production team worked on several modifications of the Reims racer as they built the new plane. Due to his wife's concern about the dangers of such a long flight over water, Curtiss installed flotation gear on the Albany Flier, as the new craft was called. This included an airtight metal cylinder placed under each lower wing and a series of five inflated air bags, made out of balloon cloth, strung out underneath the full length of the plane. The plane was to be powered by 52-hp engine of 8 cylinders, the most powerful that Curtiss had yet produced, and its wing span was increased by several feet over that of the Reims racer. A shoulder yoke, such as Curtiss placed in his June Bug, moved the ailerons, the pilot's wheel activated rudder and elevator surfaces, and his feet controlled the ignition and throttle. Once ready, the plane was tested in the air over Keuka Lake and landed cautiously near the shore. Everything seemed in good order.

Toward the end of May, Curtiss was ready to undertake his Hudson River flight. He divulged his plans to the media in Albany on Monday, May 23, then left his mechanics there to assemble his plane while he, his wife, and two close friends took the Hudson River dayboat to New York City the following day. In addition to taking a very careful look at his planned route from the bridge of the side-wheeler and questioning the captain about landmarks and weather conditions, he wished to locate two permitted landing sites along the way, and to meet Aero Club officials in New York City in order to be sure that their

35

monitoring of his flight was properly arranged. He was delighted to have his old friend and fellow pilot, Augustus Post, assigned as an official observer, with him on the train ride back to Albany on Wednesday, May 25.

Anticipating a departure on May 26, excited crowds began to converge on Albany, and Curtiss was entrusted wth a letter that Albany Mayor James B. McEwan asked him to take into the air early the following morning. The state legislature, having just wound up a session, stayed in Albany the evening of May 25 in hopes of seeing a takeoff the next morning. But it was not to be on May 26. The plane was simply not ready to go then, even though the weather was ideal. Nor could Curtiss depart on May 27 or 28 due to treacherous wind conditions.

Mostly in response to the expressions of impatience which greeted him at every turn, Curtiss was led to make these comments to newsmen on May 27:

> Some day laymen will learn enough of the air game to allow us our leisure in preparing without growing impatient. They don't understand what there is to do, and how tedious and long the task becomes. But if some of them had spent hours planning every precaution they could conceive of, and then in a trial flight had found that they failed totally because some little, insignificant thing they had overlooked went wrong, they would see the need for fussing away as we have day after day in making ready.
>
> I have never undergone the strain of so long a flight as I am now called up to make. It takes both hands and my body all the time to operate the machine, and there is no such thing as taking leisure aloft for such a task, for instance, as putting on a pair of gloves. One can't handle the craft even on the smoothest gliding with a single hand.

Curtiss had always felt that Sunday was his lucky day, and so Sunday, May 29, proved. After a hasty breakfast with his party at the Ten Eyck Hotel, he donned a brown leather jacket, his visored cap, worn backwards, and motorcycle racing goggles and took to the air from Van Rensselaer Island at 7:02 A.M. For a change, the capricious Hudson Valley weather seemed ideally calm. The aviator later recalled "It was a perfect summer day...I felt an immense sense of relief...the motor sounded like music." Only a small handful of people were on hand to witness the long-awaited takeoff.

In contrast to the Albany send-off would be the magnitude of the welcome he was about to receive at New York City. After some 2½ hours of flying, with a stop at Poughkeepsie, a pass

over West Point—where the cadets waved their caps in salute, and another stop at Inwood on the estate of financier William B. Isham, Curtiss found himself over the Hudson River with the breathtaking sight of Manhattan Island spread out to his left and the busy tidal estuary before him. He was suddenly aware of automobiles trying to keep up with him in a losing race down Riverside Drive. He saw ferryboats and great ocean liners with their railings crowded with people waving. Thousands were watching his plane from rooftops and office buildings as he circled the Statue of Liberty and made an easy landing on Governors Island. It was noon on May 29. His flight to New York City, at an average speed of 52 mph, had demonstrated to thousands of Americans that the quickest way to link two cities was through the air.

Indeed, no one surpassed that Hudson River flight through the balance of the year, and Curtiss was permanently awarded the *Scientific American* trophy. During the ceremony at the Aero Club's annual dinner in March 1911, the publisher of the magazine said: "Three names will always remain associated with the history of the river—that of Hudson, the explorer; that of Robert Fulton, the introducer of river navigation; and that of Glenn H. Curtiss, the birdman."

A letter, which Curtiss had carried from Albany on his prize-winning flight and which he had presented to Mayor Gaynor at the *New York World's* banquet in his honor on May 31, 1910, read:

> On the occasion of the first long flight by airplanes in this country, I take the opportunity of sending Your Honor greetings and good wishes.
>
> The great flight, if accomplished, as I hope, will be historic. It is possible, too, that it is but the forerunner of what may in the not too distant future be a commonplace occurrence.
>
> The speed of this new instrument of locomotion seems to fit it admirably for many purposes of service to humanity, especially in the way of rapid communication. So far, however, no letter has yet been carried by this new means, and I am glad that these greetings between us should be the first.

Mayor McEwan of Albany, his own words make clear, was anticipating the advent of air mail. Certainly, the flight of Glenn H. Curtiss between Albany and New York was a milestone in the emergence of practical aviation in America. By achieving the first sustained flight between two major cities, Curtiss was pointing the way to passenger flight and the transport of mail and packages over distances that would some day stretch across the country.

Time of tournaments

Seen in perspective, Louis Blériot's flight across the English Channel, and the Hudson River flight of Glenn Curtiss pointed to more than the widely celebrated fact that the world was entering an age of accelerating interactions due to a revolutionary new method of transport. Blériot's achievement bespoke another change that was hardly recognized in July 1909. The Frenchman's magnificent exploit hinted that the trend of progress in aviation was rapidly shifting away from the United States to Europe, and particularly to France. As one writer has said, "If America was the cradle of aviation, France was the progressive nursery school."

Certainly no nation embraced the sport and the business of heavier-than-air flying more swiftly or more creatively than did the French. And no other year served to illustrate this point better than 1909.

Hardly had the excitement of the Blériot celebrations subsided when the attention in France was focused on the historic city of Reims. There, during the week of August 22 to 29, was held the world's first great international aviation tournament, the first gathering of the world's outstanding planes and pilots. Arranged by members of the prosperous French champagne industry, the meeting was billed as La Grande Semaine d'Aviation, and it provided a full range of tests and competitions that demanded the utmost of men and machines. The lure to participants was a dazzling 200,000-franc prize kitty.

The meet was held on the spacious, open plain of Bétheny, just to the north of the famed cathedral where some of the kings of France had been crowned. Thousands of people swarmed to the sidelines of the landing field, coming on foot and by bicycle and carriage. Almost 3,000 Britons came on a special excursion. Approximately 2,000 Americans made their way to the week-long spectacle. One visitor described the event in these words:

> Thrills we had in plenty. Paulhan flew in a wind blowing at 25 miles an hour, a feat considered astonishing at the time. The spectators seemed to go almost frantic over it. Rougier lost control of his machine, which dashed into the crowd, knocking one man down without injuring him seriously. Blériot, flying in the speed race, had a petrol pipe broken and his machine crashed and burst into flames. Fournier had an accident which destroyed his machine. Both were unhurt.

> That Reims meeting marked a gigantic step towards the conquest of the air and dispelled the doubts of even the most skeptical as to the future of aviation.

If Reims was the social occasion of the season for French society, it proved also the crowning moment for thrills for the aviation fraternity. Not only did the pilots recall their personal wonderment and elation at seeing, for the first time, as many as seven planes in the air at once, but they also remembered the unrestrained and spontaneous response of the spectators before whom they performed their awe-inspiring feats of daring and skill. The pilots would relive, too, the meetings and exchanges that they had with each other about their machines, their experiences, and their ideas.

During the meet, an attrition took place. At the conclusion of the week, a small percentage of the original registration of thirty-five different aircraft were still flying. Pilots had either pushed planes and their power plants beyond limits or had demonstrated a scantiness in assortment of skills. Reims was truly a school of hard knocks, where learning was taking place each moment. During one circuit of the course, Curtiss remembered seeing "as many as twelve machines strewn about the field, some wrecked and some disabled and being slowly hauled back to the hangars by hand or by horses." Because of balky equipment, some pilots never left the ground the entire week. But to everyone's relief, not a single life was lost, not a serious injury was incurred.

Since Reims was the world's first aviation meet on a grand scale, it is not surprising that records were set in almost every event. Often records were made, then exceeded in successive flights. In the altitude competition, Hubert Latham set a new record by taking his Antoinette up to the then astonishing height of 155 meters (508.5 feet). On August 27, Henri Farman, flying his own plane but with a new French Gnôme rotary engine, turned in a remarkable flight of 180 kilometers (112 miles) that required 3:05 hours to win the distance event.

On the final day, attention centered on a special speed race that involved a trophy, a prize of 25,000 francs, and an international championship that was to be contested annually. As a counterpart to a trophy that he had given for ballooning, the wealthy American publisher of the English-language Paris *Herald*, James Gordon Bennett, had now offered a magnificent silver cup to mark the establishment of speed records in a yearly airplane competition. At Reims, much to the surprise of everyone, the Gordon Bennett Trophy was won by Glenn H. Curtiss, the lone American entrant. Curtiss completed his two laps in 15 minutes and 50.4 seconds, traveling at an average speed of about 47 mph in his Reims racer. The French, having been allowed three entrants, the right of every country, fully expected one member of their team to garner the important prize. However, Latham and Eugène Lefebvre turned in considerably slower times on the course than Curtiss. Only Louis Blériot, the final competitor, gave Curtiss a run for his money. Flying his large Model XII, with a new 60 hp British engine installed, Blériot nearly caught the leader. When his time for the course was found to be just 6 seconds longer, the American flag was raised at the judges' stand and the band rendered the American national an

Pioneer air labels and modern stamps together effectively document early aviation history. Shown above are the promotional vignette prepared for the first great aviation tournament at Reims (1909), and a 5-lira commemorative stamp from San Marino (1962) showing the biplane used by Henri Farman to win La Gran Prix de la Champagne at Reims. The trim little cover below was not flown, but prepared as a souvenir of an aviation meet held in Nice in April of 1910. This cover sports a bisected French stamp, a special aviation date stamp, and a promotional vignette, but lacks the organizing committee's special circle cachet.

them. "I cut corners as close as I dared and banked the machine high on the turns," reported Curtiss about his strategy. He also followed a steadily descending flight path.

His triumph represented the first victory for a biplane and the first victory for an American-built craft in international competition. Contrary to American hopes, the first award of the Gordon Bennett Trophy did not presage a bright future for the United States entries in such competitions. The American contribution to aviation's future continued, of course, yet during most of the pioneer period Europeans would lead the way.

The French postal authority was blind to neither the implications of nor the opportunity provided by the Reims attraction. For the duration of the meeting, a special cancellation was made available and used on mail posted at the airfield. This cancellation was hexagonal in shape and carried the words BÉTHENY AVIATION—MARNE, with the date appearing in the center. Today it is much sought after by collectors, for it represents the first official postal recognition of aviation in France. Also, in aerophilatelic collections can be found specimens of an attractive vignette that was sold in conjunction with the Reims week. Not a substitute for regular French postal franking, and in no sense an indicator that a letter was flown (when it appears on an envelope), the vignette was issued by air meet officialdom solely for promotional and souvenir purposes. The design portrays the cathedral at Reims with a biplane flying overhead.

The Reims assembly was the forerunner of many other such events. On a small scale, Italy hosted—in northern Lombardy— her Circuit of Brecia, attracting the likes of Blériot and Curtiss. Won by Curtiss in a splendid effort, this event occurred only days after the proceedings at Reims were concluded. During the same month, September 1909, three aviation meetings were held in Germany: one at Berlin; the famed long-term International Aviation Exhibition at Frankfurt-am-Main; and a week-long tournament at Cologne. The event of Cologne is of enduring interest to aerophilatelists because of an official postal card that was issued there. The card displayed a vignette-like cachet printed in the upper right corner next to the printed postage stamp. While vignettes were found printed on German postal stationery and postal cards as early as 1908, especially in conjunction with lighter-than-air Zeppelin flights, none had been granted space on the card in the area normally reserved for the postage stamp and the cancellation.

A second special French aviation cancellation was prepared for an event that took place from October 3 to 17, 1909. It was the first meet to take place in the vicinity of Paris, and it was held at the airfield of Juvisy, on the railroad line that ran from Paris to Orléans. While undistinguished compared to Reims, the Paris meet did produce one bit of excitement when the pilot of a

Wright biplane, Count Charles de Lambert, departed from the prescribed circuit and carried out the first airplane flight over the French capital. After twice circling the Eiffel Tower, Lambert returned to Juvisy, completing a trip of about 29 miles. For exercising his imagination at the possible expense of the admiring throng below, Lambert received a stern reprimand from the Paris press. His former teacher, Wilbur Wright, thought he should be sent to a home for lunatics. "Everybody has the right to risk his own life, but," said Wright, "not that of other people."

In October 1909, a commercial rivalry of sorts led to simultaneous events being undertaken in Great Britain. The Royal Aero Club sponsored an aviation tournament at Blackpool, attracting the likes of Farman, Louis Paulhan, and Latham. Another group of promoters staged a meeting at Doncaster, which they claimed as the first in Britain, and this was attended by Delagrange, Hubert Leblon, and Roger Sommer. Present at Doncaster was Hélène Dutrieu, one of the earliest female flyers, who would soon establish many records for women in her Farman biplane. Weather hampered both of the English events, but they were instrumental in showing the British public the head start the French had in aviation.

The first important aviation meet in the United States took place between January 10 and 20, 1910. Held at Dominguez Field, a former ranch near Compton, several miles south of Los Angeles, the gathering attracted a few talented flyers including Paulhan from France, the millionaire balloonist Clifford B. Harmon, Glenn Curtiss, and two members of the Curtiss exhibition flying team, Charles K. Hamilton and Charles Foster Willard, the first man Curtiss taught to fly. While balloons and dirigibles filled the air and a large grandstand filled daily with 25,000 cheering spectators, Paulhan was winning the largest share of prize money. On January 12, he set a world's altitude record of 4,164 feet, especially remarkable in view of Latham's winning mark of 508 feet at Reims. On the final day, Paulhan won the endurance contest by completing a 64-mile flight with a few side trips over the Compton plateau in a bit over 1¾ hours to the applause of the crowd. Spectators swarmed around his plane at the meet's end, carrying him from the flying field on their shoulders.

The winter weather in central Europe early in 1910 led the pilots to warmer climates or to indoor work on their aircraft. In February, an aviation meeting was held at the Heliopolis Airfield near Cairo. This, the first tournament on the continent of Africa, attracted nine French pilots, including Hubert Latham, who came with three different Antoinettes. The famous German pilot Hans Grade was also present with a plane of his own manufacture. The postal officials of Egypt cooperated with the sponsors of the meeting and made available a special postal

cancellation, reading Heliopolis Aerodrome in both Egyptian and English. Promoters even raffled off a Blériot machine and offered a secluded observation gallery for harem ladies in order to assure the gate.

Beginning with two events in April along the French Riviera, at Cannes and at Nice, where visiting Russian pilots took the top prizes, the French aviation scene of 1910 was off to a busy start. Almost every other week a city somewhere in France was promoting a local tournament, leading up to a repeat of the great Reims international meet in July. With all of this activity in France, it is ironic that a small meet at Lanark, near Glasgow, Scotland, produced two important world's records in August—a 77.67 mph speed mark and a 6,621 foot altitude record.

It is clear that the European aviation tournaments and meetings of the 1909–10 period helped to accelerate the progress of airplane design and to create an ever-growing supply of trained aviators. Through these important events, the world had come to realize, as Lloyd George remarked; "Flying machines are no longer toys and dreams; they are an established fact. The possibilities of this new system of locomotion are infinite."

OFFIZIELLE POSTKARTE N° 1

ILA

INTERNATIONALE
LUFTSCHIFFAHRT
AUSSTELLUNG
FRANKFURT A/M 1909

39

3

Era
of pioneers

A flying mail dream comes true Early in the year this entry appeared in an Indian newspaper: "Rudyard Kipling dreamt of a *great flying mail* through the sky to New York, but Capt. Windham has succeeded in actually reproducing this movement on a small scale." Windham's small-scale replica of Kipling's imaginative dream was small indeed. It involved an airplane flight (with mail) of about five miles. But it was witnessed by thousands, and it had the blessings of a government.

The ties between man's unfolding history in the air and his transport of written messages have always been close. Despite the fact that airplane development centered itself in the United States and Europe, the first officially flown mail in a heavier-than-air machine occurred deep in the heart of Asia. It is surprising but true. Behind this evolutionary anomaly was an Englishman, who believed deeply in the commercial future of aviation.

Walter Windham, a motor-car producer and racer, was one of a handful of men in England who had taken aviation quite seriously from the start. In addition to building a biplane of his own design and founding the first airplane club in Great Britain, Windham also took an active interest in aviation as it developed across the Channel in Europe. He was one of two Englishmen present in Calais to observe Latham's and Blériot's preparations for their flights, and he formally participated with the organizers of the first international aviation meet at Reims in 1909. As the official who registered the pilot entrants there, he publicly decried the fact that only one of these flyers—George Cockburn—was British.

At the time of his cross-Channel triumph, Louis Blériot had been presented, in addition to his many other awards, a gold cup, offered by Captain W. G. Windham to commemorate the occasion. Windham, in a revealing insight into his thoughts about the 1909 era, expressed these views of the Blériot achievement:

> This crossing had an immense influence on the public mind, particularly in Great Britain. All through the centuries we had been effectively separated from the Continent by the Channel. When Blériot sped through the sky to Dover we had to realize that the "silver moat" was no longer defensive in the older sense. The people of England had to realize, whether they liked it or not, that the world was moving into a great phase of flying, and that it would be imperative for us to devote ourselves just as energetically to airfaring as, in the past, we had done to seafaring and the motor-car.

Toward the end of 1910, Walter Windham was invited by the government of the United Provinces of India to take part in their annual commercial and cultural exposition at Allahabad in February of 1911. He was asked to bring planes and pilots and to make demonstration flights to help advance Indian understand-

41

Far right: Three applications of Sir Walter Windham's special postal marking identify this cover as from the world's first official transport of mail by airplane. Properly backstamped at Allahabad on February 18, 1911, the cover made its way from the tiny post office at Naini through the regular Indian posts to its destination. With the cover is the high value of a three-value commemorative series issued by India in 1961 to mark the golden jubilee of her historic first aerial post; the low value appears above.

lem in the form of large, sharp thorns which were found abundantly in all corners of the landing field. Tires on the planes punctured easily and had to be repaired after almost every landing attempt.

During the course of his stay in Allahabad, Walter Windham was approached by the chaplain of the Holy Trinity Church in that city. "The respected clergyman...asked me if I could help him to raise funds for his new hostel, and it occurred to me that this could be done by inaugurating an aerial post." And thus the idea of the world's first official airplane mail was born.

The Postmaster General of the United Provinces, Sir Geoffrey Clarke, and the director-general of the post office in India both granted approval for mail to be officially received and specially cancelled prior to transport by one of Windham's planes. The public was invited to deliver stamped and addressed mail to the chaplain of the church, enclosing either sixpence or six annas with each letter to be posted by air. Or it was possible to hand a letter to a postal official at the tent hangar at the parade ground, paying the extra cost at that time. The surcharge was donated to the Oxford and Cambridge Hostel for Indian students. The letters all received the special cancellation and were readied for a flight that was supposed to take place on February 20.

The special mail flight was actually made on February 18, 1911, two days earlier than planned. Thousands of Indian citizens viewed Pequet's takeoff, as did United Provinces' governor Sir John Hewett and his wife. The departure was well attended for reasons other than advance publicity and the attraction of the exhibition itself. At least one million Indian visitors were in Allahabad at the time to observe the religious festival of Hartel, the occasion for the washing away of sins in the sacred waters of the Ganges. Further, Indian people were greatly drawn to aviation happenings because of a legend, very much alive in their cultural tradition, which emanated from the sacred Vedas; the final days of the earth's existence were supposed to occur one thousand years after a man descended to earth in a mode of flight.

Flying one of the two Sommer-type biplanes from the parade ground, Pequet made history by carrying approximately 6,500 letters and cards on the first authorized air mail carry. The flight itself, for reasons of safety and convenience, was limited to about 5 miles, Pequet coming down near the jail in the town of Naini, on the outskirts of Allahabad. Here the mail was turned over to postal officials for surface transport to destinations all over the world. Pequet's journey to Naini had required all of 13 minutes.

The special postmark used on the Allahabad mail was quite distinctive. "The die for it," wrote Windham, "was cut at the insistence of the Government of India, and I had the honor of

ing of the airplane and the young art of flying. "Confident as to the future of aviation," wrote Windham, "I decided to give up my motor business and booked a passage to India in 1910, taking with me two flyers, Messieurs Pequet, a Frenchman, and Mr. Keith Davies, an Englishman." He also took with him eight airplanes—two Sommer-type biplanes with 45 and 50 hp engines and six Blériot-style monoplanes, powered by 35 hp 3-cylinder Humber engines. One of the monoplanes eventually received a gold medal award, being on public display throughout the Allahabad exhibition. Except for the display model, the planes were housed in a tent-like canvas hangar situated on the parade ground that overlooked the Ganges River.

Henri Pequet actually made the first airplane flight from Indian soil while testing one of these planes at Allahabad in December 1910. Other flyers arrived in India about this time. Baron de Caters flew in Mysore and Rangoon, and Jules Tyck in Madras in February 1911. After the Allahabad stay the Windham team proceeded on to Bombay for other appearances before they departed India for home.

Several flights were made by Henri Pequet and Keith Davies in keeping with the wishes of the United Provinces Exhibition Committee. The biplanes performed well at Allahabad, but the monoplanes, with engines of lower power outputs, did not seem to operate well in the heavy warm air made increasingly turbulent at ground level by the landing field's proximity to the Ganges and Jumna rivers. The flyers encountered another prob-

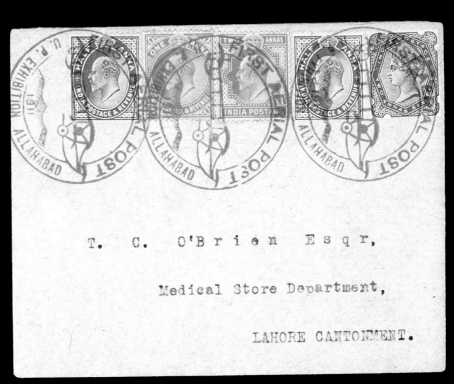

drawing the design, the silhouette of a biplane in flight over the mountains of Asia." The postmark had been made at the postal works in the city of Aligarh and was reported to have been destroyed immediately after Pequet's mission was accomplished.

Among the mail carried were a number of picture postcards depicting Pequet and his biplane. These were autographed in advance by the pilot and sold at a price of one rupee each, again for the benefit of the Oxford and Cambridge Hostel. The signed cards are extremely scarce and much coveted by aerophilatelic collectors the world over.

The organizing committee of the United Provinces Exhibition used the occasion of the air mail to send letters of greeting to European royalty and to prominent people in Great Britain. Walter Windham sent the following letter concerning the Allahabad air mail to the man who had just ascended the throne of England, King George V:

May it please Your Majesty:
I have the honour to request that you will be graciously pleased to accept the enclosed as a souvenir of the first official air post which was dispatched from the United Provinces Exhibition at Allahabad, and carried by aeroplane under the Government Post Office regulations, 20th February, 1911, under cover bearing the impress of the first air post.

I have the honour to be, Sire,
yours most obediently,
Walter Windham

Within a short time, the following reply was received:

Dear Sir,
I am commanded by the King to thank you for the letter received from India by this mail bearing the inscription 'First Aerial Post,' which will be an interesting addition to his Majesty's collection of stamps.
Yours truly,
Clive Wigram

Among the congratulatory letters sent to Windham after Pequet's flight was one he valued greatly and which reached him almost at once. It was dated the very day that Windham's creative idea for air mail was carried through, and was written on the stationery of an Allahabad hotel. It read:

Dear Captain Windham,
Allow me to congratulate you and your associates upon your successful demonstration of the practicability of establishing a postal service through the air.
Yours sincerely,
Alexander Graham Bell

In 1961, India issued a series of three postage stamps on February 18 commemorating the fiftieth anniversary of Henri Pequet's brief but momentous flight with mail and the first official cancellation prepared for mail to be flown. Pequet, who became France's eighty-eighth licensed pilot in 1910, lived to be 86 years old, dying at Vichy in 1974.

First Nordisk Flyvepost

That the world was ready to embrace heavier-than-air craft early in the new century, there can be no question. Within forty-eight hours after his celebrated Channel crossing in 1909, Louis Blériot's aircraft factory had received close to a hundred orders for planes like the one that had made history. It was inevitable that demonstration flying events would continue to multiply around the world. First airplane flights were recorded in no less than twenty-five different nations in the years of 1909 and 1910. Blériot planes alone made the first flights in Hungary, Romania, Spain, and Norway. Other flights were made around the globe from Brazil to Japan.

For one very good reason, however, commercial use of the flying machine had to wait a year or two. The reason was horsepower. Initially, the horsepower ratings of the earliest aircraft engines were so low that they provided barely enough power to lift the plane and the pilot. In fact, the lighter the pilot, the better his chance of getting airborne. As engines increased in power, the added weight factor became less critical.

Europe's first experience with air mail took place in Denmark, some six months after the Pequet flight in India. Denmark had been the first nation in the world after the United States to witness sustained flight in a heavier-than-air machine. Just eleven days before Santos-Dumont thrilled Parisians with his epic free-flight of September 1906, Danish engineer Jacob C. H. Ellehammer achieved a tethered flight of 42 meters with his semi-biplane on the little island of Lindholm. Second into the air, the Danes would now claim a second in terms of air mail.

The pioneering effort with flown mail coincided with a flurry of aviation excitement that was sweeping across Denmark in August of 1911. For most of that month a popular German aviator named Robert Thelen had been making headline news with a series of demonstration flights. On September 2, his successful completion of a flight of 2½ hours from Aarhus to Copenhagen stirred the emotions of the Danish public anew. The aviator had traveled 115 miles in his Wright biplane and was surrounded by a wildly enthusiastic crowd who had gathered to watch him land. Copenhagen's chief newspaper *Politiken* gave lead space to this triumph.

In small print, on the same front page that acclaimed Thelen's feat, appeared a brief announcement of the first Danish air mail flight. The same day that the German had performed so admirably, a Danish pilot, also named Robert, was carrying in his biplane some promotional postcards printed by a newspaper in Middlefart. The trip of Robert Svendsen from the city of Middlefart terminated at Fredericia, less than ten miles away across the Little Belt inlet of the Baltic Sea. Although the flight did not actually involve an official transport of mail, Svendsen's plane did participate in the delivery of these cards, which were franked with ordinary Danish postage stamps and which eventually received ordinary postal cancellations when redispatched at Fredericia.

The 150 to 200 cards flown by Svendsen therefore represent Europe's first experimental air mail. Eighty cards were reportedly carried on his return flight to Middlefart, and all of the cards carried in both directions pictured the plane and were signed by the pilot.

This card is a rare specimen of Europe's first experimental air mail. Danish aviator Robert Svendsen carried at least 150 such cards, all signed by him, over a narrow channel of the Baltic Sea to Fredericia on Sept. 2, 1911. The notation at the bottom of each card reads "Fra Belt flyvingen 1911" (from Belt flight 1911).

From London to Windsor

The first United Kingdom aerial mail was conceived as part of the celebrations surrounding George V's ascension to the throne of England in 1911. This temporary service of mail by air has long been termed "The Coronation Air Post."

When Windham returned from Asia to Britain early in the spring of 1911, he was enthusiastic about the possibility of a trial air mail in England and went at once to see the British Postmaster General, the Right Honorable Herbert L. Samuel. Though Samuel favored the idea and was willing to help, he pointed out a technicality that seemed a substantial hindrance to any such effort. A special charge would be required if letters were to be flown in order to help underwrite the experiment, much along the lines of the Allahabad plan. British postal regulations, however, forbade any changes in postal rates without an Act of Parliament.

Faced by this apparently insurmountable obstacle, Windham devised a scheme whereby special postal stationery (envelopes and postcards) would be printed by an Aerial Mail Committee, sold in major London retail shops, stamped with regular postage by the purchaser or the store, dropped in special collection boxes at the point of purchase, and then transported to the Western District Post Office on Wimpole Street for processing. The fees collected at the retail locations for the special stationery would pay all costs, with any excess being given to charity. Processing by the postal service simply meant applying a unique commemorative cancellation to each piece of mail. The committee would then see that the collected mail was taken to the landing field, carried in planes of their hire and, finally, placed in the regular mail stream at the selected landing place. The postmaster general was even to be absolved of any responsibility for loss, delay, or damage to the mail by virtue of a small printed notice in the lower left-hand corner of each piece of air mail stationery.

In a letter to Windham dated May 15, 1911, the General Post Office granted approval for the "conveyance of letters and postcards, [but not of registered correspondence] by aeroplane between the Post Office and the Festival of Empire, Crystal Palace, and certain places in the United Kingdom to be hereafter agreed upon." The letter, signed by one Matthew Nathan, further specified that "the postage stamps would be obliterated by means of a special dated stamp which would include the words '1st U. K. Aerial Post'," and added, "You will no doubt be so good as to call here at an early date to arrange the necessary details."

The necessary details were many. Windham was joined in his enterprise by D. Lewis Poole, Secretary of the Royal Aero Club, and together they arranged for an artist, William W. Lendon, to create the pictorial design for the envelopes and cards. They then arranged to have eleven different commercial firms handle the sale of the special stationery, each firm being supplied with a bright red, wooden aerial mail collection box, manufactured by Windham's own airplane factory at Clapham Junction.

The route of the flights, the choice of pilots, and calendar matters were then considered. Originally, it was felt that the Crystal Palace vicinity in London would be a good terminal point for the post because the coronation-related "Festival of Empire" was to take place in this noted exhibition hall over a number of weeks in the summer of 1911. In line with this plan, Windham obtained royal permission to land the mail at Windsor Great Park in the shadow of Windsor Castle, located just over twenty miles from the center of London. However, when it was realized that the preparations for the post would take more time than expected, the London terminus was shifted from Crystal Palace to London's only air field at the time, the Aerodrome at Hendon. The date for commencing air mail flights between London and Windsor was finally set for September 9.

The organizers wanted to secure the services of the colorful American flyer, Colonel S. F. Cody, who had only recently obtained British citizenship. Unable to do this, Windham and Poole approached the Grahame-White Company, a firm that owned and operated the Hendon aerodrome. Directed by the handsome, well-to-do exhibition pilot, Claude Grahame-White, who had succeeded in winning the second international Gordon Bennett trophy race in the United States the previous year, the Grahame-White Company, it was agreed, would put together a team of pilots and a small fleet of planes that over a period of days would carry whatever air mail was collected from the public.

The team of pilots lined up for the Coronation Air Post included Gustav Hamel, Clement Greswell, Charles Hubert, and E. F. Driver. Windham was elated over Grahame-White's choice of fliers. He later said, "I reckoned we had the best team that could be assembled at the time." Hubert and Driver, a Frenchman and a South African respectively, were well known around Hendon for their fine piloting skills; Greswell, a graduate of the Grahame-White flying school, was then an instructor using a biplane produced by Windham's firm. As for Hamel, Windham respected his ability in the air and considered him the equal of any pilot then active.

For the use of these flying postmen, Grahame-White obtained four planes, two Blériot monoplanes and two Farman-built biplanes. All the aircraft were carefully readied for their important postal task. 45

The design prepared by Lendon and accepted with favorable comment by the organizing officials featured a silhouette treat-

ment of a Farman-like biplane flying over Windsor Castle. The copy-line above the pictorial portion of the cachet read A. D. Coronation 1911/First U. K. Aerial Post/by Sanction of H. M. Postmaster General. In order to encourage multiple purchases of the envelopes and cards bearing the cachet, Windham had them printed in different colors—violet, scarlet, purple-brown, dark brown, deep brown, black, bright green, dull-dark green, and gray. The violet stationery was used at the discretion of the committee, but all the other colors were sold to the general public. On September 8, the first collection of this mail was made by Macnamara's postal van and taken to the Wimpole Street Post Office for the official aerial post cancel. All mail collected in advance of the first flights was dated September 9, the date of planned inaugural flights.

Once the first collections of mail were processed, it was evident from the volume of letters and cards that the first United Kingdom aerial post was going to be a great success. Windham observed that "people were so keen to send letters and cards by this first British Air Mail that in some places I found them queuing up." The public paid sixpence for the cards (or 6½ pence, if stamped) and one shilling for the envelopes (or 1 shilling, 1 pence with stamp).

Six different cancellation devices were used on the mail, all showing the same information except for the die number. Those pieces processed at the Wimpole Street office bore die numbers one through four and were most likely purchased at one of the nine announced store locations in London or at the Aerial Post Committee Secretary's Office, General Buildings, Aldwych. Dies five and six were used at the regular Hendon Aerodrome Post Office for the special mail collected there or for mail sold and deposited at two retail locations on the road from downtown London to Hendon.

Windham wrote later about the mood of people as the day of Great Britain's initial air mail experiment dawned.

Many wanted to take part in this first experiment, but there was skepticism since much was being written about the unreliability of aeroplanes, constant forced landings, and cancelled flights. But there need not have been doubts. The first day of our flying post gave striking proof that a plane handled by an expert could even at that stage of aviation be flown through a wind approaching gale force.

And so it was, when the motor van delivered twenty-three sacks of mail weighing just over 600 pounds to the Hendon Aerodrome shortly after noon on Saturday, September 9. A stiff breeze blew and it was not at all certain that airplanes would fly that day. After an hour's delay beyond the 3:30 P.M. departure time and a trial flight by another pilot, Gustav Hamel had one of the Blériots rolled out to the field to undertake the first flight.

46

Green and white semi-official stamp employed privately to seal tobacco samples flown in February, 1913. Pilot B.C. Hucks, an early exhibition flyer, delivered tobacco tins in northeastern England for the Robert Sinclair Co. of Newcastle-upon-Tyne. Right: An air mail essay of 1923 that almost became Great Britain's first air mail issue.

After receiving the routine papers (a waybill and time sheets) and one bag filled with "privileged" mail—the violet-colored envelopes and cards being sent to the king and queen, other reigning sovereigns, ambassadors, and notable individuals all over the world—Hamel was on his way. All hats were respectfully doffed and a band on hand for the occasion swung into "God Save the King." After a quick pass over Hendon and the assembled crowd, Hamel turned his plane toward Windsor, with the blessing of a rigorous tailwind that pushed him swiftly through the air. The time was 4:58 P.M.

A large crowd at Windsor awaited his arrival. Among those was a postman with a bicycle, ready to carry the incoming mail to the Windsor Post Office for sorting and further dispatch. Less than fifteen minutes after departing Hendon, Hamel completed a tricky landing near the Royal Mausoleum at the Great Park in Windsor. A telegram was sent at once to the king informing him of the safe arrival of the first air mail in his realm.

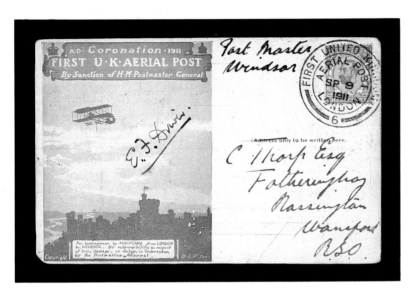

The Farman biplane in flight over Windsor Castle readily identifies cards and covers from Britain's first trial air mail. Though displaying a September 9th cancellation, this slightly worn reddish-brown card flew at a later date from London to Windsor—only violet cards and covers in a "privileged" mail were carried on the first flight on the 9th. This card's special appeal is the signature it bears near the plane, E.F. Driver being one of four pilots who carried mail between Hendon and Windsor in 1911 and the pilot of South Africa's first airmail.

As Hamel's mail was being unloaded at Windsor, aviator Charles Hubert was attempting a second carry of a portion of the mail waiting for transport to Windsor. He was piloting one of the Farman biplanes. His trip, however, was aborted when he was unable to control the plane in a freshened wind.

Since there was no intention to carry mail on Sunday, the next flights were attempted on Monday, September 11. Three airmen—Hubert, Driver, and Greswell—were prepared to make early morning flights that day, hoping to make a dent in the large pile collected at Hendon. Hubert went off first with eight mail bags, but met with misfortune during his takeoff. His machine crashed from forty feet in the air and he was very seriously injured in what would prove to be the only accident of the entire exercise. Rushed to the hospital, he was found to have two broken legs along with other less serious injuries.

Hubert's injuries were to lead to a temporary disruption of the air mail delivery on Tuesday, September 19. With three final bags of London to Windsor mail waiting to be flown, Hamel refused to fly until the organizing committee had paid Hubert 500 pounds in compensation for his injuries. It took several days for notes and authorizations to pass back and forth on the matter and as a result, the delayed bags of mail were not flown to Windsor until September 25 and 26. On the latter date, all the mail processed at the Wimpole Street Post Office had been successfully delivered and the Coronation Aerial Post came to an end.

Mail flights were made on ten different days between September 9 and 26, with a much smaller mail being carried from Windsor to London on two of those dates. The Windsor mail was handled similarly to London's, with "Windsor" inserted in place of London on the two cancelling devices. Windsor had two die numbers, with number one being reserved for privileged mail that originated there and which filled the first bag flown to London by Greswell on Sunday, September 17. Hamel also carried one bag of mail from Windsor on the afternoon of that same day, and both he and Greswell received silver matchboxes with an engraved view of Windsor Castle from the Deputy Mayor of Windsor as a memento of their service.

In all, sixteen flights were made from London to Windsor during the period of the experiment, involving 37 bags and approximately 113,000 pieces of mail. The Windsor mail amounted to about one-tenth of the London mail.

After all expenses and the payment to Charles Hubert were deducted, the first British air mail showed a surplus of 937 pounds. This money was presented to the King Edward VII Hospital at Windsor to endow a bed, over which a brass tablet was placed recalling The Coronation Aerial Post of 1911. Aerophilatelists find that specimens of the flown cards and covers serve today as excellent reminders of an historic series of air mail flights. Especially coveted are the violet cards and envelopes that rode with the first mail carried in each direction. Also prized are the cards that bear the signatures of the Grahame-White pilots and the cards that display commercial advertising on the reverse side. Among the companies that utilized the first air mail for advertising purposes were Schweppes, Ltd., Wright's Coal Tar Soap, and the Gramophone Company.

More than twenty years after this first extended experimental transport of mail by airplane, Lord Herbert L. Samuel, who as Postmaster General of Great Britain had authorized the temporary service, said about the effort. "It was the first airpost to be flown in the United Kingdom, and that was an event worthy to be commemorated in the history of the world's communications." A few years after the Hendon-Windsor flights the talented Gustav Hamel, Britain's first air mail pilot, flew off into the English Channel mists and was never seen again.

An incredible aerial journey

A tall, robust, cigar-smoking pilot named Cal Rodgers stole the spotlight from America's better-known flying heroes at the Chicago International Aviation Meet, the most prestigious aviation event that country had yet to see. At the conclusion of the program, it was discovered that the thirty-two-year-old unknown had copped the grand prize offered by the Aero Club of Illinois for spending the most time in the air during the nine-day meet. The Pittsburgh native won $11,285 and people had noticed. "Who is this Rodgers?" they asked.

Calbraith Perry Rodgers was born into a staunch Navy family in 1879. He was a descendant of Captain Oliver Hazard Perry, hero of the Battle of Lake Erie, and Commodore Matthew Calbraith Perry, who opened Japan to the outside world in 1854. His grandfather, Rear Admiral Christopher Raymond Perry Rodgers, in the Union Navy during the Civil War, had risen to the Superintendency of the Naval Academy, Annapolis. Cal would have followed his illustrious forebears into military service except for one factor—he was almost totally deaf.

Always fascinated by speed, Cal went from a pony to a yacht to a motorcycle to the challenge of a flying machine. He made a beeline for the Wright School of Aviation in Dayton shortly after it was formed and displayed such an aptitude for flying that he soloed after an hour and a half of instruction, a record of long standing. He became the first individual to own and operate a Wright biplane outside the circle of Wright employees. And it was from National Cash Register Company's aviation field in Dayton in August 1911 that Cal flew to test his skills in Chicago.

About the time of Rodger's prize-winning performance in Chicago, another Wright-trained pilot, Harry Atwood, passed through the same city en route to a world cross-country record. Atwood made a trip of some 1,265 miles, going from St. Louis to Governors Island, New York, in 9 days. The press coverage of that marvelous jaunt, following Atwood's arrival in New York on August 25, kindled a spark in the minds of the aviators in Chicago, reminding them of William Randolph Hearst's generous prize announced on October 9 of the previous year. Hearst had declared that $50,000 would be awarded to any pilot who flew from Boston or New York to either Los Angeles or San Francisco (via Chicago), providing the trip was made in less than 30 days and completed prior to October 10, 1911.

With his prize money in hand, Rodgers hurried to enter the transcontinental competition. He felt that he stood a fair chance of winning. He was energetic, determined, and had extraordinary physical stamina, a quality that had helped him win the Chicago endurance prize. Other announced contestants included Robert G. Fowler, James J. Ward, Harry Atwood, and Earle L. Ovington. Fowler was the first to get under way in the Hearst competition, heading eastward from San Francisco's Golden Gate Park on September 11. Jimmy Ward left Governors Island two days later, going west. Rodgers at about this same time was loading a new custom-made Wright racing plane on a train for transport from Dayton to New York. The new biplane, one of two that he bought for the flight, cost $5,000, plus an additional amount for spare parts. Slightly smaller than the Wright Model B, it had a wingspan of 32 feet. This faster type, known as the Model EX, and the only one of its kind ever built, was powered by a 4-cylinder, 4-cycle, 35 hp water-cooled engine and could achieve a speed of 55 miles per hour. By September 17, Rodgers was prepared to leave from Sheepshead Bay on his transcontinental attempt.

Meanwhile, Harry Atwood, unable to find a sponsor, had to withdraw from the race for financial reasons. Rodgers had already taken care of such matters by successfully making arrangements with the Armour Meat Packing Company of Chicago to promote its new carbonated grape drink, Vin Fiz. He would display the product's name and logo on all the flat surfaces of his plane. Armour, in turn, agreed to pay him five dollars for every mile he flew east of the Mississippi River and four dollars for every mile completed west of the river. Armour also contracted to cover the expenses for a private train that would trail the *Vin Fiz Flyer* and carry Cal's wife, his mechanics, Armour personnel, reporters, the second plane, and spare parts. Rodgers assumed financial responsibility for all his own fuel and repairs to the planes. Thus it was, after a hasty negotiating session between the Armour people and the young pilot, that the stage was set for the most ambitious flight yet tried and the most creative promotional campaign yet devised by a company to introduce a new product.

In a brochure to promote his flight, Rodgers wrote:

I obtained the services of Charles Taylor, Master Mechanic of the Wright Company, who has long been associated with the Wright Brothers and assisted in the development of the flying machine from its earliest conception. I have also two expert mechanicians in my employ, Frank Shaffer and C. L. Wiggins, who have been with me during the past summer. Mr. Fred Felix Wettengel of Appleton, Wis., takes care of my business interests and, by faithful and hard work, relieves me of the details on the ground. With this material and personnel, I feel sure of my ability to show the American people that the Wright Brothers are not only the inventors of the flying machine, but the inventors of a vehicle capable of carrying an American citizen throughout the length and breadth of this vast country.

After the takeoff from Sheepshead Bay, Cal flew over Brooklyn at an altitude of 800 feet and crossed the East River by the

Brooklyn Bridge. Flying directly over Manhattan, he followed Broadway up to Madison Square, then headed west toward New Jersey where he met the *Vin Fiz* train on the Erie Railroad tracks. He followed the tracks north as far as Middletown, New York. His landing at the fairgrounds there was so smooth, as Cal said, that "it didn't knock the ashes off my cigar." The 84-mile flight had taken 105 minutes.

Instead of reaching Chicago in 4 days as he had hoped, it took Cal 21, and within that time he had survived 3 crashes. The first occurred while leaving Middletown when his undercarriage snagged a willow tree. The plane momentarily stalled, then recovered, but too slowly to gain sufficient altitude to clear some power lines. Cal quickly cut his engine, whereupon the plane dipped, striking a hickory tree and plunging into a chicken coop. The *Vin Fiz* was all but destroyed. Under Taylor's guidance, however, the mechanics were able to repair the plane in about forty hours.

On September 21, Rodgers left Middletown and flew to Hancock, New York, covering 95 miles in 78 minutes at a speed of 74 mph. On Friday the twenty-second, the day a crash at Rathbone, New York, took Jimmy Ward out of the race, Cal departed Hancock shortly after 11 A.M., still following the railroad tracks. Unfortunately, he made an error at a junction and flew several miles on the wrong course. By midafternoon, he had again found his route, but arrived in Elmira delayed by six hours.

Later, back in the air, a troublesome spark plug that had been popping out started acting up again. Cal had to fly the rest of the way to Canisteo with one hand on the plug and the other on the controls. Not quite reaching Canisteo, he landed nearby at Hornell. There, his left skid was snagged; the plane veered violently, smashing the left wing. This time, used to such mishaps, the mechanics were able to have the craft repaired for takeoff at ten the next morning.

On Sunday, October 8, just two days short of the deadline for the Hearst prize, Rodgers reached Chicago, the intermediary stop specified in the contest regulations. In three full weeks, Cal had spent only 23 hours and 37 minutes in the air and barely completed 1,000 miles of his 4,000-mile journey. Assailed by reporters who wanted to know if he was going to quit at this point, he answered in his usual taciturn manner. "I am bound for Los Angeles and the Pacific Ocean. Prize or no prize, that's where I am bound, and if canvas, steel, and wire together with a little brawn, tendon, and brain stick with me, I mean to get there. The fifty-thousand dollar prize, however, seems to be practically out of the question. But, anyway, it doesn't matter much. I'm going to do this whether I get five thousand dollars or fifty cents or nothing. I am going to cross this continent simply to be the first to cross in an aeroplane."

To emphasize the point, he took off from Chicago late that afternoon on a course to the southwest. On Tuesday, October 10, the day the Hearst prize expired, Cal left Springfield, Illinois. With a strong wind at his back, he overflew St. Louis and reached Marshall, Missouri, by evening. His speed exceeded 70 mph on this journey of over 200 miles. In total now he had flown 1,398 miles, surpassing Harry Atwood's cross-country record set in August.

When he landed at Tucson on November 1, Rodgers met up with Bob Fowler, who on September 11, almost a week before Cal's departure, had been the first to start the transcontinental race. Fowler, having started from the West Coast, had had to return to Los Angeles for a second start, but was still intending to move eastward. (He eventually did reach the Atlantic coast, arriving in Jacksonville, Florida, on February 9, 1912, 112 days after his start.)

Rodgers then flew to and stayed overnight in Maricopa, Arizona. The next day, while flying over the desert, he ran out of gas at Stoval Siding, on the other side of Phoenix. By the time his train caught up with him, it was too late to continue the next sixty miles to Yuma. Early Friday morning, he left Stoval Siding and flew over the Salton Sea. Suddenly, there was an explosion, and a sharp pain pierced Cal's right arm. Ignoring the pain, he made a perfect landing near the Southern Pacific station at Imperial Junction, California, where his mechanics determined that the number one cylinder in his engine had exploded. sending metal shards to tear into his flesh. A local doctor spent over two hours removing splinters from Cal's right arm. Charles Taylor reinstalled an engine he had removed in Kyle, Texas, and the next day the dauntless Rodgers pushed on to Banning, California.

With the Pacific Ocean only seventy-five miles away, it seemed that nothing else could go wrong. Rodgers knew that his dream had nearly come true; it was almost too good to be true. Granted, the replacement engine still had the problem of spark plugs coming loose, and the radiator continued to leak. Shortly after takeoff at Banning, though, he was forced down into a plowed field because of a broken gasoline line, a connecting rod problem, and a loose magneto. On Sunday, November 5, Rodgers finally landed in Pasadena, having survived no less than 15 major accidents.

So far, Cal had been flying for 49 days, of which 3 days, 10 hours, and 4 minutes were actually spent in the air. By following the railroad lines instead of flying directly cross-country, he had traveled a total of 4,321 miles at an average speed of 51.5 mph. 49 Even after the tremendous ovation he received upon landing at Tournament Park in Pasadena, Cal felt that a short flight to the ocean was in order before he could consider his flight finished.

50

Departing Sheepshead Bay, Long Island, New York on September 17, 1911 (left), Cal Rodgers begins his transcontinental flight. Cal's wife (in light dress, opposite page, below) served as self-appointed "Postmistress" along the way. The plucky aviator survived 15 serious crashes, finally reaching Pasadena, Ca., 49 days later. On Sunday, Nov. 12, he sought to fly with souvenir mail from Pasadena to Long Beach but experienced his worst accident of the long trip instead. Rodgers' final and fatal plunge happened at Long Beach at 2:50 p.m., April 3, 1912 (bottom right).

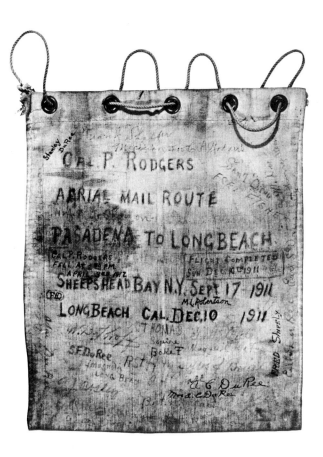

Perhaps he should have left well enough alone. On November 12 as he lifted off from Tournament Park, he visualized the transcontinental flight ending in just a few moments. Halfway to Long Beach, however, he encountered difficulty. A broken control wire forced him to make a nasty crash landing. When he regained consciousness the next day, he'd endured a concussion, both legs broken, several cracked ribs, burns, and a multitude of bruises. "I don't know what may have caused it," he said, "but it's all in the ball game. I am going to finish that flight and finish it with the same machine."

Just how much of the original machine remained was in question. As far as Rodgers himself knew, only the rudder and the drip pan from the engine, with a possible interplane strut or two, were original parts. The important point is that on December 10, 1911, exactly two months after the Hearst prize expired, Cal, who had spent almost a month convalescing, strapped his crutches behind the seat of his famous *Vin Fiz Flyer* and took off from an alfalfa field near Compton, California. When he landed on the beach at Long Beach, over 40,000 people lined the boardwalk to cheer him. Acting in defiance of the odds against him, Rodgers taxied his biplane across the wet sand. Then aides pushed the wheels into the Pacific surf. After landing in Pasadena, Rodgers had commented, "My record won't last long ...with proper landing places along the route and other conditions looked after, the trip can easily be made in thirty days or less." The total numbers of days it had taken Calbraith Perry Rodgers amounted to 84, including the month he needed to recover from injuries.

Rodgers remained in California. But on the afternoon of April 3, 1912, as he was flying over the shoreline, a flock of seagulls flew into his path, causing his craft to fall out of control. Nearby swimmers rushed to the wreckage and pulled him out. It was clear that his neck was broken; he expired almost immediately. This final plunge had taken place, ironically, a few yards from where Rodgers's wheels had touched the Pacific Ocean for the first time almost four months before.

An air mail historian finds much of interest concerning this historic pioneering venture. Sometime in 1911, during Rodgers's transcontinental flight, a special adhesive label, somewhat larger in size than an official postage stamp, appeared that related to the flight. This black-on-white stamp depicts a Wright airplane with the words Vin Fiz Flyer on the underside of the vignette. Above the oval design picturing the Wright Flyer, there are printed the words "Rodgers Aerial Post." A value of 25 cents appears in the four corners.

Apparently, somewhere during the course of the flight, Rodgers had offered to carry letters between towns. This is believed to have been organized by his wife, Mabel, who announced the "Rodgers Aerial Post" (Mrs. C. P. Rodgers, Postmistress) in a leaflet that read:

Postcards delivered to me at the special train or the aeroplane will be carried by my husband's aeroplane to his next stopping place for 25 cents. There they will be stamped by me:

Carried by Rodgers' Aeroplane *Vin Fiz.*

From_____ To_____ October_____, 1911 and delivered to the local postmaster who will send them to the person addressed. A card addressed and stamped, sent to me care of the Plaza Hotel, Chicago, with 25 cents, will be forwarded to me, given a ride in the aeroplane and posted as described. In this way it will be possible for anyone to send a postcard to himself or friends, part of its route at least, in an aeroplane.

Just when the adhesives first began to be used is unclear, but none have been discovered on letters postmarked earlier than Rodgers's landing dates in Texas. A date appearing on Mrs. Rodgers's brochure suggests that the labels were printed in advance and sent onto her as soon as it became clear that her husband would realize his cross-country flight.

On his way, Rodgers advertised the carbonated Vin Fiz beverage by dropping leaflets across the country. To help finance the journey he also sold his special stamps and peddled picture postcards of himself and his plane. Because he had no permit to carry mail and no government sanctioned mail-route number, his carries were entirely unofficial, and all letters bore regular government postage stamps in order to reach their postal destinations. Mrs. Rodgers' use of the term Postmistress was also unofficial.

Vin Fiz covers are extremely rare and only a handful are known. To date, only one mint, unused copy of the "stamp" has been found. The postmarks known are from Waco, Dallas, San Antonio, Imperial Junction, and Pasadena. There also exists one known crash cover that is rubber-stamped with this three-line cachet: Machine wrecked/at Compton/Aviator injured. Each cover is a prized reminder of a remarkable aviation feat.

1911

Aeroplane Station No. 1 As the year dawned, attention in Europe began to swing away from aviation tournaments and toward distance races. These competitions, starting with a Paris–Madrid race in May, took the headlines from the less sensational local air meets. A race of international stature in late May 1911 saw several of Europe's top flyers reaching for the best time between Paris and Rome. Then in June it was the circuit of Europe (Paris–Brussels–London–Paris), followed by the circuit of Britain, starting July 22. In between the circuits, the British did host a tournament centered around the third Gordon Bennett race, brought to Britain by virtue of Claude Grahame-White's capture of the trophy at Belmont in New York the previous October. This British tournament was held at Eastchurch on the Isle of Sheppey, located at the mouth of the Thames River.

Aviation attention in the United States in the "year of races" still centered on tournaments, Cal Rodgers's epic flight notwithstanding. The great Chicago Meet of August 1911 at which Rodgers won the endurance prize saw Lincoln Beachey set an altitude record of 11,642 feet and achieved an attendance of 75,000 spectators each day. It also provided an opportunity for the introduction of new European aircraft, for example the Morane Borel, into American competitions.

Considering the gradual shift in emphasis to distance flights and the grand scale of most prestige meets, a $40,000 prize must have seemed a rather sparse outlay to the frontline pilots of the day. Still, that amount was held out to entice flyers to an international aviation meet on Long Island on September 23, just one month after the Chicago event. The Nassau Aviation Corporation of Long Island, hired as planners of the meet by a group of real estate developers, obtained the use of the large airfield owned by the Aero Club of New York and located on Nassau Boulevard near Garden City.

Although the meet attracted several celebrated pilots from England, France, and the United States, it proved an event of minor importance save for one fact. Before the assembled crowds, the United States flew its first experimental air mail; it had been arranged to have an air mail flight on the daily schedule throughout the gathering.

It appeared that the United States was following the lead of the British, who had begun their special flights of mail between Hendon and Windsor just two weeks earlier. In fact, except for a quirk in the weather, the United States might easily have led the world in air mail experimentation. In November 1910, even before the Allahabad mail flights in India, Postmaster General Frank Hitchcock had approved a ship-to-shore flight of mail to see if the use of an airplane could expedite the delivery of letters, papers, and small valuables from arriving and departing transoceanic vessels. Weather squelched one such attempt on Novem-

Duly sworn in at Garden City, New York, as "First Aeroplane Mail Carrier" on Sept. 23, 1911, Earle L. Ovington, 32, successfully carried out the first authorized air mail flight in U.S. history. Writing about his experience 20 years later, Ovington said, "Guess I'm still an air mail pilot . . . I've never resigned (and I've) never been fired." Pictured here in his French crash helmet, Ovington poses before his Dragonfly.

The plane displays the number thirteen on its rudder and carries a mascot-doll named "Treize" (13 in French).

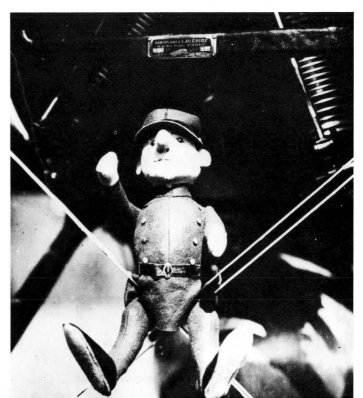

Above: An unusual specimen of the inaugural mail. Bearing both the special date stamp and the straight line cachet, this cover traveled to London (by ship) for 2¢ instead of at the existing 5¢ overseas rate set in 1885. Below: Ovington flew the mail only once again after 1911 before his death in 1936. He and Frank Hitchcock joined in a 20th anniversary round-trip flight between Los Angeles and Tucson. Both signed this cover with the rare Tucson cachet. Ovington's cachet appears on the back.

ber 3, and a broken propeller blade halted a second attempt a week later.

The authorizations for ship-to-shore trials, based on Eugene Ely's successful landings and takeoffs from naval ships in 1910, did indicate that Postmaster General Hitchcock was entirely receptive to the idea of air mail. He, in fact, initiated contacts with the organizers of the Garden City meet and helped develop the proposals that led to the experimental mail carries of September 23–30, 1911. Hitchcock wanted not only to see United States mail flown for the first time, he also had ambitions himself of going along on the historic first flight.

Before September 23, the opening day of the meet at Garden City, the forthcoming trials with air mail were announced to the public. This constituted yet another inducement for people to take the special trains from New York City to the new Long Island Railroad Station built near the edge of the airfield, and as the spectators entered the aviation-field enclosure, they were handed leaflets promoting the use of air mail. They also encountered near the grandstand strategically placed mailboxes ready to receive their stamped and addressed postal souvenir. Nor could they miss a large white tent with the legend U. S. Mail/ Aeroplane Station No. 1 stenciled on its canvas top.

The mail deposited in the various boxes in the spectator areas was to be collected regularly and taken to the tent for processing that involved application of a special circular date stamp with the words "Aeroplane Station No. 1—Garden City Estates, N.Y." set around the date. Processing also meant the addition to each cover of a straight-line, rubber-stamped cachet reading AERIAL SPECIAL DESPATCH. The mail was then collected in a mailbag until the time came for lift-off.

The organizers of the meet sought out pilots to carry the mail. Two prominent British flyers were approached but declined politely when they learned that there was no remuneration. A young American exhibition pilot stepped forward, however, and was waiting to be sworn in as an official carrier on opening day by the Postmaster General. The pilot's name was Earle L. Ovington.

Ovington, who had just pocketed $5,900 for a sixth place showing at Chicago, learned to fly at Blériot's Aviation School in Pau, France. Prior to that training, he had worked as an engineering assistant to Thomas A. Edison in New Jersey. After his return from France his reputation as a skilled pilot began to spread throughout the northeastern United States and he began to win prizes. He was the first pilot to fly a plane over Boston and also the first to fly over portions of Massachusetts, New Hampshire, and Rhode Island. Although he flew a Curtiss-type pusher biplane at Chicago, he preferred a tractor-type monoplane and came to Garden City with an American-made Blériot Queen, a plane similar to the first aircraft built by Clyde Cessna. Ovington's Blériot was named the *Dragonfly* and bore a bold number 13.

Postmaster General Hitchcock arrived at Garden City fully expecting his mail carrier's plane to be a two-seater, with one seat reserved for him. "Not until I arrived at the field at Nassau Boulevard did I learn that his Blériot was of a small pattern capable of carrying no more than one person. Not wishing to surrender the distinction of being the first air mail carrier," reported Hitchcock, "I immediately decided to postpone the flight until a two-seated plane could be procured."

Eventually, Ovington's pleading and the possibility of embarrassment to the postal service if the mail did not fly as promised on the opening day persuaded Hitchcock to reconsider. "I handed the pouch to Ovington...and permitted him to proceed on that first flight alone. For a time," Hitchcock recalled, "I felt rather deeply disappointed of thus failing in my ambition to become the first [air mail] carrier of record [in the United States]. Afterwards, when I became better acquainted with Earle Ovington and began to appreciate more fully his fine qualities, I ceased to begrudge him the honor he wrested from me."

So it happened that Ovington took off on September 23, 1911, with a load of 640 letters and 1,280 postcards in a mail bag tucked between his legs—the first airplane carry of United States mail authorized by postal authorities. Ovington flew to Mineola, about three miles away, where, as agreed, he dropped the bag in a prearranged spot for waiting postal officials to claim. The drop landed on time and on target, but unfortunately the bag broke upon impact with the ground, scattering the mail hither and yon. After a scramble, all the letters and cards were retrieved and sent on their way via regular postal channels. Sturdier bags were obtained for later flights.

Except on September 29 and October 1, when bad weather made flying impossible, Ovington flew at least one load each day until the meet ended. And on the days when the loads were too heavy for a single flight to Mineola, other pilots pitched in as mail carriers. Among these were H. H. "Hap" Arnold, a young army lieutenant, and Eugene Ely, the Curtiss pilot who had successfully landed on navy ships the previous year. On September 26, Postmaster General Hitchcock returned to observe his air mail experiment and was, in fact, able to carry his own bag as there was need for a second flight that day. Flown in an army biplane piloted by Lieutenant Paul Beck, Hitchcock displayed prowess by dropping his bag directly at the feet of postal employees waiting below.

Over 43,000 pieces of mail were processed and flown during the Garden City event. A very small percentage of this mail was signed by the pilot either at the time of the temporary service or in later years after he had moved to Santa Barbara, California.

Nassau Boulevard landing field from the air—a photo believed taken by Earle Ovington himself. This is the same flying field mentioned in a letter which Earle Ovington wrote during his second air mail carry at Garden City.

The exciting moment of takeoff for U.S. Air Mail! "As I had no baggage compartment," wrote Ovington later, "I put the bag of mail on my lap . . ." Below: Adele Ovington, the lady on the right, and friends see her husband fly off to Mineola and into history.

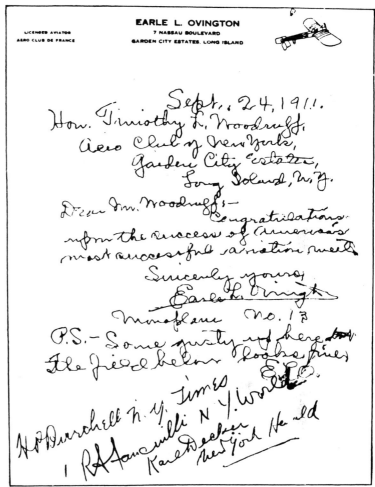

Ovington subsequently designed a personal cachet that he used along with his signature. Picturing a Blériot-type monoplane, the cachet read "Earle Ovington—Santa Barbara, Cal./First U. S. Air Mail Pilot/Flying since 1911." A clue to any Garden City mail signed on the spot would be the absence of Ovington's special cachet. Also, all of the mail he signed during the aviation tournament included his middle initial, L, which he later dropped.

Following the Long Island tournament, Ovington planned to take off for the West Coast in pursuit of Cal Rodgers in an effort to earn the distinction of being the first to achieve the transcontinental distance. Because the Post Office Department had granted him the first temporary route number, #607,001, it is

clear that he and the Postmaster General expected mail to be transported on this extended flight. This temporary route failed to be placed in service, however, when the engine of Ovington's special new cross-country plane proved inadequate for its task.

A specially prepared postcard was sold at the Garden City meet that advised the recipient to retain the card, as it had historical value. The worth of this advice has been proven many times over, as cover and cards today displaying the Garden City Aeroplane Station No. 1 postmark are becoming as increasingly valuable as they are hard to find. Much rarer still are multicolored vignettes prepared by the organizers of the Garden City meet to promote the event. Only three are known to exist.

Hail the pioneers

Most countries of the world can point to a time when their air posts were transported unofficially in airplanes by pioneer pilots. The period for such posts varied from country to country; some nations began their experiments with air mail quite early and carried on their unofficial systems much longer.

The pioneer years of air mail coincided with the romantic epoch of early aviation. Pilots generally rode their craft in the open, perched on the leading edge of the lower wing. They were flying frail machines with underpowered engines and short ranges. Some said they were reckless young men and women. Yet the public was enamored with the prospect of flight, the flying machines and the flyers. The names of outstanding pilots became household words. Their exalted status seemed to produce the kind of special aura that surrounded clipper ship captains of an earlier age.

In the United States the pioneer period of air mail began with Earle Ovington. When he took mail aboard his monoplane at Garden City and flew it to Mineola, it was an historic event; at the same time, Ovington inaugurated an era that would continue until 1916, a period when letters were flown experimentally and without expense to the Post Office Department.

According to guidelines established long ago by the Aero Mail Club, predecessor of the American Air Mail Society, pioneer air mail in the United States means mail that was flown, or, in a few cases, prepared for flight under the auspices of the Post Office Department and processed through regular postal channels. Ninety-four such instances in the United States between 1910 and 1916 have now been identified, with fifty-two of them taking place in 1912 alone. The lone pioneer flight recorded for 1910 was the unsuccessful ship-to-shore flight arranged by Postmaster General Hitchcock permitting Ovington properly to claim to have been the first official United States air mail pilot.

An outstanding authority on pioneer mail flights in the United States, Thomas J. O'Sullivan of Connecticut has described the largest category of these postal ventures in this way:

Typically,...a pilot would be under contract to give a flying exhibition at a local fair. His manager would persuade the postmaster (alone or with authority from Washington) to permit the pilot to fly mail from the fair grounds to the post office. The mail would be dropped in flight; it would be picked up, taken to the post office and forwarded in the regular channels. This fit into the economic situation of the pilot. He was trying to earn a living by flying or perhaps to repay the money he had borrowed to buy his airplane. He might be competing with other pilots at the fair for prize money in various aerial events or he might have only a guaranteed amount for his flying exhibition. He could expect to pick up some additional money by selling post cards picturing himself or his airplane. If he could advertise that these cards would be flown in the mail, he would hope to sell so many more. Thus, a poster...might be put in the windows of the local dry goods store, the pool hall, or the tonsorial parlor, to announce the flying exhibition and the mail-carrying and to bring the crowds out to the fair.

The voluntary transport of mail, with pilots and postal officials working together, was a productive cooperation. It pleased the officials because it allowed them to garner air mail experience without any commitment of money. And it pleased the airmen insofar as it presented them with another means of supporting their aerial activity. Pioneer air mail in the United States proved to be a laboratory wherein pilots and postal authorities alike could begin to explore the commercial possibilities of the airplane.

In addition to mail carried at aviation meets and fairs, pioneer air mail was also generated from early demonstration flying between two separate points, such as two cities, and from various commemorative flights. There was tremendous variation in the volume carried, ranging from the 43,247 pieces counted during the nine-day Garden City meet to some occasions when fewer than 10 items constituted the load.

Pioneer covers usually display special postal markings, date stamps, or cachets or both, indicating their status as pieces of flown mail. Beginning with Ovington's projected cross-country flight in October 1911, the Post Office Department initiated a system of numerical identification for the temporary air mail routes that obtained authorization in Washington. Not all of the pioneer flights could claim a specific route number because many of the authorizations were supplied by local postmasters. However, those that did have Washington's approval, for the most part, were identified with a 6-digit number in a 600,000 series. Under this scheme the first three numbers indicated the state in which the flight was made (for example, 607 was New York; 650 was Texas; 633 was Indiana), and the last three numbers identified the chronological order in which the routes were approved. Thus, the pioneer mail flight in Dubuque, Iowa, in July 1912 received #643,001, and the flight at Cedar Falls, Iowa, in September of the same year was assigned route #643,002. In one instance, where the route number was incorporated in the wordage of a cachet, the numbers were transposed and incorrectly shown on the mail. The South Amboy, New Jersey, flight of July 4, 1912, was granted route #609,001, yet all the mail relating to that occasion sported a bold cachet that read AERO PLANE/ROUTE NO. 900006. It must be added that rarely were the route numbers of importance to the general public or even known outside of Post Office circles.

Air mail crosses the Mississippi

Between October 4 and 8, 1911, approximately 25,000 letters and postcards constituted the first mail flown not only west of the Mississippi River (or west of the Allegheny Mountains, for that matter) but the first flown across the river itself.

The flights that carried this mail were all part of a five-day aviation program sponsored by the active Aero Club of St. Louis, Missouri, and held in connection with the Veiled Prophet's Week celebrations in that city. St. Louis Postmaster Thomas J. Akins had secured approval (but no route number) from Washington to have ordinary mail carried each day of the meet. Two post office stations were set up at opposite ends of Kinloch Field to collect and process the mail that was to be flown to Fairgrounds Park near downtown St. Louis. There, the mail would be off-loaded, retrieved, and transported to the main post office in St. Louis for redispatch.

Walter Richard Brookins, who was born in Dayton, Ohio, and who later became the first American aviation student of the Wright Brothers in 1910, was the pilot of record on October 4. Flying in a Wright biplane, he accomplished the round-trip flight to Fairgrounds Park without incident, leaving Kinloch Field at 4:18 P.M. and landing the mail precisely at 4:32 P.M. There was so much mail deposited at the air field on subsequent days that the pilots gave up the downtown trip and simply flew the mail into the air over their own landing field. Once on the ground, they turned the mail over to the postal station at the opposite end of the field from which they had received it.

On October 8, the final day of the meet, Hugh Armstrong Robinson, a native of St. Louis, carried a small quantity of mail in his Curtiss hydro-aeroplane, in which he had taken off from the St. Louis side of the Mississippi River. In a vivid demonstration of his dexterity, Robinson passed over and under several bridges spanning the river in the area. Robinson's mail had a distinctive marking that read HYDRO-AEROPLANE/MAIL SERVICE/ST. LOUIS, MO. The marking also included the date of Oct. 7, 1911, although, as mentioned, the Robinson flight took place on October 8. Because Robinson did pass over a small portion of Illinois on his flight it can also be said that he flew the first mail across the Mississippi.

Robinson, a Curtiss-trained flyer who centered his interest in hydro-aeroplanes and flying boats, was credited with one other carry of mail during the pioneer era. He was asked by the Aero Club of St. Louis and some Minneapolis businessmen to make a flight down the Mississippi from Minneapolis to New Orleans. This flight, which began on October 17, petered out at Rock Island, Illinois, on October 21 when the necessary financial aid was not forthcoming. Covers are known from this venture from Red Wing and Winona in Minnesota, La Crosse and Prairie du Chien in Wisconsin, and from Rock Island. All display a manuscript notation in the lower left corner of the cover, which reads: "Care Aviator Robinson, Hydro-Aeroplane route," and they remain among the rarest of the pioneer flights series. After his exploits with air mail, Robinson became the sole American competitor in the world's first hydro-aeroplane meet in Monaco in March of 1912. There, his plane crashed in a spectacular dive into the sea. Robinson miraculously escaped injury.

Walter Brookins gained a share of aviation fame prior to his air mail stint at St. Louis. By age twenty-two he had already twice set world altitude records, reaching a height of 6,259 feet at Atlantic City on August 7, 1910. That same year, as the chief United States hope in the second Gordon Bennett trophy race at Belmont, he entered with a new Wright Model R—called the *Baby* because of its small size. Brookins' chances to win were dashed when he had a minor accident while giving the racer a warm up. He carried the mail again in a listed pioneer flight at Wilmington, North Carolina, early in 1912, but cancelled out of a mail assignment in May on route #610,001 at Altoona, Pennsylvania. Because police were unable to keep spectators off of the landing field, Brookins wisely chose not to fly in the interests of everyone's safety. The Altoona covers, prepared but not flown, are among the few non-flown specimens given pioneer status by aerophilatelists.

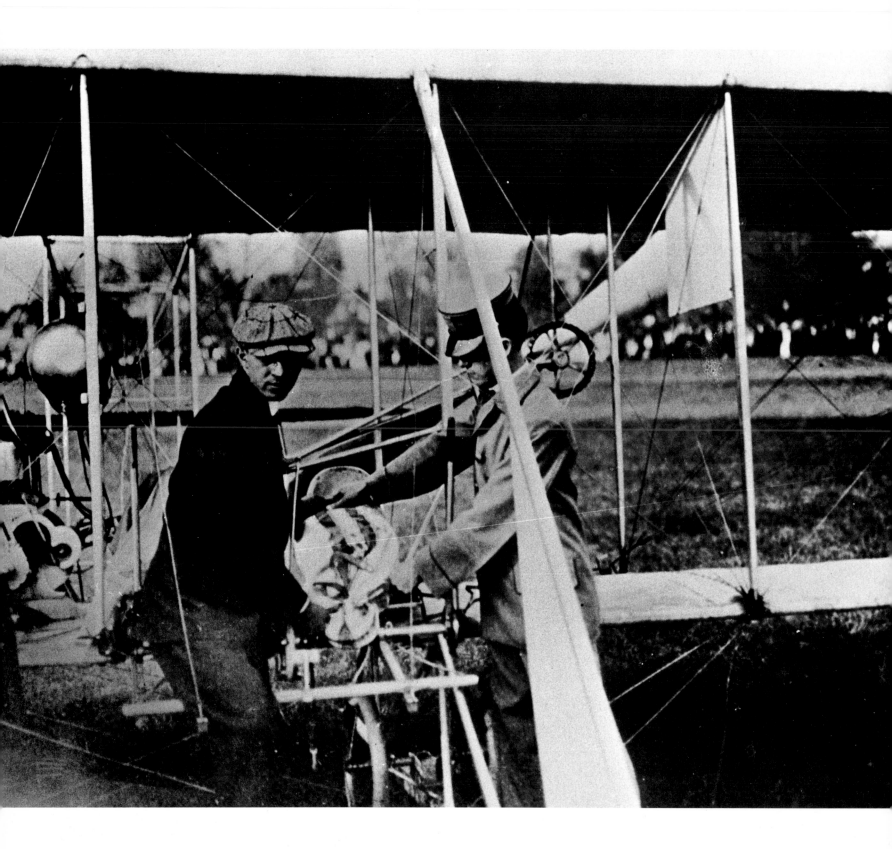

Pioneer aviator Walter Brookins and a postal aide on-load St. Louis's first air mail at Kinloch Field, just before take-off on October 4, 1911. The 6,000 pieces of mail, mostly postcards, were contained in two regulation mail sacks strapped to the plane for the 12-mile ride downtown to Fairgrounds Park.

Right: A ground supervisor checks the wind velocity at Kinloch Field just before Walter Brookins' departure. Below: Brookins prepares to land at Fairgrounds Park before 25,000 spectators.

Pioneer par excellence

Among pioneer air mail flights, Rochester, New York is especially remembered by aerophilatelists not because the event there was outstanding or early, but because of one man, Lincoln Beachey.

A member of the Curtiss exhibition team that, like the Wright and Moisant teams, toured the country continuously, moving from fair to fair, from exhibition to exhibition, Beachey eventually commanded more than $5,000 for free-lance performances. His boss, Glenn Curtiss, who frowned upon stunt flying for any reason, once said of Beachey, "I consider Lincoln the most daring and skillful aviator under any and all conditions that I have ever seen." Orville Wright called Beachey "...the greatest aviator of them all."

During his unusual career as a pioneer airman, Beachey barnstormed in balloons and motor-driven airships; he flew 11 pioneer air mail assignments; he established an altitude record of 11,573 feet in August 1912, dead-sticking to earth when his fuel supply was exhausted; he flew planes around the dome of the Capitol in Washington and did loops over the mall while President Wilson looked on; he piloted a plane over Niagara Falls, barely missing the lip of the falls as he hurtled through spray and foam to the gorge below; he flew a biplane into San Francisco's gigantic Machinery Hall—in through one set of hangar-like doors and almost out the other. He thrilled millions at air shows with death-defying stunts.

Beachey's first air mail flight and the sixth listed pioneer flight in the United States, took place at Rochester's Crittenden Park Race Track on October 21, 1911; it went off routinely. Mail was collected at a temporary post office belatedly set up at the meet on October 20. The pilot made two trips with air mail in his Curtiss pusher-type biplane, flying about two miles to Genesee Valley Park where he dropped the pouches to waiting handlers. It is believed that about 15,000 letters and cards were flown that day, much of it being stamped with a two-line cachet that reads, GREETINGS—ROCHESTER'S/FIRST AERIAL POST.

After leaving Rochester, the Curtiss exhibition flyers moved on to Fort Smith, Arkansas, then to Atlanta's Speedway Aviation Meet, and finally to Beachey's home state of California for the third annual International Air Meet at Dominguez Field near Los Angeles. Beachey carried mail at each of these locations.

In the parlance of modern-day test pilots, Lincoln Beachey "pushed the outside of the envelope" once too often. During a power dive in a new light monoplane, that had been built in San Francisco especially for him and which he had not flown before, his wings collapsed and he plunged to his death in San Francisco Bay on March 14, 1915. Fifty thousand spectators attending the Panama–Pacific Exposition were looking on. Beachey was only thirty-one years old when he drowned.

Like his teacher Glenn Curtiss, Lincoln Beachey followed the airship route before learning to fly heavier-than-air planes in 1911. The Californian became America's most famous aviator, joining the Curtiss exhibition team and flying the greatest number (11) of U.S. pioneer mail flights. He teamed up with auto driver Barney Oldfield, the pair racing and stunting together at country fairs. The contemporary photo shows the last and fatal Beacheys crash.

Pacific Aerial Delivery Route 1

Another California pilot, this one a graduate of the self-taught school, who built his first airplane in an abandoned church near his home, found himself in the limelight as the first official carrier of air mail at Los Angeles. The day after the opening of the international tournament at Dominguez Field on Saturday, January 20, 1912, a page-one article in the *Los Angeles Tribune* carried the headline: "Pacific Aerial Delivery Route Number 1 Opened by Glenn Martin." Less than a week after his twenty-sixth birthday, Glenn Luther Martin from Santa Ana had been picked from among some of the best-known American aviators to inaugurate air mail deliveries that would be a daily feature of this meet for the first time. In being selected, Martin also flew the first experimental mail on the West Coast.

The great success of the first international aviation tournament at Reims, France, in 1909 was the chief reason that the Dominguez International Air Meet came into being one year later. Located on a wide plateau between Los Angeles and Long Beach, the meet attracted many flyers (including Curtiss, Paulhan, Lincoln and Hillary Beachey, Charles Hamilton, and the "Boy Wonder of the Air," Charles Willard) and large, enthusiastic crowds of spectators, who had come to the field on the Pacific Electric Line from San Pedro. It was during that first meet in 1910 that Charles Willard coined a phrase into the annals of aviation vocabulary. After a particularly difficult ride in turbulent air, Willard was asked about his flight by a copy-hungry reporter. "Looked bumpy from here," the reporter offered. "Bumpy for sure," Willard replied. Then he added with a smile, "The air was full of air pockets, as a Swiss cheese is full of holes." The term air pockets, referring to a down-draft of air, appeared in the reporter's column and soon came into common usage.

The meet at Dominguez grew. By its third year, a large grandstand had been built to hold more than 25,000 spectators and permanent wooden hangars lined one end of the field. More importantly, a large troupe of aviators had gathered, along with the balloonists, to vie for the prizes. In 1912, the year that twice-a-day Aerial Mail deliveries were added to the program, the entry list—a veritable who's who in American aviation—included Lincoln Beachey, then called the "California Flying Fool," Blanche Scott, William B. Atwater, Horace Kearney, Phil Parmalee, Farnum Fish, and many others, besides Willard and Martin. Such a star-studded field attracted more than 40,000 people on Sunday, January 21.

To allow the transport of United States mail from the field by plane, meet officials had received a go-ahead from Los Angeles' Postmaster Harrison. A small postal substation was set up in a tent near the grandstand, and during the nine-day event it processed close to 16,000 pieces of mail, which were then flown four miles to Compton where the pouches were dropped in the vicinity of the post office for relay by train to the central post office in Los Angeles.

An unusual feature of the pioneer covers and cards from Los Angeles relates to the three different special date-stamp canceling devices that were used. The circular date-stamp portions identified the mail as emanating from the "aviation" or "aeroplane" station, but the killer bars that were meant to mark the postage stamp varied. One set of killer bars was composed of six wavy lines, a second had five wavy lines and the words Aviation Field, and the third set had four straight lines, with the second and third lines being interrupted by the words "Dominguez Field." It was mandatory for postal officials to destroy all temporary postal marking devices following the occasion for their use, which explains why these three different devices seemed a bit extravagant. Besides the expected postal markings, most of this mail also carried a four-line cachet: "This piece of mail was carried by/Aeroplane from Aviation Field/Postal Station to nearest regular/Post office at Compton, Cal."

A number of pilots were utilized for these flights. In addition to Glenn Martin, who flew the mail on the opening and closing days of the meet (January 20 and 28), Willard and Clifford Turpin each acted as an aerial postman on more than one occasion. This was the only Pioneer mail event that Charles Willard ever participated in, but Beachey, Martin, Fish, and others would fly more mail before the era ended. Martin's second and final experimental air mail carry took place less than two months after the Dominguez meet. On Sunday, March 3, he carried a portion of the mail collected at a small air meet at Agricultural Park in Sacramento. Two months after that he was flying his new float plane from Newport Bay to Catalina Island. Though he carried no mail on that 68-mile round-trip venture, he traversed for the first time the route of the famed Catalina Island carrier pigeons that had hauled the mail several years earlier.

A report on the Los Angeles pioneer air mail event would be incomplete without the mention of one other surprising fact. Farnum Fish, who had been taught to fly at the Wright Brothers' school in Dayton, Ohio, flew the mail at Dominguez Field in his Wright biplane when he was only seventeen years old. The following year this amazing adventurer would be in Mexico serving as a general in the army of Mexican rebel Pancho Villa. Fish became, during this period, the first war pilot to suffer a wound while in flight, and, along with Alexander the Great, he shares the distinction of being one of history's youngest generals.

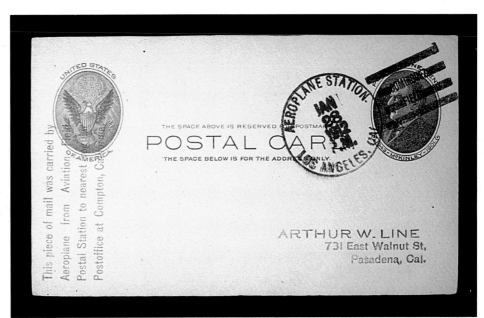

Above: One of 16,000 items carried aloft at Los Angeles early in 1912, this card displays the large circular date stamp used on January 27 and 28. It is the only cancellation to mention Dominguez Field (see the second and third killer bars over McKinley's face). The lower cover displays Glenn Martin's signature on an officially recognized Kitty Hawk anniversary.

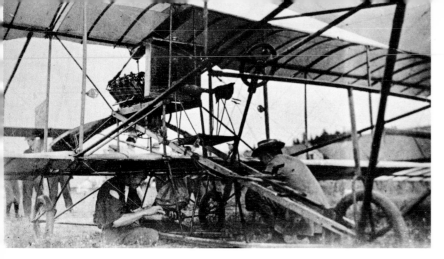

U.S. pioneer air mail flight #48 was a first for the Pacific-Northwest. Granted temporary route #673,001, pilot Walter Edwards twice flew from Portland, Oregon, to Vancouver, Washington, on August 10 and 11, 1912, carrying over 1000 pieces of mail each day. In addition to focusing on the well-advertised service, undertaken in a Curtiss biplane, these views of the Portland pioneer air mail event record the attendants wiring the mail bag to the landing gear and show the temporary postal sub-station established at the take-off point on Portland's Country Club Fair Grounds.

U.S. Aeroplane
Mail Service
THIS LETTER CARRIED BY
AVIATOR WALTER EDWARDS
FROM PORTLAND, OREGON TO
VANCOUVER, WASH.

PORTLAND
AUG 10
4 PM
OREGON.

U.S. POST OFFICE
AEROPLANE MAIL SERVICE
PORTLAND, ORE. TO VANCOUVER, WASH.
Stamps for Sale

67

The experiment travels

The air mail process that began in India, Denmark, Great Britain, and the United States continued apace throughout the world and the idea, itself, gained ground as aviation spread its wings, growing by modest leaps here and unexpected bounds there.

In 1912, American aviation, which had not progressed much beyond desultory tournaments and playful one-man exhibitions, was beginning to recognize the need to keep up with the competition. English aviator Claude Grahame-White found time in 1911 to co-author a book on aviation that startled many people by demonstrating how far ahead of the rest of the world France was in aviation matters. Grahame-White's scorecard of "trained pilots" showed France with 387 aviators, followed by England with 128, Germany with 46, Italy with 38, Russia with 37, and the United States with 31. In terms of the airplanes used by the listed pilots, the nod still went heavily toward France and French models. For biplanes, Farmans were favored by 135 to 59 and 39 for Voisins and Wrights, respectively. In the monoplane category, there was not a single United States type mentioned. The French Blériots (158) and Antoinettes (47) were runaway favorites.

Clément Ader, a well-respected French inventor, once remarked, "Whoever will be master of the sky will be master of the world." French actions were inspired by this belief, and French pilots began to seek every important world aviation record.

But thanks to men of vision like Northcliffe, Sopwith, and Windham in Britain, Martin and Curtiss in the United States, and Hans Grade in Germany, not to mention a host of enterprising pilots of other nationalities, the pull to develop aviation along practical, useful lines to the benefit of mankind was not solely up to the French.

1911

Norway In a land that hosted no international competitions, but held small local flying meetings only, the air mail trial occurred remarkably early. During the course of one of these meets on October 2, 1911, two days after the Garden City flights were completed, Baron Carl Cederstrom, a Swede, dropped some copies of the newspaper *Tidens Tegn* over the airfield at Trondheim. People rushed forward to claim the souvenirs that had fallen from the sky and discovered that the wrappers hold-

The Japanese are among those nations that have celebrated their aviation and air mail history on postal issues. This 10-yen regular issue from 1960 marks 50 years of Japanese aviation. German (Berlin) and South African issues mark air mail milestones by illustrating together pioneer planes and modern jets. The 1978 French airmail is a tribute to a particular pioneer mail flight, and the German semi-postal pictures an early Grade eindecker (monoplane), forerunner of the Bork mail plane. The top stamp commemorates the first air mail flight in Australia.

ing the newspapers were identified as Norway's first air mail. The finders of the pre-addressed wrappers were asked to deposit them in the nearest letter box for delivery to destination. This particular demonstration (or promotion) does not seem to have been followed up, as the next recorded postal flight in Norway took place years later.

The Flying Baron, as Cederstrom was known, was an aviation pioneer, best known for his exhibition flights throughout Scandinavia. Trained in France, he flew a Blériot named *Bilbol*. Eventually he established in Sweden a flying school and a factory for hydro-aeroplanes.

1911   South Africa   South African people evidenced

an early enthusiasm for flying. Flights were attempted at Johannesburg and East London as early as 1909 and 1910. The first real exhibitions, however, began in the final months of 1911. With them developed the first South African Aerial Post.

As an attraction during the holiday season, an African organization syndicate known as the Cape Peninsula Publicity Association arranged to have two experienced flyers give a series of exhibition flights at Kenilworth, near Cape Town, in 1911. To enliven the proceedings and insure a good turnout at the airfield, the organizers planned an experimental aerial post between Kenilworth and Muizenberg, a nearby town. Special cards were printed for the program and sold for one shilling each. Purchasers were advised that if the cards were properly addressed and bore the required "stampage," they would be posted to any place in the world. The cards, which had a pictorial cachet showing a monoplane of the Blériot-type in flight, stated very clearly that the First South African Aerial Post was sanctioned by the Ministry of Posts and Telegraphs.

Of the pilots secured for the Kenilworth exhibitions, one had already flown mail. E. F. Driver, a Blériot owner and pilot, had only recently returned to his native South Africa after taking part in the First United Kingdom Aerial Post between Hendon and Windsor in England. Driver's associate was Compton Paterson, and the two were to divide the duties on the eight days of planned flights. No flying was scheduled for December 25 and 26, nor for December 31, or for New Year's Day of 1912.

An accident on December 26, a day when no flights were to occur, took Paterson out of the picture. The newspaper *Cape Argus* gave this report on December 30:

Mr. Paterson, who on Christmas morning had set up a South African flying record by soaring 2000 feet up and covering a

69

distance of about 30 miles in 35 minutes, essayed to give a demonstration on the Green Point Track on Tuesday morning (the 26th Dec.). There was a large crowd present, but the consternation of all around the enclosure may be imagined when, after ascending a height of about 50 feet, his biplane was seen to turn turtle and came down to the ground with a great crash. The brave aviator retained his presence of mind under these most trying conditions and shook himself free from the machine so as to allow himself to fall free. But he fell heavily, nevertheless, and at first it was feared that he had sustained very serious, if not fatal, injuries. Willing hands at once rushed to his assistance and he was carried to the Hospital, where it was happily found that although very greatly shaken, he was not permanently hurt.

E. F. Driver carried on alone. It is likely that two round-trip flights were required to transport the mail which had been collected. One round-trip journey between Kenilworth and Muizenberg took place in the early evening of December 27, 1911. The other trip apparently required two days. Mail went to Muizenberg on January 2, and mail returned to Kenilworth on the final day of the exhibitions on January 3. Special circular date stamps indicate on which flight a particular card was carried. It is estimated that 2,597 cards were processed for the First South African Aerial Post, and E. F. Driver remains one of the few pilots in history to participate in the initial air mail flights of more than one country.

1912 Germany On February 18, 1912, the anniversary of the world's first air post flight at Allahabad, another inaugural flight of mail was taking place between the German towns of Bork and Bruck, about an hour's train ride from Berlin. The famed German pioneer flyer, Hans Grade, who had built Germany's first power-driven airplane in 1909 and flown that craft at the International Aviation Week at Heliopolis (Cairo) in 1910, was the prime mover of the Bork-Bruck flight. What made this flight significant is that it signaled the beginning of a semi-regular *private* airplane mail service that continued well into June of 1913. It was also the first such enterprise to issue *private* air post stamps.

By initiating his own service, Grade, working in cooperation with the local chamber of commerce, was trying to draw attention to an airfield at Bork where he had located his factory and where he believed that effective commercial and real estate development could occur. In a promotional brochure that he produced in 1910, he described the area and landing field as ideal for "any additional airplane factories."

When the mail flights began on February 18, Grade sent along letters of greeting to the German emperor and to various members of the national cabinet, including the minister of posts. His pilot on the first carry, named Pentz, departed Bork at 3:30 P.M. and arrived at Bruck, approximately four miles away, at 3:45 P.M. On landing, Pentz accepted the greetings of the mayor, who hailed the start-up of this first German air post service (unauthorized though it was) and gave his mail to Bruck postal officials for redispatch.

A portion of the written agreement between the Bork Chamber of Commerce and a regional postal director from nearby Potsdam read in part:

> The air transport flights from Bork Railroad Station to Bruck are scheduled to take place in the future as often as possible ...The Bruck Post Office is to be informed by telephone in advance of the planned flight. The cooperation of the postal services is requested to consist in the sending of a postal clerk of the Bruck (Post Office) to the landing field, where he will have to accept the mail flown in by the airplane...

The agreement specified that the aviators were not to be paid.

Before Hans Grade's early mail service lost momentum and disbanded in June 1913, it issued three unofficial air mail adhesives that were sold to cover the cost of moving the letters or cards by air to Bruck. The first stamp, which seems to have appeared at the time of the second flight on February 26, 1912, was an air post vignette intended to be affixed to the letter directly beneath either a regular 3-*pfenning* or a regular 5-*pfenning* postage stamp. All three of these unofficial stamps, and especially flown covers bearing them, are prized aerophilatelic items.

1912 Canada Sometime prior to 1950, a Canadian cover was discovered bearing an intriguing cachet that read, FROM WINNIPEG/BY FIRST AERIAL ROUTE/THOMAS McGOEY, AVIATOR. The envelope was postmarked at Winnipeg, Manitoba at 9:30 A.M. on May 10, 1912, and was addressed to Toronto. To it a date stamp was also applied at Grand View, Ontario, on May 14. This cover stirs many questions. Was it actually flown? If so, it is an extremely early pioneer example from Canada. Who undertook the flight? Pilot Thomas McGoey was ill in Grand Forks, North Dakota, at the time the letter is supposed to have departed Winnipeg.

Whether the McGoey letter flew or not, it remains clear that the air mail bug had bitten at least a few Canadians as early as May 1912.

William B. Atwater, pictured above, ultimately received the Order of the Rising Sun from the Emperor.

1912 Japan

Several European flyers, including the Frenchmen Hubert Latham and R. Vallon, were visiting the Far East in late 1910 through 1911. Another pilot who was also making an appearance in the Orient at this time was the American, William B. Atwater. Early in 1912, he sailed to Japan to introduce the Curtiss hydro-aeroplane to officials there who had already seen a number of land planes in their country. During his visit Atwater made history by carrying Japan's first air mail.

Beginning on May 6, Atwater made several flights over the harbor area at Yokohama for the benefit of Japanese naval officials. On one of his two flights on May 11 he carried a message from Admiral Saito, Minister of the Japanese Navy, to the commanding officer of a destroyer anchored in the bay. Delivery was effected by making a low pass over the vessel and dropping the message to its deck. After receiving the message, the destroyer's captain responded by signal that he had received and understood the instructions.

On June 2, 1912, after a false start from Yokohama, Atwater undertook Japan's first official flight of experimental mail, this time at Shibaura, a section of Tokyo. Fireworks signaled the takeoff before thousands of spectators. After a short run in the water, he lifted his craft, circled once over the crowd, and turned toward Yokohama.

The American plane traveled at a speed of 65 mph and had aboard a mail bag containing an estimated 10,000 picture postcards that had received a special Japanese Aerial Post date stamp. Also in that bag was a special letter of greeting from the Mayor of Tokyo to the Mayor of Yokohama. Before landing at 5:12 P.M., Atwater took time to circle the S. S. *Mongolia*, the ship that had brought him and his plane to Japan. Greeted by deafening cheers, he taxied to a pier in Yokohama. After a brief pause, he was once again airborne, this time with about 600 cards and the second letter of exchange between the mayors. Upon arrival the Tokyo mail was rushed to the Edobashi post office for immediate handling.

The cancellation applied to the special postcards had the number 45 as part of the date: in 1912 the Japanese were celebrating the forty-fifth year of the Meiji era.

An editorial in *Scientific American* (June 5, 1909) discussed the great proportion of failures then facing innovators in the field of aviation. "...the experimentalist does not (always) realize the extreme difficulty of the problem, both from the theoretical and mechanical standpoint." For some of the same reasons that explained why only a very few of the hundreds of flying machine designs worked, only a very few of the early air mail experiments could survive. Yet each time a letter was flown, the chances for sound air mail systems improved.

71

The Stinson sisters, busy making history! Below: Marjorie, a Wright-trained pilot, flew pioneer air mail at Seguin, Texas on May 19 and 20, 1915. Her mother and relatives see her sworn in as carrier on temporary route #650,004. Right: The Japanese postcard picturing Katherine in her Partridge-Keller biplane recalls Katie's successful Far Eastern tour of 1916–1917. She was especially adored by Japanese women, who saw her as their emancipator. Opposite: Katherine's "school-girl" look, and a view from Helena, where she made air mail history.

米國女流飛行家　スチンソン嬢　ライト式機上

The flying schoolgirl

It was a warm summer's day in 1911 in Kansas City when a diminutive, frail-looking girl, along with three other women, climbed into the gondola of Lieutenant H. E. Honeywell's balloon. They had been selected from a group of over two hundred and fifty applicants who, when told that the Army balloonist would take four female passengers for the first time in his lighter-than-air machine, vied for the honor. While all eyes on the ground were on the ascending balloon, the big brown eyes of slender Katherine Stinson were ablaze with a vision of things to come. Almost at once she decided to give up her plans for a career as a music teacher. She believed that if she could obtain a pilot's certificate she could earn a living as an exhibition pilot. At that time, flyers were able to earn as much as a thousand dollars a day.

Persuading her parents to allow her to take flying lessons was easy, but coming up with the required $500 was another matter. Somehow knowing that she would never need it again, Katherine decided to sell for $200 the piano she had won in a Canton, Mississippi, high school popularity contest. Mr. Stinson, urged on by his strong, independent wife, Emma, gave Kate the balance. January 1912 found the determined young woman at Tom Benoist's factory and flying school, located on Kinloch Field near St. Louis, Missouri. She was thrilled to be at the same field those famous airmen—Walter Brookins, Arch Hoxie, Ralph Johnson, and others—had flown from the previous October.

On a bitter cold day, made colder by an uncharacteristic cover of snow still on the ground around St. Louis, Katherine Stinson experienced her first airplane ride with her instructor, Tony Jannus, a celebrated cross-country flyer and exhibition pilot. Jannus warmed up the Roberts two-stroke engine of the Benoist Model 12 biplane, then proceeded to take his passenger up to approximately 1,000 feet before banking sharply in a circle around the flying field. The unexpected spiral effect startled Kate, who thought the pilot had lost control, and she shouted above the engine's noise to "level those wings!" Noting the urgent tugging on his sleeve, Tony laughed, misinterpreting his passenger's confusion as fright, and gently landed the plane. To prove that she was misunderstood and not afraid, Katherine demanded a second flight immediately.

Although he did offer Katherine several cursory lessons the following week, Benoist was still unsure about carrying the liability of a young female pilot, who would probably either be unable to control an aircraft or, at best, catch cold and die of pneumonia. Eventually, Katherine was asked to not only leave Kinloch, but also to leave the business of flying to the men. In their estimation, ladies belonged "under a roof, not in the air." Although Benoist and Jannus greatly underestimated Katherine Stinson's capabilities and fierce dedication to her hopes, thereby

depriving themselves of the honor of teaching her to fly, they did, nonetheless, retain their special place in aviation history. On New Year's Day 1914, Tony Jannus, flying Benoist's *Flying Boat*, made the first scheduled air passenger-service flight in the world. This was the inaugural flight of a charter service operated for a short time between Tampa and St. Petersburg, Florida.

After leaving St. Louis, Stinson was not to be deterred from her goal, however keenly disappointed she was by the Kinloch experience. In March 1912, when the flying Mills brothers came to Hot Springs, Arkansas, for an exhibition, her mother, continuing to plead her cause, cornered George Mills and told him in no uncertain words that her daughter wanted to become an aviatrix. Would he be the one to teach her or not? George glanced at the young lady. He couldn't believe she was 20 years old nor the 101 pounds she claimed to weigh. Like Benoist and Jannus, he declined the invitation to be her instructor.

73

In May, while visiting Chicago's Cicero Field, Kate met through George Mills, as fate would have it, a genial Swede named Maximilian Theodore Liljestrand, known simply as Max Lillie. Lillie at the time was organizing a flying school, and he good-naturedly accepted Katherine as his first female pupil. She flew with him as a passenger on Memorial Day to Grant Park where, upon landing, he was arrested. According to a Chicago ordinance, landing an aeroplane in a public park was legally forbidden. Kate had to take a trolley back to the boarding house where she was staying. After paying his fine, her pilot was allowed to fly his Wright Model B biplane back to Cicero. Soon after, Stinson was beginning her primary lessons in aeronautics.

Because she was an eager, alert, and self-confident pupil who listened well, she was able to grasp the fundamentals of flight after two and a half hours of dual instruction at $1.00 per minute. Her solo attempt finally came on July 13, 1912. Dressed in a pair of young boy's trousers, a middy blouse, and laced boots, she taxied across the field, and took her Wright Model "B" smoothly into the air. After climbing to about three hundred feet, she circled back to the field to complete the required banks and figure-eights. Suddenly her engine quit. Max Lillie shouted frantically for her to land. Very calmly, she did—as if nothing out of the ordinary had happened. On the 16th of July, she flew to an altitude of five hundred feet and qualified for the Fédération Aéronautique Internationale pilot's certificate. She was the fourth American woman to win this license. Of the other three only Blanche Scott was still actively flying.

Throughout July and August, Stinson polished her skills at Cicero field. With the cold weather coming, she went briefly with the Lillie company when it set up quarters for the fall at Kinloch Field and then spent the winter with her relatives in Hot Springs, Arkansas. It was here the Stinson family began to talk in earnest about the future of the aviation industry. Kate planned to contribute her earnings from exhibition flying to help her mother incorporate the Stinson Aviation company, which finally came to pass in April of 1913. In May, Kate went back to Cicero Field and invested $2,000 in a modified Wright "B," which had been engineered by Max Lillie; this became the aircraft that carried Katherine Stinson to fame and fortune.

On two weekends in July, Stinson was the feature attraction at Cincinnati's Coney Island Park, where she filled the grand-stands and thrilled the public. From there, she went to Columbus, Indiana, under contract to fly for three days during August.

The turning point of her career came on Labor Day 1913. She landed at Pine Bluff, Arkansas, a lady, and left a "legend." Bill Pickens, Lincoln Beachey's shrewd manager, had overheard Katherine respond to a reporter's question about her age. With a twinkle in her eye, she admitted, "I'm not old enough to vote."

Seeing her standing there, petite even in her flying coat and cap, with her black curls tied in pink ribbons, her narrow face and slender shoulders accentuated, no one could doubt it. Even though twenty-two at the time, Kate looked like a high school girl, and a young one at that. Pickens was given charge of her publicity, and immediately touted her as "The Flying Schoolgirl."

Three weeks later, Katherine Stinson was in the headlines. Mr. A. J. Breitenstein, secretary of the 1913 Montana State Fair, which was to be held in Helena from September 22–27, arranged to have Miss Stinson undertake exhibition flights each day of the fair. Along with her plane and her mechanic, Richard Wagner, Stinson traveled by train to Helena, where she registered at the Placer Hotel on September 16. Local headlines and fair publicity proclaimed aviation's foremost attraction—The Flying School-girl—to be in town. Secretary Breitenstein, intending to capitalize further on the situation, urged George W. Landstrun, Helena's postmaster, to allow Katherine to realize her dream of becoming America's first lady air mail pilot. Permission from Postmaster General Albert S. Burleson was quickly forthcoming, as was the designation for a temporary Pioneer route, #663,002.

Landstrun then set up an aerial post substation on the fairgounds. Collection boxes were put out where mail for the intended flights could be deposited. Postal employee C. B. Anderson was placed in charge. As the fair opened on September 22, Katherine was sworn in by Landstrun as America's first authorized woman air mail carrier.

On the opening day of the fair and on September 25, the winds proved too strong for any flying. But on the other days, Katherine would take off with a mail bag and fly over the rolling hills surrounding the Helena Valley. Then she would drop the pouch at the fairgounds for Anderson, who had cancelled it before it flew, using a special circular device reading AERO POST/HELENA, MONT. with the date in the center. After retrieving it from the drop zone, he would forward it on. Katherine carried a total of 1,333 letters and postcards during her visit to the Montana State Fair. Many of the postcards pictured The Flying Schoolgirl.

Even airborne, Katherine did not overlook her friends below. One card written in her hand (undoubtedly on the ground) was addressed to Mr. A. J. Breitenstein. Given an Aero Post cancel on September 24, it read:

Here's hoping we have good weather and attendance that will surpass any previous Fair weeks.
[Signed] Katherine Stinson

Not only did Katherine help the Montana State Fair set new attendance records, she also made the occasion of the seventy-third listed United States pioneer air mail flight an historic one. Never before had a woman flown official mail.

Oskar Bider and the Flugspende

In spite of Switzerland's proximity to the continental European cradles of aviation, France and Germany, she got off to a very slow start in the area of practical aeronautics. On March 13, 1910, she became the twenty-seventh nation to achieve an airplane flight within her borders. Even at that, the Swiss needed a German pilot flying an American-style biplane to join the other countries on the list.

That first powered flight of a heavier-than-air craft in Switzerland was performed by a touring German military aviator, Captain Paul Engelhard, who had flown with Wilbur Wright during his celebrated demonstrations before Kaiser Wilhelm II in 1909. Engelhard's first flight for the Swiss was made from the frozen surface of the lake at St. Moritz; he flew a German-made Wright biplane. As if in a final display of resistance to the airplane, many Swiss opposed Engelhard's attempt, stating that the thin atmosphere of St. Moritz might not sustain flight. Engelhard persisted in his intentions, however, and eventually proved that the ring of mountains in the area was especially helpful to flyers because it shielded the lake surface from the most treacherous winds.

It is not difficult to understand why aviation was slow to make headway among the Swiss. With high mountains covering 61 percent of her 15,944 square miles, the small nation simply did not possess topography that invited experiments with flight. Moreover, the Swiss were somewhat addicted to ballooning, no doubt as a result of a series of spectacular trans-alpine balloon flights made between 1898 and 1913 by a St. Gallen native, "Captain" Edward Spelterini. In 1909 the Swiss hosted the fourth International Gordon Bennett Balloon Competition, and the Swiss Aero Club was greatly preoccupied in carrying off that event with precision and success.

With practical applications of the airplane being difficult to distinguish from joyful occasions for sport and competition, it was natural that the air mail idea was slow to germinate in the Swiss mind. However, once the world's airplane technology evolved, providing the vehicle with greater speed, range, and control, the flying machine was seen in an entirely new light. Now it could begin to crack certain barriers of isolation. Now it could even prove an effective tool in the military machine. It was this final consideration that led the once uneasy Swiss into the field of experimental air mail, not to fill a communications need, but rather to raise money for a military aviation branch.

The Swiss moved with extraordinary swiftness to make up for lost time. They issued an impressive series of semi-official airmail stamps in 1913, an output exceeding that of any other nation during the pioneer period. These stamps, all featuring stylized or actual monoplanes in flight, are highly esteemed by aerophilatelists everywhere.

Why the Swiss, with the cooperation of their postal authorities, produced their air post stamps when they did, requires a brief explanation. When the Swiss General Staff was alerted to the advisability of creating an air arm to operate in support of Swiss military units, it determined that its primary need was for planes and airfields. Pilots were not a problem. A good many Swiss had already received flight training both in France and Germany. The problem was fiscal; the machinery and real estate demanded by an aeronautical program had to be financed somehow. With the national budget locked in place early in 1913, and a large increment already granted for defense needs, the Swiss General Staff could not rely on federal aid to support its aims. The staff promptly opted for a characteristic Swiss solution; it turned to the Swiss. A Flugspende—a massive voluntary national collection—was decided upon to underwrite aviation development.

A two-pronged approach was chosen by most regions for the collection. In the first place, there were direct pleas for voluntary aviation contributions, with extra cajoling about the national-security needs. The second thrust involved a broad-scale educational effort—Swiss Aviaton Days—when Swiss flyers would conduct brief regional aviation meetings to show the populace just how far aviation and the plane had progressed. To enhance the educational experience as well as to expand the revenues, an air mail flight was planned as an adjunct of the aviation days. The Swiss postal service made it mandatory to use special air stamps, issued by the regional collection authorities, on all mail flown during these demonstration flights. The air post stamps, however, were not to be used without regular Swiss postage. It was intended that the bulk of the income generated by the semi-official air mails would be placed right into national collection coffers. While the stamps themselves were actually issued by civilians in the areas where the postal flights were staged, the Swiss postal service did contribute special air post cancelling devices appropriate to each flight. The first such die, used at Basel on March 9, 1913, was not destroyed, but given to the Swiss Postal Musueum in Bern for permanent care.

The pilot selected to carry this experimental air mail was Oskar Bider, a Blériot specialist and a native of Langenbruck, a town near Basel. Bider, born in 1891, had traveled to Argentina in 1911 to take up a life of farming. But the lure of aviation became too great, and he returned to Europe, enrolling in the Aviation School at Pau in France. Upon obtaining his license, Bider bought a 70 hp Blériot and promptly undertook a flight from Pau to Madrid, thus becoming the first airman to cross the Pyrenees. Later, headquartered in Bern, he was invited to take part in the various shows and meets in support of the national fund.

75

The card above was aboard for Oskar Bider's second National Flugspende effort, March 30, 1913. Bearing the semi-official Bern-Burgdorf stamp in the upper left corner, of which 13,000 were sold, the card also displays a special cancellation reading, "Erste Flugpost–30 III 13–Bern–Burgdorf" Flugspende airmail from the fifth (Aarau–Olten–Lenzburg) pioneer mail flight is shown here. The oversize yellow/brown label from 1913, and the 40-franc stamp issued by Switzerland in 1977, honor Bider, who flew over the Central Alps to Milan one day after his twenty-second birthday.

Basel aviation week began on March 1, 1913, but the corresponding air mail flight did not take place until March 9. At 5:30 P.M. on that day, Bider, with his brother and two full mail bags crammed into the passenger seat, took off from the field at Basel before a cheering crowd and headed at once toward Liestal, some twenty miles away. Once over the Gitterli parade ground at Liestal, before several thousand spectators, a bag of mail was dropped. During his second circuit of the parade ground, Bider dropped the other bag, which like the first, was retrieved by Swiss soldiers and taken at once to the Liestal Post Office for forwarding. Oskar Bider collected no fee for flying this mail; his reward was to see the national collection benefit to the extent of 5,030 50-centime stamps reportedly sold. Moreover, he was delighted to undertake six more postal flights for the cause.

The special air mail date stamp supplied by the Swiss postal authorities read ERSTE SCHWEIZERISCHE FLUGPOST—9.III.13. The second air mail flight in this pioneer series would take place three weeks later at Bern. Oskar Bider would again be the pilot of record, but more than twice as many semi-official air post stamps would be sold. Swiss aviation seemed to be on its way at last.

Bider died early in a crash at the Dubendorf-Zurich airfield in 1919. He was a national hero, known to old and young alike for having piloted most of the Swiss Aviation Day flights, and especially, for flying over the Central Alps from Bern to Milan— the first such crossing ever recorded.

An air mail stamp is born Leaning against the wooden roof support of an open storage shed in the aviation camp in Turin, the young pilot looked somber. Never had he seen so much rain. Five consecutive days of it had forced his mission to be postponed. Through a sheet of wind-driven rain Lieutenant de Bernardi glanced toward the huge hangar where his two-seat Pomilio PB–1 biplane waited. With a slight nod to a nearby mechanic and a shrug of the shoulders, the disappointed airman turned to leave the camp. The date was May 21, 1917.

During this crucial year of the Great War, it might be imagined that Mario de Bernardi's mission had something to do with an expected Austrian offensive on the gradually thawing northern front. On the contrary, the twenty-four-year-old pilot was increasingly impatient to undertake a flight that appeared to be entirely unrelated to Italy's war effort. His job was simply to fly a few sacks of non-priority (civilian) mail from Turin to Rome, a distance of some 500 kilometers. Then, he would carry more mail on the return. A round-trip flight of regular mail, that's all.

The mission, however, had been authorized by no less an official than Signor Fera, the Italian Minister for Posts and Telegraphs, and Lieutenant de Bernardi was convinced that his projected flight was more urgent than he knew. His suspicions were correct, in fact; he was about to fly for the very first time mail franked with an official air mail stamp.

With the outbreak of World War I, pioneering experiments with flown mail were, for the most part, quickly put aside. Especially in Europe, aviation resources were turned to offensive military purposes. Pilots were trained to haul bombs and become proficient in using constantly improving machinery and armaments instead of transporting mail and parcels.

Then, almost without warning, the air mail process reappeared. Suddenly it became a live possibility on both sides of the Atlantic, and oddly enough, the war, which to this point had inhibited such an evolutionary advance in communication, had much to do with the change. The United States was on the verge of initiating the world's first regular air mail service over an

An unused copy of the world's first official air mail stamp. Clearly seen are its 25-centesimi value, its portrait of Italian King Victor Emmanuel III, and its special black overprint. Beneath the 1917 issue is a 40-lira stamp of 1967 that points to the 50th anniversary of the earlier stamp. Of three commemorative cards prepared for the first Turin–Rome flight, this one is most commonly found. Featuring an allegorical figure of "Italia," it displays both special postmarks and a faint arrival stamp.

established route, with the primary aim of giving the pilots added experience in cross-country flying techniques. And, with a minimum of fanfare, Italy had issued the world's first air mail stamp because the government wished to undertake a test flight of mail between two distant cities—Rome and Turin. The advent of an official adhesive postage stamp designated exclusively for aerial delivery was an unexpected and long-awaited endorsement of the entire air mail enterprise.

Italy's reason for pursuing the air mail flight was clear; her intent in regard to the stamp was less so. She was seeking a viable means of communication with her islands of Sardinia and Sicily in the event that German submarine activity separated them from contact with the mainland. An inland test would prove whether or not the transport of mail by plane over such a distance was feasible. In the case of the stamp, it was thought that the Italian government issued the world's first airmail for prestige (semi-official air post stamps had been produced before—e.g., in Germany in 1912 and in Switzerland in 1913) and as a means of diverting the attention of Italians at a time when the fortunes of war were hardly smiling upon them.

The new stamp was made available officially on May 16, 1917 in the post offices of Rome and Turin. Not a new design, the stamp was an overprint of Italy's then-current rose-red twenty-five-cent special delivery (ESPRESSO) stamp, which had been issued in 1903. The black overprint read: ESPERIMENTO POSTA AREA/MAGGIO 1917/TORINO—ROMA ● ROMA—TORINO, and it was applied to 200,000 copies at the State Printing Works, Turin. This first air mail was a "provisional" issue intended for temporary use only on the single round-trip venture between Turin and Rome. Sales were restricted to three per customer. Special mail boxes to receive the mail were set up in both cities a few days before the announced date of the flight on May 19, 1917.

Following postponement of the flight due to bad weather, de Bernardi prepared to depart for Rome the next day and, indeed, it did appear as if the clouds were beginning to lift the next morning. Consequently most of the mail was ordered cancelled that day in both Turin and in Rome. However, the weather again closed in as the day advanced, and another delay was forced upon the operation. Finally, on May 22, it seemed possible to attempt the flight.

When de Bernardi and his general purpose biplane rose into the air from the Turin Aviation Camp at about 11:20 that morning, history was made. The pilot would later describe his flight in this way:

> I crossed Turin at a low altitude because the clouds were low and I was in the midst of them when I had climbed to only one thousand meters.

The wind was against me at that height, so I descended to 800 meters, and directed my machine toward the Apennine mountains. Subsequently I climbed again to 1,300 meters, and as the clouds were thick, and I could not see the ground, I directed myself entirely by compass. In this first trip, instead of flying direct to Genoa which is in a straight line from Turin, I flew to Savona. Turning to the right and flying over the sea, I had below me the most magnificent view of that industrial zone and the high smoke-stacks of the many factories gave me a synthetic impression of the tremendous work that is being done in Italy to win the present war.

The port of Genoa, with its innumerable vessels at anchor, the masts of which have from high, the aspect of a great forest of trees without branches or leaves, present a fantastic appearance.

Following the route, I passed Portofino, then over Spezia, meeting better weather, but my machine and myself being beaten every now and then by showers and wind.

Keeping the sea on the left, I passed over Livorno, and there finally saw the sun. But before I reached Piombino, the persistent rain was back and was with me until I had passed Civita Vecchia. Towards Rome the weather was better. I passed over the city at not over 500 meters altitude, with a strong wind shaking my aeroplane. I found later that the velocity of the wind was 34 meters a second.

I descended over the Centocelle aviation camp when a violent puff of wind struck my aeroplane as I landed, and caused one of the wheels to strike a pile of rubbish in the field. I suffered a few scratches, not serious enough to prevent me from starting back to Turin that evening.

I had accomplished the trip, with a detour over Savona, with a further deviation over the sea at Livorno, in four hours and three minutes, having covered the distance of 635 kilometers in that time.

Some four-hundred-eighty pounds of mail were transported, much of this weight being composed of large numbers of specially prepared commemorative cards and one hundred copies each of two newspapers. De Bernardi was greeted at the Centocelle airfield by General Marieni, Italian Military Aviation chief, and by the Postmaster of Rome. One of the mail bags was taken from the plane by the pilot and ceremoniously handed over to the postmaster, this mail being distributed in Rome by four o'clock that same afternoon.

If Lieutenant de Bernardi's slight mishap on landing in Rome was not sufficiently harmful to plane or pilot to cause a delay in the return flight, the weather was. The Rome to Turin mail was eventually on its way on May 27.

> I started from Rome [on the 27th], again in horrible weather. There were, however, no incidents as far as Genoa; but in the

vicinity of the Apennine mountains the clouds were so dense that although I climbed up to 4,000 meters, I did not succeed in finding blue sky. Instead, I was buffeted by gales, which prevented all progress. Twice I pointed the machine towards Turin in different points, but it was in vain. The gale forced me back each time. So I decided to turn back and I flew along the Ligurian rivers looking for a landing place. Flying at about 200 meters from the ground, I finally saw a beach that seemed adequate for landing; I circled over it and landed at Lavagna, where I was given a hearty reception.

The reception must have been a hearty one and long lasting, for the flying postman's northbound mail was not delivered in Turin until June 3, and, understandably, was never given a receiving stamp by postal workers. Most of the Rome–Turin flown mail, of course, was franked with the new provisional stamp and bore a May 20 cancellation date. A very small number of pieces of the mail destined for Turin are dated May 27, indicating that they were cancelled just before the flight.

Only a portion of the overprinted first airmails of Italy were used on the de Bernardi flights of 1917. Remaining copies were available for sale through the Italian Postal Administration for many years, being sold for slightly more than face value. But shortly before the outbreak of World War II, supplies of the stamp were either exhausted or destroyed. Fortunately, many were preserved on cover as a continuing reminder of the historic dimensions of the Turin–Rome flights of 1917.

This photo shows the type of Pomilio biplane used by Lt. de Bernardi in 1917.

Military courier airpost Shortly after Italy's war-related trial air mail flights of 1917, which saw a second provisional stamp issued for a seaplane flight between Naples and Palermo, the Austrians began a remarkable military air courier service in Central Europe. This service was initiated on March 31, 1918, involving the transport of military dispatches as well as civilian mail, and continued until mid-October of the same year.

While little publicized because of its military connection, the Austrian courier service boldly demonstrated that the long-range planes then in use could be employed for communications purposes regularly, over long distances, and with a high degree of success. Only two small loads of mail were reported lost in the six months in which the service operated. The service also was the occasion for the issuance of a new three-value set of overprinted provisional air mail stamps, Austria following Italy's lead in the matter of franking air mail letters.

The courier service operated from its inception between Vienna, capital of Austria, and the cities of Cracow and Lemberg, though the Vienna/Cracow leg alone excluded civilian mail. The Lemberg leg was frequently extended all the way to Kiev, since that city was serving as headquarters for the occupation forces of Germany and Austria, and therefore, of considerable strategic importance at the time. Schedules called for the Cracow route to be flown in four hours, the Lemberg route in seven hours. A plane going beyond Lemberg to Kiev would require another six hours, making the full Vienna-Kiev flight an amazing thirteen-hour marathon. Although there were intermediate stops on all legs of the courier network, the aforementioned stops were the only ones involved with the transfer, exchange, and processing of mail.

The dramatic nature of the Austrian military courier service can be imagined. A small three-wheeled motorcycle, with a mail-chest to the side in place of the passenger seat, would race to the airfield under armed guard each morning just before dawn. There in the shadows of a large aircraft, the urgent dispatches and mail would be loaded aboard. Soon the lumbering plane would lift from the field, always carrying aloft a military officer, an "observer" assigned to oversee the flight. The communications and mail were the responsibility of a senior non-com who would see to their delivery into proper hands upon arrival.

The mail that came to and departed from Vienna's Aspern Aviation Field was impressive. Usually, the envelopes bore regular postage for surface transport in addition to the new air mail stamps and were heavily decorated with both ordinary circular and air post cancellations. The air post cancellation of the destination city was, as a rule, applied on the back of the envelope to verify the arrival date. It is known that 184 covers were flown to Cracow on the first day of operations (March 31, 1918) and that 264 covers went from Vienna to Lemberg the same day.

The final run of this very ambitious courier service took place on October 15, 1918, just prior to the war's end. The service itself offered the world an auspicious hope of things to come in terms of governmental sponsorship of air post systems.

The cover at the right, with considerable foxing (browning), traveled with the Austrian air courier service that operated for about six months in 1918. First cancelled at Lemberg on April 14, the cover also displays a special Lemberg airpost cancellation (April 15) at the right edge, and a Vienna airpost date stamp (April 16) as a backstamp. The three provisional airmails at the top of the cover are the first-printing gray-paper ones; the mint set off cover are of a later white-paper printing. A 5-schilling blue commemorative from 1961 pictures the first Austrian mail plane, a 1918 Albatross of German design.

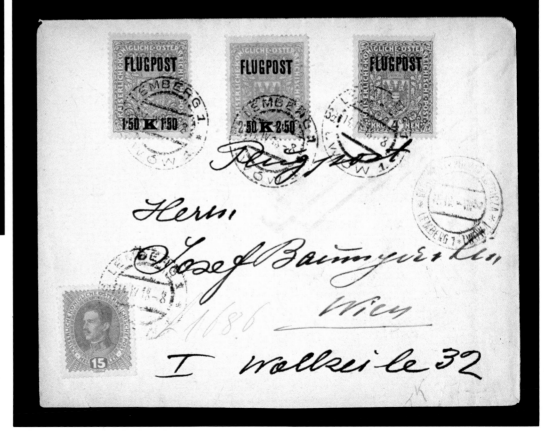

4

Growth under government

The great breakthrough "Let the trains carry it! We've got a war to win!," cried a young American Signal Corps pilot in dismay and disbelief at his latest orders. He had been sure that reassignment from Ellington Field near Houston, Texas, to Long Island meant an overseas posting at long last.

But here were the orders carrying a date of May 8, 1918: First Lieutenant Howard P. Culver is assigned to Hazelhurst Field, Mineola, Long Island, New York, "for duty in the Training Department in connection with the aerial mail service. By order of..." With keen disappointment sweeping over him once again, Paul Culver struggled to fathom how such an ill-timed directive could have come to pass.

In the early months of 1918, instructor pilots with Culver's depth of experience and hours aloft were not thinking air mail. Nor was hardly anyone else. World attention was riveted on the war. Americans were, for the most part, intent on obeying stern-visaged, top-hatted Uncle Sam, who pointed his finger at them from billboards, and they were busy mobilizing their personal and collective resources to support their country's participation in the war.

Mid-1917 had seen Lieutenant Colonel William "Billy" Mitchell join the staff of the Commander-in-Chief, American Expeditionary Forces (A.E.F.), to carry forward the overseas organizational task of building a military air service to support the A.E.F. Construction of American war planes in France began at Romorantin the following February, and simultaneously, the 94th Squadron of the 1st United States Pursuit Group began its operations across the fighting lines. In April 1918, Lieutenant Edward V. Rickenbacker shot down his first enemy plane. At home, President Wilson had just proclaimed (among other things) a licensing requirement for all civilian pilots.

Almost no one, it seemed, was concerned about air mail early in 1918. The world was saddled with far more pressing matters. Yet 1918 was destined to become the birthing hour for the world's first regular air mail system. In the midst of Liberty Loan drives and Red Cross benefits and countless other distractions, and in spite of all the reasons why not, Woodrow Wilson announced that May 15, 1918, would be the day to begin the ambitious new service. Undoubtedly, few persons were more surprised by this decision than the tiny contingent of Army Signal Corps pilots who were about to assist as midwives at the birth.

On the surface it appeared that Paul Culver's cry of dismay about the aerial mail was well founded. Weren't the powers-that-be off on a wild flight of fancy when they consented to the initiation of a flying postal service right in the midst of a national emergency? Critical resources in terms of planes and pilots would have to be diverted to an apparently non-essential task.

83

And who could be sure that an all-weather daily mail service by plane was even possible in 1918, considering the performance capabilities of the aircraft then available? The whole venture seemed questionable, filled with unnecessary risk. Yet, there were other factors that convinced Wilson and his Postmaster General that air mail was an idea whose time had come.

For one thing, Congress was already prepared with the funding: $100,000 had been appropriated for fiscal 1917–18 for the creation of an aerial mail route, this amount being tacked onto the allotment for steamboat and power-boat service for the year. Very few observers in or out of government ever expected to see the money used for its expressed purpose. A similar grant had been all but ignored the previous year. No takers had advanced bids to operate experimental routes in Massachusetts and Alaska in 1917, simply because no company could obtain planes to accomplish the specified jobs.

A far-sighted Texan named Morris Sheppard was principally responsible for the Congressional actions in behalf of air mail. As early as 1910 when in Congress, and later in 1916 as a senator, Sheppard introduced bills seeking authorizations and appropriations for the conduct of experimental routes. Support for his proposals in 1916 came from the influential National Advisory Committee for Aeronautics. Thus, Congress saw fit to provide $100,000 for each of the two fiscal years between 1916 and 1918. Passage of the Sheppard bills proved one very important point— that serious attention to aviation's commercial possibilities was gradually replacing a tenacious indifference in the United States, an indifference based largely on a viewpoint that classified the airplane as a plaything for daring but frivolous young men of means.

Insofar as technological advances are concerned, kinder welcomes and appraisals often come with increased familiarity, and Americans were feeling increasingly at home with the flying machine. Visits to carnivals, fairs, and air meets permitted young and old alike to witness exciting demonstrations of flying skill. The pioneers eagerly served as unpaid aerial mailmen, taking off with thousands of souvenir cards and letters, then as now prized symbols and nostalgic reminders of the dawning age. But the early birds did more than prove that airplanes were fit to haul the mails. They also contributed to a particular mood about the future of flight, and their mail-carrying sorties inevitably had an impact in Washington as well as in remote country hamlets.

President Wilson had more to go on than a heightened grassroots awareness and appropriated dollars as he set the air mail wheels in motion. He was flowing along with particular currents that the war itself had produced. There was a continual race among the combative nations to improve their hardware, in-

cluding their flying machines. Indeed, a steady stream of modified and newly-developed airplanes moved to the fighting fronts from both sides, giving the air power advantage a see-saw effect. Almost weekly, the lead changed from one side to the other, depending upon whose plane was making its debut in the skies over France. The improvements in aerial capability at this juncture of the war were frequent and dramatic. Moreover, the war produced an urgent need for trained flyers. One of the chief arguments for the air mail route—the argument that eventually earned Paul Culver's enthusiasm for his assignment—was that it would impose a strict and challenging regimen upon some inexperienced pilots, by forcing them to learn cross-country flight techniques at an accelerated pace. Lastly, the conflict spawned a clear recognition of the value of speed in communication. The government and its widespread supply network urgently required the fastest possible means of moving critical papers and materials over great distances.

Overshadowing most factors was the matter of personnel. In this regard Woodrow Wilson felt supremely confident. Postmaster General Albert S. Burleson supported the air mail concept with unqualified enthusiasm and desired very much to see this emerging section of his Post Office Department blossom and succeed. Under his direction there was the short, cigar-smoking Otto Praeger, who was cut out for his task of overseeing the transport of all mail. A visionary, Praeger contributed both enthusiasm that speeded up events, and hard-driving competence that by-passed or cut through the masses of red-tape surrounding the start of the service. Second Assistant Postmaster General Praeger was uniquely prepared to tackle this new opportunity. Finally, President Wilson was fully aware of an enlarged pool of skilled military pilots and mechanics from which he could draw for the air mail in the post-war period.

Thus it transpired that the United States, in response to the President's directive, initiated the world's first regularly scheduled air mail service. The United States also prepared to issue the world's first definitive air mail stamp, designed and intended for continuous use on an established air post route.

Relative to the operation, there ensued some furious days in May 1918. For several months preliminary conversations about an air mail venture had been taking place between the War and Post Office Departments, and they led on March 1 to a tentative agreement to jointly operate an air mail service whenever the time seemed right. However, it was not until May 3 that a War Department order actually put the plan in motion. This directive, under the signature of Secretary of War Newton D. Baker, instructed the department's air service to begin as early as May 15 daily two-way carriages of mail by plane between New York and Washington, D. C., with an intermediate stop in Philadelphia. Accordingly, a slightly earlier date of the 13 was chosen by the Post Office Department for public introduction of its new 24-cent air mail stamp.

Two promising young Signal Corps officers were selected to put the service together. Major Reuben H. Fleet, then Colonel "Hap" Arnold's assistant in charge of all Air Service pilot training, took command of the air mail and assumed responsibility for securing and maintaining the planes. He also supervised the team of pilots, which included Paul Culver and five other less-experienced men. Captain Benjamin B. Lipsner, a non-pilot from Air Service Production, became Fleet's chief aide. He was to handle all supervisory detail.

Major Fleet learned of his new assignment (he did not relinquish any of his other duties) in Secretary Baker's office on Monday morning, May 6. He and Captain Lipsner were informed that they had nine days in which to assemble the pieces of their little miracle. Fleet made a spirited plea for additional time, and this was promptly turned down by Postmaster General Burleson. The take-off date, Burleson emphatically let it be known, had just been fed to the media. Major Fleet had no choice, and went to work on the spot. In his own words:

Without leaving Secretary Baker's office [on the morning of May 6th], I telephoned Colonel E. A. Deeds of Air Service Production and requested him to order six JN–6H's from the Curtiss Aeroplane and Motor Corporation at Garden City, Long Island, New York, which firm was manufacturing trainers for the Army, leaving out the front seat and the front control, and substituting in the front cockpit a hopper to carry mail; also installing in each airplane double capacity for gasoline and oil, the six airplanes to be delivered to us at Mineola Air Field in eight days.

Curtiss accepted the telephonic order and agreed to have ready the six such airplanes at the sacrifice of suspending delivery of trainers during this period. They proposed to use two regular nineteen gallon gasoline tanks to double the fuel capacity. The normal range of a Curtiss JN-6H airplane trainer with a gasoline tank carrying 19 gallons was 88 miles in one hour and twenty minutes at cruising speed of 66 miles an hour, reduced by head-winds and accelerated by tail winds.

The JN–6H "Jenny" referred to was powered by a 150 hp Hispano-Suiza engine.

The historic day was Wednesday, May 15. A small band of dedicated men shared an exciting enterprise, one that was geared to speed communications and help shrink the world's size yet another notch. It was a mission that would in time precipitate the growth of a great commercial aviation industry in the United States, the very industry that was to "loft the common man toward hitherto undreamed of destinations."

By day's end, a short roster of names—Fleet, Webb, and Burleson; Edgerton, Lipsner, and Boyle; Culver and Praeger—were front-page news. For this team of Signal Corps airmen and Post Office Department administrators inaugurated, under the authority of a Presidential decree, the world's first regularly scheduled air mail service. Beginning that day, mail-carrying flights in both directions between the nation's capital and its center of commerce at New York City, with intermediate stops in Philadelphia, commenced daily (except Sundays), weather conditions notwithstanding. It was a rather tall order for these flyers, considering the level of aviation technology just fifteen short years after Kitty Hawk!

By midmorning, a large and excited crowd had gathered around the perimeter of the Polo Grounds in Potomac Park in Washington, D.C. A festive air reigned.

Lieutenant Jim Edgerton, the United States Army Air Service pilot who would be landing on the field the same afternoon with the first flown mail coming into the capital, later described the Polo Grounds this way:

It was an area about one thousand feet long and four hundred wide, oval in shape and entirely surrounded by sixty foot trees. To make the situation more enjoyable, a covered bandstand stood out about one hundred and fifty feet from the southeast end, the hangar occupying the opposite end. Forced landings were well taken care of. One approach was a city of barracks. The other side of our two-way field led directly to the War and Navy Buildings. On each side the field was sandwiched in by water.

Hardly an ideal landing site, the Polo field on the edge of the Potomac river had been selected as the Washington terminus of the air mail because there was no better flying field in the city.

Hastily arranged plans for that morning called for almost simultaneous departures of mail planes from Washington (11:00 A.M.) and from Belmont Park on Long Island (11:30 A.M.), which had been selected as the New York area terminus in order not to interrupt war-time pilot training at the nearby Army field in Mineola. In Washington, as well as in New York, a brief ceremony preceded takeoff.

About 9:30 A.M., on what proved to be a warm and sultry spring day, the excitement was mounting in Washington. A plane had just swooped down to a graceful landing on the turf of the Polo Grounds. It was a spanking new Curtiss "Jenny," bearing the bold, black numerical designation 3–8–2–6–2 on both sides of its fuselage. The pilot was Major Reuben H. Fleet, officer-in-charge of the Air Mail Service, who had flown the plane in from Philadelphia for its first mail assignment.

No sooner had the plane taxied to the end of the field near the crowd, when it was surrounded by an army of mechanics, photographers, and officials. In a few moments, a police-escorted mail truck arrived with a boldly lettered sign reading UNITED STATES AIR MAIL SERVICE. The mail had made a dramatic entrance. After greeting many of the officials present and making a quick estimate of the load, Major Fleet and Lieutenant George Leroy Boyle put their heads together to study maps and review route features. Lieutenant Boyle was to fly the first load of mail out of Washington. Because the military road map strapped to Boyle's right leg was sketchy at best, the trip was to be a "contact" flying exercise for him; Fleet was anxious to key in the young pilot as completely as possible to those topographical features that would serve as his check points on the flight.

With a minimum of fanfare, an elegant, shiny, black limousine then drove to planeside with a police escort. A new excitement swept over the crowd. The President and Mrs. Wilson had just arrived from the White House.

Among the noted individuals present to greet the President and to celebrate the inauguration of the Service were the Postmaster General of Japan, Secretary of War Newton D. Baker, Postmaster General Burleson, and Assistant Secretary of the Navy Franklin D. Roosevelt. Members of the Senate and House Committees on Post Office and Post Roads were also there, as was Second Assistant Postmaster General Praeger, who was in charge of the transportation of all mail in the United States and who had worked long and hard to bring this occasion into being. While mechanics continued to attend to the aircraft, Major Fleet greeted the President and his wife and was asked to come with Secretary Baker to the White House immediately following takeoff.

As the crowd pressed forward, Woodrow Wilson wished Boyle success and then drew from his pocket a personally autographed envelope addressed to the Honorable T. H. [the initial should have read G] Patten, Postmaster of New York City. After this letter was carefully placed in the last mail bag to be loaded aboard, the President stepped back solemnly to watch. The full mail load weighed close to 140 pounds. Most of the individual items displayed the bright, new red-white-and-blue 24-cent adhesive that had been issued for the thrilling first trips. The stamp design, if carefully studied under a magnifying glass, reveals a Curtiss Jenny #38262.

The mail was about to be on its way. Boyle shouted the familiar, "Contact!," heard clearly by the jubilant crowd. Sergeant E. F. Waters of the ground crew moved toward the plane, grasped the Jenny's large wooden propeller, and pulled it through a complete arc. Then he whipped it part-way into a second revolution, and deftly released his hold while stepping back. The prop snapped around...then came to a stop. Once more the husky sergeant tried with an identical result. Repeated efforts to get the

engine to turn over were futile. In its moment of glory, the 150 hp engine had balked. A cadre of khaki-suited mechanics swarmed around the plane. Five...ten...fifteen minutes passed. The President impatiently fingered his pocket watch.

It was 11:15 and still holding! Derisive laughter began to spread through the restless crowd. A now visibly annoyed President paced back and forth.

Suddenly, while Major Fleet continued to review procedures with George Boyle at planeside, Captain Lipsner, following his intuition, asked whether anyone had checked the gas tanks. No one had! And upon investigation, they proved to be bone dry. In all the excitement, no one had remembered to refuel the Jenny.

With understandable haste, Waters and his men borrowed gasoline from some nearby planes and filled the tanks. The "Hisso" sprang to life on the first swing through...the prop instantly became a shiny blur. The tail skid bounced across the rutted turf during the takeoff run, and, with a surge of power, the machine separated from earth, skimming perilously close with its landing gear to tall trees that bordered the far edge of the field. The crowd erupted with a cheer of approval. This was the grand moment when air mail truly became airborne for good.

Sadly, however, Boyle and his mail were not Philadelphia-bound as planned. In one of those intrusions of fate, which make historic events often outshine even the cleverest of fictions, #38262 flew off to an unforseen and unfortunate set-down in a plowed field just southeast of Washington.

Confused by the number of railroad tracks leading from the capital, Boyle had followed the wrong set. He realized after several passes over unknown terrain, and after missing the water that he was supposed to keep on his right, that he was hopelessly lost. His forced landing, near Waldorf, Maryland (and ironically, right next-door to the rural home of Otto Praeger), was made with the intention of securing directions from anyone he might encounter. But he splintered his propeller tumbling over some rough ground, and his takeoff capability was instantly and irrevocably compromised. The Boyle portion of the nation's first regular air mail was stranded some twenty miles from its starting place!

Preparations for the first flight from the Washington terminus
include a route briefing for pilot Boyle (above, with map), on-
loading of 6,600 first trip letters—of which 300 are to be deplaned
at Philadelphia, and posing—as Reuben Fleet does in the photo at
upper right—for the ubiquitous photographers. Finally, JH-6H
#38262, one of twelve planes modified for air mail duty, moves to
its takeoff position well after 11 A.M.

With ground personnel positioned at both lower-wing tips, Lt. George Leroy Boyle shoves his throttle forward and begins his takeoff run over the mottled surface of the Potomac Park Polo Grounds. Moments later the craft is airborne, carrying aloft four mail sacks containing the world's first regularly scheduled air mail.

Reuben Fleet and his pilots received complimentary wristwatches to mark their historic flights. After receiving his watch at Potomac Park from Hamilton Watch Company President Charles F. Miller, the Major proudly shows it to Mrs. Fleet upon arriving home.

Fortunately, the comic—almost melodramatic—happenings attending the inauguration of the service were reserved exclusively for the Washington end of the line. Elsewhere, things were on track and on time. The honor of flying the world's first *successful* regular-service air mail flight fell to Lieutenant Torrey H. Webb, a former student of mining at Columbia University. After hearing most of the ceremonial speeches at Belmont Park, New York, and after receiving a Hamilton wristwatch (as did all of the first-trip pilots), Webb departed precisely at 11:30 A.M. from the infield of the racetrack and set his course for Bustleton. In just over an hour's time, Webb and Jenny #38278 arrived in Philadelphia...right on schedule.

Lieutenant James Clark Edgerton received Washington-bound mail from Torrey Webb at Philadelphia and promptly departed from Bustleton in his Jenny #38274. He arrived at the Polo Grounds at 2:50 P.M., with a small but enthusiastic crowd still on hand to greet him. The southbound leg of the Air Mail Service thus achieved a perfect score on opening day. Edgerton's load of mail comprised some 150 pounds of letters, parcels, and copies of *The New York Times* from the day before.

The officer-in-charge at Bustleton, Lieutenant H. Paul Culver, rounded out the first-trip performances with a delayed, but otherwise uneventful, flight to New York, using Webb's plane #38278. With the northbound load from Washington temporarily grounded, Culver carried only Philadelphia mail bound for New York and points beyond. This involved some 350 letters, of which 200 were addressed to New York City locations. Several planes from the Army field at Mineola were in the air to welcome Culver over Long Island, and a throng of happy schoolchildren were at Belmont Park to greet his landing. The children had been excused from classes in order to witness history being made.

In later years, after he had received the honorary designation of Air Mail Pilot #1, Fleet made these points about the Washington–New York challenge:

All the aerial mail planes were doped fabric covered as to wings and fuselages, structure being wire-braced...the front cockpit had a covered hopper for mail...there were no parachutes...every pilot rode his airplane down to earth on a forced landing...there were no maps of much value; they showed only political divisions with nothing of a physical nature except cities, towns, rivers, harbors, etc....the magnetic compass was inaccurate and was affected by local metal on the airplane and there were no compass bases to use in compensating each compass.

Little wonder that he would add, "We should, therefore, not criticize Lieutenant Boyle too severely."

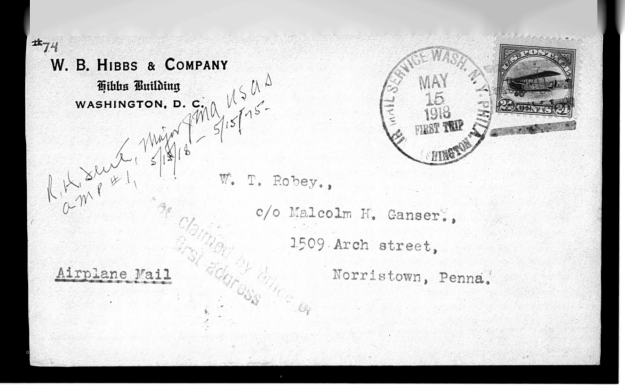

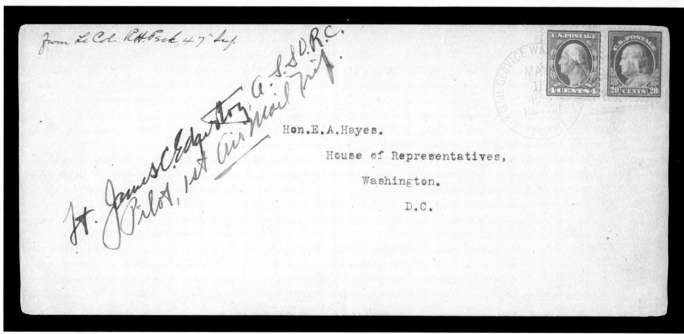

Two covers from U.S. air mail's first trips. The above cover, signed by Major Fleet on the 57th anniversary of the 1918 inaugural flights, bears the 24¢ red-and-blue airmail issued on Monday, May 13, 1918, just in time for the opening of the pioneer route. This Boyle-flown cover was prepared by William T. Robey, the young Washington stock clerk, who on May 14, 1918 found the full sheet of 24¢ inverted-center airmails. The lower cover, carried from New York by Torrey Webb and into Washington by James Edgerton, is a scarce, pilot-signed cover of May 15th with ordinary franking.

After receiving official blessings and a "good luck"
horseshoe from visiting French airman Lt. Henri Farre,
1st Lt. Torrey H. Webb departed promptly at 11:30 A.M. from the
infield of Long Island's Belmont Park race track. Carrying 182
letters addressed to Philadelphia and 459 for Washington, Webb's
brief flight to Bustleton on May 15, 1918, proved the first successful
mail run over a permanently established air mail route.

Using Webb's plane #38278, Lt. H. Paul Culver inaugurates the Philadelphia–New York leg of the new route. On the afternoon of May 15, he turns over 350 letters to a welcoming postal offical at Belmont Park. Jim Edgerton's Jenny #38274 (below) is readied at Bustleton for its Philadelphia–Washington mail carry, including Washington-bound mail just flown by Webb.

The upside-down "Jenny"

Twenty-four hours before the inaugural flights on the air mail route between Washington and New York, the newly issued red-white-and-blue adhesive had caused a furor that had captured the headlines. On Tuesday, May 14, 1918, one sheet of 100 copies of the 24-cent stamp was discovered with inverted blue vignettes or centers; the Jennys pictured on this sheet were all flying upside down! This find by a Washington, D.C., stamp collector named William T. Robey instantly shook the philatelic world. It even caused the Army to fear that the postal error might somehow interfere with the launching of the service on the following day.

A collector of plate-number blocks of stamps at the time, Mr. Robey bought the sheet across the counter of a local branch post office near his office in Washington. It seems likely that he spotted the inverted blue plate number before he noticed the upside-down planes. Only one sheet of the entire first printing had a plate number, and that sheet was the very one handed to Robey by the postal clerk. The perforating machines used for the first printing of this hastily produced stamp had automatically trimmed off the margin where the blue plate number appeared on all the other correctly printed sheets.

Operating on the belief that other similar sheets might turn up, Robey sought at once to sell his treasure. Within the week, Philadelphia stamp dealer Eugene Klein purchased the $24.00 sheet intact for $15,000. Later, Klein sold it for $20,000 to a well-known collector, Colonel E. H. R. Green of New York. Green eventually had the full sheet broken up so that other collectors could obtain some of these stamps, but retained the principal position blocks for his own collection.

The first United States air mail stamp had a lot going for it. It was the world's first definitive airmail...the first air mail issue of the United States and the Western Hemisphere...the first air mail issue to picture an aeroplane...the first bi-colored airmail ...the first stamp associated with a regular civil air mail service ...and, the first air mail stamp to be printed with an error. That error occasioned the most valuable philatelic discovery ever made in the United States. Single copies of the 24-cent inverted-center stamp of 1918 now obtain a price in excess of $100,000.

A right-margin copy of the 1918 inverted-center airmail. Designed by C.A. Huston, the 24¢-issue was hastily produced for the inaugural air mail flights. Microphotographic analysis has shown that the blue press run followed the red, thus confirming the "inverted-center" description.

The famous Taussig letter

The last envelope placed in the mail bags in Washington on the morning of May 15, 1918 was destined to become first among cherished mementos of that important occasion.

This letter, sent from Postmaster General Burleson to the Honorable Thomas G. Patten, Postmaster at New York City, bore President Wilson's signature at the top of the cover near, but not on, a freshly cancelled 24-cent airmail. Burleson referred to this particular stamp as "the first aeroplane postage stamp to be sold by (his) department." Six high Post Office officials also placed their initials on the white selvage, which adjoined the stamp on the cover.

Often called the Taussig letter in aerophilatelic circles because it resulted from an idea of Noah W. Taussig, New York businessman and life-long stamp collector, the letter in the cover became the property of Postmaster Patten. However, the envelope with the President's signature and the cancelled stamp was to be delivered upon receipt to Mr. Taussig. He in turn had arranged for the cover to be auctioned off for the benefit of the war-involved Red Cross. When nobody topped Taussig's guaranteed opening bid of $1,000.00, to his great disappointment, the cover came into his possession. An exciting piece of philatelic detective work in 1978 by Philip Silver, then President of the American Air Mail Society, determined that the cover still remains with the Taussig family and the letter still resides with New York City's incumbent postmaster.

Among the first letters to be airborne on May 15, 1918, the Taussig letter ended up being among the last to be delivered, due to Jenny 38262's surprise landing in the Maryland meadow. ". . . and the first shall be last."

Washington Postmaster Merritt Chance holds the famed Taussig letter at Potomac Park before it is placed in the bag by President Wilson. Like other "first trip" mail, this letter received the special air mail service date stamp that indicated the city of origin at the bottom of the circle under the date.

From poetry to mathematics

With the inaugural flights between New York and Washington a matter of record, the challenges of the air mail enterprise became immediately clearer to those involved. No one has described this settling-in period better than Captain Ben Lipsner, who played a major role—first as Major Fleet's second-in-command and then as his successor, when Fleet was transferred to other duties early in June. Lipsner remarked:

With the inauguration of the Air Mail Service on May 15, 1918, the aeroplane entered the commercial field.

It is not now a question of experimenting to determine the usefulness of aeroplanes as a commercial carrier. The Air Mail Service is a success, operating without interruptions by weather conditions and carrying the mail by schedule.

The aeroplane has developed marvelous efficiency as a fighting machine, its flights have outdistanced the flights of imagination . . . but aeronautics is not food for the mere imagination . . . we pass from poetry to mathematics . . . the utilization of power with the least possible waste of lifting energy, the details of construction (of aircraft), and the consumption of fuel are things which attract our attention.

The air mail route is the first step toward the universal commercial use of the aeroplane . . . The Air Mail Service is the mechanical laboratory for the advancement of commercial aviation. The wonderful acrobatic feats necessary to aerial combat are not a feature of the flying in this service, but in their place is the necessity to make ordinary flying commonplace, and to do everyday commonplace things efficiently.

United States Army pilots would fly the mail for almost three months, until Saturday, August 10. Although George Boyle was moved to other duties after his second try with air mail led to a crash landing near Philadelphia on May 17, 1918, Paul Culver, Jim Edgerton, and Torrey Webb continued with the service as long as the Army was in charge. These trail-blazing pilots were joined by Lieutenants Stephen Bonsal, E. W. Kilgore, and Walter Miller. A second type of plane was also pressed into service without delay. Jennys continued to amass route miles between Philadelphia and Washington, but the Curtiss R–4 was placed in service on the New York–Philadelphia runs. The R–4L was powered by the Liberty 400 hp engine.

In addition to inaugurating southbound flights out of Philadelphia on opening day, Jim Edgerton completed on May 16 the first successful carry of mail in the opposite direction out of Washington, taking with him Boyle's delayed load from May 15. That afternoon Edgerton became the first pilot to fly two sections of the route on the same day. When Walter Miller's Jenny developed engine trouble shortly after departure from Bustleton, Edgerton volunteered to take the mail into Washington, the city from which he had just come.

Edgerton later recounted how important it was that the pilots solve the weather problem. If they had not done so effectively and with all possible haste, he suggested to one audience, postal authorities might have closed up the entire air mail venture in 1918, branding it as totally impracticable.

One of two Post Office Department appointees on Major Fleet's initial roster of air mail pilots (Boyle was the other), Jim Edgerton had the most outstanding record during the Army's stint on the pioneer route. He completed 52 flights in 106½ hours of flying time over 7,155 route miles. He died in October 1973 at the age of seventy-seven, after having served as the superintendent of all flying operations for the Post Office Department in Washington. He also helped establish the first permanent ground-to-air radio stations in the United States.

The man who handed James Edgerton approximately 100 pounds of his first load of mail at Philadelphia on May 15 remains another unsung hero of the Army's days of experimentation with air mail. Even though he made almost as many flights, Torrey H. Webb never challenged Edgerton's statistical lead among the pilots, logging during the period between May 15 and August 10 about half the hours in the air and close to half the miles flown by his fellow airman. One reason for the difference in totals is that Webb did all his flying on the shorter New York–Philadelphia leg. Another reason is that on the strength of his superb performance record he was called upon to undertake an assignment that kept him away from his regular postings for several days early in June 1918.

To Webb goes the credit for having flown the first extension of the initial route. On June 6, he carried mail experimentally from New York to Boston under instruction from Postmaster General Burleson. Just as it was accidental that Webb and his Jenny #38278 achieved the world's first *successful* regular service air mail carry, so also was his making the first official flight of mail into Boston.

Special mention must be made of Edgerton's leadership in contending with violent summer storms. Though the pilots encountered thunderstorms as expected, with no fewer than four scheduled flights being scrubbed in the first two weeks of operation on the new route due to weather, their instructions were to avoid risk to themselves, their planes, and the mail by landing in the first open field and sitting it out. Almost from the start, the pilots all quietly stretched the rules and dared to tackle, bit by bit, the weather problem.

Edgerton was the first to force his way completely through a violent weather system. Sustaining hail damage to his propeller on the occasion, he was rewarded for his brashness with increased knowledge concerning his plane's capability in severe turbulence.

Torrey H. Webb, mining student turned oilman, who
piloted both the first successful scheduled air mail flight and the
first experimental extension of the original route.

A soft field at Saugus on June 6, 1918, left Webb's Curtiss R-4 mail plane
in nosed-over condition. However, pilot and plane were fit, by June 11,
to transport 64 pounds of mail to New York. Opposite: The return mail
from Boston bore a large distinctive date stamp and a three-line
cancelling device reading "Boston-to-New York." The 10¢ 1975
U.S. stamp features Torrey Webb's first mail plane.

The initial New York–Boston assignment had been granted, as an honor, to a French military aviator who was serving as a flight instructor at Mineola, New York's Army Aviation Field No. 1. Lieutenant Gustave Vannelle was scheduled to depart for Boston with his mechanic and with air mail on Monday morning, June 3. Unfortunately, the Frenchman encountered problems with a control wire during his takeoff run and his plane flipped over before becoming airborne. He sustained no serious injuries, but the mail did not go through to Boston that morning. Instead, it was trucked over to the Belmont Park field to wait another day... for another pilot, Torrey Webb.

At noon on June 6, Webb, with his mechanic, R. Heck, and seven full bags of mail, braved an untried route, nasty weather, and an inadequate landing site to make the delayed mail flight to Boston. "The weather was awfully bad and that flight to Boston was a 'dinger,' " Webb reported many years later. "It was raining cats and dogs when I got to the landing strip. They had marked out an old race track near Boston and the track was covered with holes that they had filled in with ashes." One of those holes nearly ended two promising careers, and came close to obliterating one R–4 mail plane.

On landing at the Franklin Park Aviation Field, part of the Godfrey Cabot estate in Saugus, one wheel of the plane dipped into one of the ruts in the field, now made softer by the down-

pour. The plane flipped up on its nose in a violent arc. Fortunately, Webb and Heck were not hurt, but the plane needed extensive repair. The trip from Belmont Park had taken 3 hours and 22 minutes, with one landing en route, in Connecticut, for a compass correction.

The return trip, with 64 pounds of mail, was another hair-raising experience, which Webb handled with great equanimity. Delayed by repairs, Webb and Heck finally departed on June 11, carrying with them Postmaster William Murray of Boston. Again, the weather was bad all along the route to Long Island. "Visibility was zero-zero," according to Webb, "and I just skimmed over the telephone poles all the way." When aerophilatelists view covers from this flight, with their distinctive "Boston, Mass" circle cancellations, they silently salute a careful and brave pilot, who received hearty congratulations from a welcoming group of field attendants at Belmont Park.

Up until his death at eighty-two in November 1975, Torrey Webb never received the full recognition that his air mail feats should have earned for him. He and his Jenny #38278 did appear on a United States commemorative postage stamp issued three months before he died. Ironically, however, the stamp was part of a bicentennial salute to the United States Postal Service, and no publicity identified the pilot or the plane used by the illustrator for his stamp design.

101

Curtiss JN-6H

The famous "Jenny," designed by B. Douglas Thomas of England for Glenn Curtiss, achieved fame in the United States all out of proportion to its capabilities. Essentially an Army trainer in World War I, the craft was used after the war by almost every civilian flying school in the United States and the great post-war surplus of Jennies supplied the aerial barnstormers of the 1920's. On May 15, 1918 the "Jenny" became the first carrier of air mail on the route between New York and Washington. The airplane used in May of 1918 was actually a hybrid, comprising features of the JN-4H "Jenny" then in production and the JN-6H about to go into production. The first planes to carry mail on a daily basis were complete JN-6H's except that their lower wings were still without ailerons.

Speed: 80 mph (high)
Range: 175-185 miles
Payload: 300 pounds
Engine: Wright Hispano-Suiza 150 hp

De Havilland DH-4B

Geoffrey de Havilland's branchild, the DH-4, that came along just in time to rescue Britain's Royal Flying Corps in 1917, was built on both sides of the Atlantic. In the United States the 4's were equipped with Liberty engines and flown by both the Army and the Navy. With their front cockpits transformed into cargo compartments and flight controls shifted into the rear cockpit, the American DHs were prepared for their role as carriers of mail for the U.S. Air Mail Service. In late 1918, 100 DH-4s were requisitioned for the Service, and on July 1, 1921 the plane became "standard equipment" for all air mail routes in the United States. Several modifications of the original plane were built and some are shown here.

Speed: 115 mph
Range: 350 miles (at outset of air mail use)
Payload: 500 pounds
Engine: Liberty 400 hp

DH-4 with radial aircooled Ashmussen engine

DH-4 equipped with Loening wings

The so-called "Pregnant Cow" version

An all-civilian service

Following the experimental flight between Boston and New York on June 11, 1918, Post Office officials were ready to abandon any plans for a permanent extension of the New York–Washington route. It was better, they now realized, to concentrate attention and energies on improvement of the existing service. Webb's trial run to Boston clearly demonstrated the complications an extension would entail, and few now felt the extra leg could be navigated on a regular basis with any acceptable degree of safety or reliability.

Yet Captain Ben Lipsner, officer-in-charge of the Aerial Mail Service, remained discontented with the service as it was. Through his contacts in Washington with several potential large users of air mail, Lipsner came to understand that its future profitability would depend upon faster planes, larger payloads, longer routes, and more frequent carriages of mail on the established routes. His civilian commercial training had taught him that his primary task, as long as he was connected with the air mail, would be to further the search for operational profitability while insuring pilot safety.

Lipsner, of course, knew that the Post Office Department was preparing to relieve the military of air mail duty at an early date. He also could predict the problems that would confront anyone who sought to operate the world's first regular civilian commercial air mail service. What he didn't know, however, was that Otto Praeger had already tabbed him as the man to take charge of the operation after it reverted to Post Office Department control. Praeger believed that Lipsner's dedication to profitability, growth, and safety were ideally suited to air mail administration.

So it was that on July 15, 1918, Otto Praeger, following discussions with Lipsner and the War Department, issued the following statement to the news media from his office in the Post Office Department building:

> In anticipation of the ultimate taking over of this service by the department, with its own equipment and personnel, Captain Lipsner has been appointed Superintendent of the Aerial Mail Service. . . .

That very morning a change was made on the air mail route that coincided with the new Superintendent's desire to increase payloads. As of July 15, the air mail rate was lowered to 16 cents (from 24 cents) for the first ounce. In the mail sacks that day were letters franked with a bright green air mail stamp that had been issued on July 11, in reponse to an order of the Postmaster General dated June 26. Special delivery handling at the city of destination was included in the new rate, as it had been previously. The stamp itself utilized the Curtiss Jenny design of the first United States airmail and was simply a one-color version of it with a new value indicated. Three hundred ninety-three pounds of mail were carried on all legs of the pioneer route as the reduced rate went into effect.

Action had also been initiated, prior to Lipsner's appointment, on the matter of faster planes, another priority item. Under development at the Standard Aircraft Corporation of Elizabeth, New Jersey was Standard's model JR–1B, a biplane that would offer the Post Office Department improved characteristics over the Army's JN–6H and R–4. The JR–1B, with its fuel capacity of 60 gallons, could carry slightly more payload at 100 mph over a considerably greater distance than the other planes. These Standard planes were examined, tested and approved for Post Office Department use on August 6, and their purchase expressly for the air mail service was seen by Lipsner as the true beginning of commercial aviation in the United States.

Army pilots brought their chapter of this historic event to a conclusion on Saturday, August 10, 1918. Edgerton, Webb, and Kilgore accomplished the final flights under military jurisdiction in routine fashion, with Webb making a round-trip stint between New York and Philadelphia. Before leaving their mail duty, the Army aviators all received letters of appreciation and commendation from the Department of Military Aeronautics in Washington. The letter to Lieutenant H. Paul Culver, dated July 25, 1918, said in part:

> This office extends its appreciation (for) your service as a pilot, flying mail planes . . . the (Aerial Mail) Service represented pioneer work in many instances, especially in aerial navigation, and constitutes arduous and hazardous service in so far as the regularity of mail deliveries frequently necessitated aerial flights in such inclement weather as to jeopardize the safety of the pilot . . . your devotion to duty as an officer, and efficient performance as an aviator, render your services distinctly valuable to the Air Service of our Army.

A tally of the Army's performance between May 15, 1918, and the following August 10 shows 254 legs flown over some 28,000 route miles. Only 16 forced landings were made (at least one for each pilot), and no loss of life or serious injuries occurred. Moreover, the Army was able to complete 98 percent of its scheduled trips. All in all, the operational record for the world's first daily delivery service of mail by air was impressive.

In anticipation of the first civilian mail flights, Superintendent Lipsner was busy recruiting pilots for the Post Office Department. His first group had all been civilian flight instructors with at least 1,000 hours of flying time, and it included Max Miller, a former instructor who had taught flying at San Diego, California; Maurice A. Newton, in his forties and a compass expert from Brooklyn, New York; Robert Shank, who had been with the military aviation training program in Texas; and Ed-

The formal inspection and purchase of six Standard JR-1B biplanes for air mail use, on August 6, 1918, gave Captain Ben Lipsner the opportunity to publicly introduce his civilian air mail pilot team for the first time. Shown with him at Elizabeth, New Jersey, are pilots (left to right): Edward Langley, Ed Gardner, (Lipsner), Maurice Newton, Max Miller and Robert Shank.

ward V. Gardner, a first-rate pilot from the Chicago area who had previously been a racing driver. An aviator by the name of Boldenweck was hired at this time as a backup man. Their salaries ranged from $3,600 to $5,000 a year, and their employment contract included a railroad pass, granting them free passage to their home bases on days when they were not flying.

Mechanics and riggers were also hired by the air mail service in support of the flying team. Edward Radel, a former mechanic for Katherine Stinson, became the chief mechanic for Lipsner, and like every other man hired, he was chosen for his experience and the excellence of his work.

In addition to new planes and a complete changeover in personnel, the all-civilian air mail service utilized a different landing field in the Washington area when it undertook flights of mail on Monday, August 12. Saying goodbye, with understandable pleasure, to the tight little field at Potomac Park, the service moved its Washington terminus to an aviation field at College Park, Maryland. One of the oldest continually operating airports in the world, and certainly the oldest in the United States, College Park Airport is located just a few miles north of the Washington, D.C. line. It was here in 1909 that Wilbur Wright taught two young Army officers (Lieutenants Frederick Humphreys and Frank Lahm) how to fly—a condition of the purchase contract that brought into service the United States Army's first aeroplane. And it was here on August 12, 1918 that Mrs. Benjamin Lipsner signaled the inaugural moment of the world's first civilian air mail service by handing pilot Max Miller a small silk American flag.

With the flag in his cockpit, 222 pounds of mail placed aboard, and a warm engine, Miller took off in his Standard JR-1B mail plane. He departed College Park at 11:35 A.M., and arrived safely at Bustleton (Philadelphia) Airport at 1:00 P.M. Pilots Newton, Shank, and Gardner also successfully carried out their first flights, employing a shuttle system like the Army's.

105

The Chicago runs

With two aspects of Superintendent Lipsner's profitability package dealt with by the time the Post Office Department began to fly the mail (the lower air mail rate and a craft offering improved flight performance), the next logical focus became longer routes.

Lipsner's ambitious program for the air mail service had the full support of Postmaster General A. S. Burleson and his assistants, especially Otto Praeger. All were eager to prove the value of flying mail over a greater distance than the 218 miles between New York and Washington, D.C. It was not yet possible to attempt coast-to-coast service, although this was foremost in future planning. It was time to head west, however. It having long been assumed that an aerial link-up between New York and Chicago would become the first leg of a cross-country route, plans for an experimental carry of mail between these two cities were set in motion without delay.

Pilots Max Miller and Edward V. Gardner were tapped for the coveted first flight assignments to Chicago. Toward the end of August they were released from duty on the New York–Washington route, being granted rest and preparation time for their new undertaking, certain to be a demanding one.

The challenge, they well knew, would involve every ounce of their skill and resourcefulness as pilots; it would test their ability to navigate successfully over and around the treacherous Allegheny Mountains of central Pennsylvania and to feel their way into unfamiliar landing sites along an untried route. Lipsner and his aides also faced a task at hand. In a very short time, they had to establish landing sites along the route and deploy personnel, equipment, and spare parts. Landing fields were selected in Lock Haven, Pennsylvania, Cleveland and Bryan in Ohio, and Chicago.

Gardner and Miller were to fly in separate mail planes and follow a route that traced a straight line between the terminals in New York City and Chicago. This route was part of an aerial highway called, in aviation circles, the "Woodrow Wilson Airway." So named by the Aero Club of America, it resulted from a proposal drawn up by the club in 1917 that visualized an eighty-mile-wide corridor from coast to coast. It was a startlingly accurate forecast of where the first transcontinental route would be located once it was attempted, and had the key advantage of encompassing many of the country's major cities.

Two round-trip flights between New York and Chicago took place between September 5 and 10, 1918. As expected, they provided postal administrators with an accurate, and therefore useful, gauge of the task facing them in order to make possible such long-distance transport of mail on a regular basis. The flights also supplied two experienced and enthusiastic airmen with a sobering sample of the hazards they and their fellow pilots would encounter in early uses of the Woodrow Wilson Airway. Though Miller and Gardner approached their Chicago flights as if engaged in a private little gambol, they came to know that they had been fortunate to conclude this grueling test without any irrevocable consequences.

Max Miller led the way from Belmont Park, New York, at 7:08 A.M. on the morning of September 5. A coin toss had determined that he would depart for Chicago an hour ahead of Gardner. Miller was flying an air mail service Standard JR–1B with a 150 hp Hispano-Suiza engine, and carried close to 400 pounds of mail. Miller and Gardner were both instructed to phone Superintendent Lipsner over a special line in the Chicago Post Office whenever they touched down.

Atrocious weather and a leaking radiator ensured that Max Miller would keep in frequent contact with "the boss" on that historic trip. He encountered heavy fog shortly after takeoff as he was passing over Newark, New Jersey, and this widespread overcast made sightings almost impossible during the Pennsylvania stretch. His first landing, in the vicinity of Danville, Pennsylvania, was intended to help him zero in on Lock Haven and occurred at approximately 9:00 A.M. Eight landings and a few adventures later, Miller finished his first day's journey at 8:25 P.M. in an open field near Cleveland, Ohio.

Periodic drenching rains had plagued him for most of the day. But other memorable encounters helped him temporarily forget the weather. In his first emergency after Lock Haven, an overheated engine caused him to land on a sloping field near an isolated farmhouse. Much to his dismay, the welcome was anything but cordial. In fact, the unfriendly farmer who approached him presented the open end of a shotgun along with his "vamoose." Miller took to the air as quickly as he had landed. Needless to say, he departed without having learned his whereabouts.

Needing to locate water to cool his engine, Miller was forced down again a few moments later. This time water was obtained from a more cooperative farmer, but unfortunately his geographical input was a little off. The farmer's "Jefferson," instead of the small Ohio town east of Cleveland, as Miller surmised, meant Jefferson County, Pa. Miller's misreading subsequently took him on a new compass heading and 100 miles south of his intended course. At 6:10 P.M., he had to fly directly northward from Cambridge, Ohio, scene of his less-than-pleasurable visit. He was convinced that his navigational error had allowed Ed Gardner to slip past him on the race to Chicago.

Miller's fears were groundless. Gardner, with the top Post Office Department aircraft mechanic aboard as a passenger, had met with even more violent rainstorms than Miller had after leaving New York. Gardner also encountered engine trouble all along the way, which eventually grounded him at Lock Haven overnight. He and Eddie Radel, his mechanic, had struggled mightily to get as far as Lock Haven, having landed at Wilkes-Barre, Bloomsburg, and Jersey Shore, all in Pennsylvania, either to seek directions or to make temporary repairs on their Liberty 400 engine. Gardner had left Belmont Park at 8:50 A.M. that morning flying a Curtiss R–4 #39365. He carried three pouches holding 400 pounds of mail, and an assortment of critical spare parts for both planes.

The next afternoon (Friday, September 6), Gardner almost caught up to Miller in Bryan, Ohio, a planned service stop on the route between Cleveland and Chicago. Miller's radiator repairs at the Glenn Martin factory in Cleveland had delayed his departure from that city until 2 P.M. Meanwhile, Radel and the Lock Haven service crew had the R–4 flight-worthy by 11 A.M., enabling Gardner to push on beyond Cleveland by midafternoon.

With the air mail service unable to operate after dark at this stage of its history, the one-hour gap between the two mail planes made a tremendous difference. Max Miller owned just enough daylight to sail through to Grant Park in Chicago. But Gardner and Radel were forced to spend that night at Westville,

Indiana, when Lipsner ordered them to remain on the ground as darkness closed in. A festive welcome by the hospitable people of Westville made this easier for the flyers to swallow.

As Max Miller's JR–1B glided to earth in Chicago at 7:05 P.M. on the evening of September 6, the boisterous crowd at Grant Park gave him a rousing ovation. All were keyed up by this flight over the first third of the future transcontinental route, and eager to honor the man who had made it happen. Gardner and Radel received a similar welcome when they reached Grant Park the next morning at 8:17 A.M. Ben Lipsner and the other Post Office Department officials were delighted, of course, that their days and weeks of planning for these pioneering flights had succeeded so well. In terms of public and Congressional support, a great deal depended on the outcome of these experiments.

An indication of the public interest in air mail service was made clear by some Chicago businessmen around the time of these first flights. A group of executives had donated $15,000 to provide a hangar for use by the air mail service in Chicago. Construction of the hangar was barely underway by the time the pilots completed their initial runs into Grant Park.

After the flights, Lipsner is quoted as saying, "I had hoped that

Lead pilot Max Miller receives a farewell salute from spectators and dignitaries at Belmont Park on the morning of September 5, 1918, as he departs for Chicago in his JR-1B.

Two covers represent west- and eastbound legs of the first New York–Chicago mail flights. The cover above, with its recognizable oval handstamp, traveled to Chicago with Max Miller, arriving September 6th. Though signed by Ed Gardner (and others), the second cover flew with Miller on the return leg. Backstamps are the key to bracketing the flight times.

Gardner and Miller would be able to enjoy a good rest, to recuperate from the rigors of the first flight, and to fit themselves for the return trip. I had forgotten to consider the fact that they would be heroes. So many luncheon, dinner and banquet engagements came up that there was little time for that much-needed rest." In fact, the return flights were postponed briefly while the two planes received thorough overhauls under Ed Radel's watchful eye.

On Monday, September 9, another spirited crowd had assembled early in the morning at Grant Park. This time they were on hand to witness the takeoff of the first return flight. Lipsner had decided that Miller and Gardner would fly back to New York on separate days in order that their race would be against the clock rather than against each other. By virtue of his earlier arrival on the westbound leg, it was decided that Miller would go first. Both pilots were keenly aware that "the brass" wanted them to make it through to New York in one day on the return trips, if at all possible.

In addition to a prevailing wind at his back, Max Miller also enjoyed crystal clear weather as he left Chicago at about 6:30 A.M. He was carrying 2,974 letters and a full load of confidence concerning his ability to keep an appointment that evening in New York.

Unfortunately, he spent the night in Lock Haven, Pa., and failed to reach New York until 11:22 A.M. the next day, the same morning that Gardner and Radel were departing Chicago. As Miller arrived over Cleveland at about 9:30 A.M. on the first day of his return journey, a water connection to his temperamental radiator broke, and he was forced down a few miles short of the Glenn Martin field where repairs had been made on his westbound trip. It was not until 4:30 in the afternoon that he was able to get going again. After arriving at Lock Haven at 7:30 P.M., Miller was determined to proceed on in darkness. Lipsner, however, would not hear of it; he ordered Miller not to take off before morning, candidly voicing his fears that Pennsylvania mountains and New York skyscrapers were too dangerous to flirt with at night.

Gardner and Radel carried a comparatively small load of 68 letters, but fared better than Miller. Although departing Chicago during a torrential downpour, their plane made excellent time along the way and they left bad weather behind. Disregarding, at their refueling stops, the phone calls back to a nervous Lipsner in Chicago, Gardner and Radel pushed on with determination. They cleared the Allegheny Mountains just before dark, coasted over New Jersey at a safe altitude of 7,000 feet, and rejoiced at the sight of "lights twinkling everywhere" as they approached the New York metropolitan area.

Still, their day's work was not finished. "I knew my gasoline was running low and would give out pretty soon. I began to worry," Gardner is quoted in Lipsner's account of the arrival. "We headed for Long Island and desperately tried to find the landing flares at Belmont Park. It was like trying to pick a couple of stars out of the Milky Way. I was baffled by all the lights. They all looked alike."

Eventually, unable to locate either Belmont Park or the flying field at Mineola, Gardner made the hard decision about where to attempt a landing. He selected a large dark area that he sensed to be uninhabited. In a field, which turned out to be near Hicksville, Long Island, the R–4 pancaked down, had its undercarriage ripped loose, and slid into an unseen obstruction that caused it to flip over "in a crashing, blinding somersault."

Their minor injuries attended to, Gardner and Radel then saw to the safety of the mail. It was only hours later that these courageous airmen found time and space to assess their accomplishment. They were the first to travel by air from Chicago to New York in a single day, and they did it in only 10 hours, of actual flying time. Miller had required almost 14 hours, spread over a 2-day period, to achieve the first westbound mail flight between the same two cities.

In the fall of 1918, a decision was made in the Post Office Department to begin regular air mail service between New York and Chicago. Based largely on the success of the Miller/Gardner flights, this action involved a new three-stage projection for the route. The first leg of the new regular route would extend from New York to Bellefonte, Pa., the latter station replacing Lock Haven as the initial refueling stop out of Belmont Park. The emergency field on this leg was established at Lehighton, Pa. Cleveland, the terminus of the middle leg moving west, was linked with an emergency field at Clarion, Pa. The final leg to Chicago remained unchanged and continued to include the mail stop at Bryan, Ohio.

Ben Lipsner resigned as Superintendent of the Air Mail Service a short time before the regular service between New York and Chicago was attempted. As one of several reasons for the resignation, Lipsner cited to Assistant Postmaster General Otto Praeger his personal disagreement with the decision to implement the New York–Chicago service. He felt that, given the then-current range of air mail service aircraft, and the approach of winter's often dangerous weather, it was rushing matters to attempt to regularize a route before the service was prepared in all respects for that step. His judgment seemed vindicated when several inaugural flights on the new route failed on December 18, 1918. It would not be until May 1919 that a renewed effort to establish a New York–Chicago air mail service would succeed.

Spreading the routes

Despite severe setbacks on the New York–Chicago route in December 1918, Post Office Department officials remained firm in their determination to establish this service. Development of a transcontinental mail route would be stymied until this initial leg was put into continuous operation: to the official mind, 1919 had to be the year.

Meanwhile, completion of full year of regular air mail, on May 15, 1919, presented Postmaster General Burleson and his second assistant, Otto Praeger, with an opportunity to review some performance data drawn from their fledgling service, including non-statistical inputs.

The operations log from the first year contained entries that dramatically pointed up the risks attendant with flying mail on a daily schedule in all kinds of weather with barely adequate equipment. For example:

October 18, 1918: Maurice Newton, carrying the mail into Belmont Park from Philadelphia, suddenly lost power about four miles short of his destination. His plane glided down, finally smashing into a basin-shaped depression in the earth. Newton survived, but his plane was badly damaged.

December 16, 1918: Air mail pilot Carl B. Smith stalled out over Elizabeth, N.J., while testing a DH-4 (De Havilland) mail plane. He was killed instantly in the crash. Cost: the life of a pilot in order to produce the realization of a need for modification of his machine. After this tragic accident, the pilot's control cables were moved to the rear cockpit in the DH-4, where the mail had previously ridden.

January 7, 1919: While pulling the prop through to compression during startup of a mail plane at Belmont Park, a mechanic slipped on the grass and was brushed by the spinning propeller blade. In this accident, Auguste Thiele suffered a fractured skull which proved fatal.

There were other crashes and near-misses. But, by and large, the air mail service performed extremely well throughout its first year under Otto Praeger's inspired leadership. Much to everyone's delight, it achieved a small profit; revenues of $162,000 exceeded costs of approximately $143,000, leaving a $19,000 surplus.

Officials estimated that over seven and three-quarter million letters (many being ordinary first class mail, of course) were carried by Army and Post Office Department pilots during the first year. A 92 percent completion record for trips attempted on the New York–Washington route involved just over 128,000 route miles covered. Out of 1,261 trips projected, 1,206 were actually flown. There were 51 forced landings made to avoid the worst of the weather; 37 trips were interrupted due to engine trouble; 430 trips were carried out in rainy, foggy or otherwise inclement weather. Not a single pilot lost his life while en route to a destination with mail aboard. In spite of this impressive record, Congress and the general public were less than enthusiastic over plans to resume New York–Chicago mail flights on the anniversary of Air Mail's "first trips."

In order to reassure everyone concerned, Otto Praeger and his colleagues chose not to attempt night flights anywhere in the air mail system except on an experimental basis. Officials also decided to lay out the transcontinental route in four segments instead of three. The New York–Chicago portion was divided into New York–Cleveland and Cleveland–Chicago divisions. Ultimately, these routes were to be connected with Chicago–Omaha and Omaha–San Francisco legs to complete the eagerly awaited cross-country airway. Another key move was the assignment of military surplus De Havilland biplanes to air mail duty. A few De Havilland DH-4s had already found their way into the Air Mail fold, offering a range of 350 miles and a load capacity of 500 pounds. With the end of the war and an "available surplus" classification, the planes became readily marketable by the hundreds, and their low initial cost assured that Post Office Department procurement officers would place them on every air mail route in the country. In late 1918, the air mail service drew up a requisition for 100 DH-4s. A second order was drafted simultaneously for 100 surplus engines, the famous Liberty V-12 400 hp power plants that were to be used as spares by the service.

The DH-4 was beginning a long and productive career as the workhorse of the air mail enterprise. Modifications on the plane and its power plant were in order for the swing-over to civilian, commercial use and these were undertaken without delay. The fatal accident that took the life of pilot Carl B. Smith had instigated the shift of pilot control to the rear cockpit. The gas tank, initially situated dangerously behind the pilot, was now moved forward and located in the front cockpit area. A mail hopper or storage compartment was then placed in front of the gas tank just behind the engine. The air mail version of the DH-4, known as the DH-4B, was also provided with a stronger nickel-steel undercarriage, a heavier axle, larger wheels and tires, and a metal reinforcement of the longerons.

A careful reworking of the Liberty engine was related to the Post Office need for a low compression engine that would perform best at low altitudes. Since the military DH-4 had been primarily an observation plane that operated at high altitudes, its engine had been developed as a super-compression one and light in weight. New rings and bearings were designed, heavy stubtooth gears added, and drilled pistons installed. An improved oil pump completed the changes, which achieved for the Liberty the reputation of being the most reliable aircraft power unit of its time—exactly what Otto Praeger was seeking!

Shortly after the transcontinental route was inaugurated, the air mail service established a repair depot at Maywood Field, Chicago. Here, many surplus planes and engines were completely rebuilt into DH–4B's in preparation for their utilization. They were shipped to the Maywood facility in the same crates in which they had been packed for delivery to the overseas battle areas in France.

One of the important procedures instituted on air mail routes in 1919 concerned a pilot-saving innovation called the parachute. Post Office Department aviators were now required to wear the "seat-pack" chute, and this proved a welcome precaution that saved many lives in the course of a very few years.

When the air mail anniversary date rolled around on May 15, 1919, the service seemed well prepared to begin daily flights on the much heralded transcontinental route. As operations resumed, the "go" decision on the anniversary involved only the relatively easy Cleveland–Chicago stretch. Trains would continue to haul the mail between New York and Cleveland. It was felt that the experience gained on regular daily air mail flights between Cleveland and Chicago would prove beneficial when it was time to open the other divisions of the transcontinental route, now called the Columbia route.

With great anticipation and considerable ballyhoo, the historic flights got under way as hoards of interested spectators lined the perimeters of the airfields to cheer the pilots on. Trent C. Fry, hired as an air mail pilot the previous December, handled the eastbound fight from Chicago. He departed the Grant Park Aviation Field at 9:35 A.M. (C.T.) on May 15 with 31 pounds of mail, and reached the Bryan relay station close to 11:45 A.M. (C.T.)

Coinciding with Fry's arrival from Chicago was the arrival in Bryan of veteran Ed Gardner with the westbound mail from Cleveland. After an exchange of mail, the two pilots retraced their steps. Fry arrived back in Chicago at 1:25 P.M. (C.T.) with 6 pounds of air mail but 249 pounds of ordinary first class mail. The Cleveland-bound mail, consisting of the 31 pounds given to Gardner by Fry, plus an additional 7 pounds that originated in Bryan, reached the Woodland Hills Park Flying Field in Cleveland at 1:48 P.M. (E.S.T.), and was being taken out by letter carriers for delivery shortly after 2:00 P.M. The mail flown to Cleveland from Chicago required 3 hours and 13 minutes in transit. This time bettered by 11 hours the most advantageous schedule by rail trip. Pleased by their performance on May 15, 1919, air mail service administrators confirmed the assignment of fifteen DH–4Bs to the Cleveland–Chicago route on a permanent basis.

1919, now on the way to becoming an historic year for air mail progress in the United States, was also a signficiant year for aviation in general. While distant cities were being brought closer together by planes carrying mail, distant continents were also being linked together by virtue of extraordinary transoceanic aerial crossings.

Shortly after the Chicago–Cleveland segment of the transcontinental route was put into operation, a United States Navy aviation crew, one of three traveling in Curtiss flying boats, achieved the first aerial crossing of the Atlantic Ocean. The plane, designated the NC4 and commanded by Lieutenant Commander A. C. Read, accomplished its epic flight, going by way of the Azores and Lisbon. Reaching Plymouth, England on May 31, 1919, the NC4 had covered 3,925 miles (6,310 kilometers) and required 57 hours of actual flying time.

More Atlantic crossings took place in quick succession in June and July. British airmen Captain John Alcock and Lieutenant Arthur Whitten Brown distinguished themselves by successfully carrying out a nonstop flight from St. John's, Newfoundland to Clifden, Ireland. Flying in a twin-engined Vickers Vimy, Alcock and Brown made their island-to-island crossing on June 14 and 15 and thereby earned knighthoods from George V, as well as the *Daily Mail* prize of 10,000 pounds. This remarkable flight was followed by that of the British dirigible R34 early in July. With a crew of thirty, commander Major G. H. Scott guided his airship from East Fortune, Scotland to Roosevelt Field in Mineola, Long Island, in 108 hours. The flight, a first for lighter-than-air craft, occurred between July 2 and 6.

The day before the R34 departed from Scotland on its voyage to the United States, the air mail service initiated flights on the second leg, the easternmost portion, of the Columbia route—New York to Cleveland.

New York to Chicago service, with daylight flights only, was now a reality. Such a service would effect a substantial time saving for letters traveling between the two most important commercial centers in the United States. And because of the time saved in the east, it became possible to gain a full twenty-four hours on New York mail to the West Coast, because advantageous rail connections at Chicago could now be met.

A recap of first trips over the new route showed that W. H. Stevens and E. F. White piloted their DH–4s to Bellefonte and Cleveland (respectively) so that their mail connected perfectly with Ira Biffel's Chicago bound departure at 9:35 A.M. Biffel flew out of Woodland Hills Park, Cleveland, arriving at Grant Park in Chicago by 12:55 P.M. (C.T.). Max Miller (Cleveland to Bellefonte) and Harold T. Lewis (Bellefonte to New York) transported 265 pounds of ordinary mail into New York to round out the inaugural trips for the new division.

Two important announcements concerning air mail emanated from the Post Office Department in July 1919. Special rates for

air mail were to be eliminated on July 18. The regular first class rate of 2 cents per ounce was to apply to mail carried by airplane thereafter. "The success of the airship (that is, aeroplane) in carrying the mail, together with the great development that has taken place in speed, in quantity of mail that can be carried and certainty of operation," said Burleson, "makes it improbable that air transportation of mail, whether by the government or commercial air transportation lines, will ever be stopped, but will increase from year to year by leaps and bounds, especially over long distances." He added, "The great expedition of mail by this means of transportation constitutes a service which the public throughout the country is now demanding and in course

Various stamps reflect aerial progress in 1919. A 10-centime airmail of 1944 celebrates a 1919 Swiss air mail service between Dubendorf (Zurich) and Lausanne which began on April 30th. The pair of 5-kroner semi-official Danish airmails, produced in 1919, were used on a special mail flight from Copenhagen to Aarhus (not Skagen) in September of the same year. The covers shown are reminders of U.S. rate changes, the above cover having been franked three days before air post rates discarded a special delivery charge, and the lower cover reflecting elimination of special rates for air mail service altogether.

of time will receive, as supplementing train service. For these reasons the air mail has been placed on the same basis with all other means of transportation and the rate of postage made the same as over all other means of mail transit." The world's first definitive air mail stamps, then in three values—24 cents, 16 cents and 6 cents—were, accordingly, abandoned.

The second announcement concerned the pioneer route between Washington and New York. Effective on July 19, 1919, the Philadelphia relay stop on this route was discontinued. The use of planes with a longer range made this stop obsolete. The elimination of one landing improved the speed of delivery.

As if the American experience with air mail in 1919 were not enough proof that the world's attention regarding aviation had shifted fully to purposes of commerce and communication after the war, the British undertook on August 25 the world's first daily scheduled commercial airline flight on an international route. On that date a DH–4A, piloted by Lieutenant E. H. Lawford of Air Transport and Travel, Ltd., left Hounslow (London) with one passenger, George Stevenson-Reece, who had paid twenty-one pounds for his seat, and a load of freight. Its destination was Le Bourget near Paris.

With service well organized and smoothly operating on the first two divisions of the transcontinental route, attention turned to the Chicago–Omaha stretch. The volume of air mail had been disappointingly light. It was clear that the public needed further indications that air mail could make a difference. Longer routes would reveal the time-saving factor to best advantage. Early in 1920 the Post Office Department sent representatives along the planned route to San Francisco to promote the idea of municipal airports, and to encourage public interest.

An experimental round-trip flight between Chicago and Omaha was arranged and carried through on January 8, 1920. However, there was no intention at this point to open this leg for daily air mail service. The Post Office Department was simply surveying the route. Another experimental carry of mail between Omaha and Chicago took place on May 15, 1920, the second anniversary of air mail service and the first anniversary of the great transcontinental route's initial flights. Pilots William DeWalk and R. Benedict flew 200 pounds and 265 pounds of mail respectively, both using the field at Iowa City, Iowa, as their refueling stop. These flights transpired without incident and were the final confirmations that the third leg of the transcontinental route could be operational when needs dictated.

In just one year's time the United States air mail service had spread its wings to cover more than half the distance between New York and San Francisco. 113

Other aspects of the emerging air mail network, many in direct support of the pilots' work, are interesting to recall. As mentioned, the Post Office Department undertook a concerted effort to interest various towns and cities to build their own municpal aviation facilities. Not only would these airports serve as emergency havens along the narrow and precarious airway about to span the nation, but they would eventually become the backbone of a new and efficient commercial air transport system for passengers, mail, and freight.

Local towns and cities along the way made one further important contribution to the transcontinental route. Officials in these communities agreed to paint on the roofs of two or three prominent buildings or water towers, if such existed, the name of the town in four-foot-high letters to aid pilots in reorienting themselves in flight or to confirm at any time their whereabouts.

Another advance that took place throughout 1920 involved a ground radio network that was initiated between key airports, repair stations, and strategic weather observation points all along the Columbia route. The ground radio network, not yet involving ground-to-air capability, was the precursor of the radio-beam signal system that would help open up the airways to all-weather night flights—a goal of enormous importance and complexity to air mail planners at this time.

Experimentation in this era of governmental operation always included the planes themselves. Following the Lipsner lead of seeking economy, reliability and safety, Post Office Department officials prided themselves on keeping abreast of every aviation advance that developed in the period of rapid progress after World War I. Not infrequently, innovations in the science of aerial navigation grew right out of the air mail experience itself. But, while the DH–4Bs predominated numerically in the air mail stable, and were busy building their unmatched reputation for dependability on the routes then in existence, the search always continued for the better mail plane.

Up until 1926 when the air mail service acquired 51 Douglas mail planes (40 M–4s, 10 M–3s and 1 M–1), at least 20 different domestic and foreign types of aircraft carried U.S. air mail with varying degrees of success. These included: the three-engined Italian Caproni (CA33); the British twin-engine Handley Page; and the German-made F–13 low-wing, all-metal monoplane. The F–13 reached American shores immediately following the armistice and appeared to have the advantage of range, load capacity, and economy of operation that suited the air mail situation at the time. Powered by a single Junkers engine of 230 hp, the F–13, designed to carry four passengers and a crew of two, could handle a gross load of 5,000 pounds.

The German response to American interest in their plane led to a collaboration with Swedish aircraft designer John Larson, and this union produced a variation of the F–13 known as the Junkers-Larson JL–6, which was almost identical to the F–13 in external configuration. Internally, it was altered to accommodate mail and parcel loads, and its power-plant was changed to a lighter 180 hp BMW engine. Eight JL–6s were purchased by the Post Office Department and placed in service on the first three divisions (New York to Omaha) of the Columbia route early in 1920.

The Junkers eventually proved to have a fire-wall defect that led to several in-flight fires. One of these claimed the life of veteran air mail pilot Max Miller near Morristown, New Jersey, on September 1, 1920. The JL–6s disappeared from air mail routes for good shortly afterward.

Variations of De Havilland, Martin, and Curtiss planes were among those tried on early air mail flights. Six Martin mail planes were used on the longer runs of the transcontinental route in its early history because they had a range of 600 miles, exceptional for their time. The Martin mail plane was similar to the Martin bomber, which was also tried out by the air mail service; each biplane was powered by a pair of Liberty 400 engines with an average cruising speed of 118 mph. All of the Martins were manufactured by the company founded and operated by Glenn L. Martin, who had carried the mail at Dominguez Field, Los Angeles, almost ten years earlier.

A number of De Havillands were modified in different ways and offered to the air mail service. None, however, ever replaced the DH–4s. Two of the DH versions incorporated twin-engine biplane designs, one being powered by Hispano-Suiza engines in the 300 hp range and the other by Hall Scott 200 hp units. The latter two aircraft were tested toward the end of 1920 and through the early part of 1921 on short feeder routes connecting at Chicago with the transcontinental flights.

None of the experimental aircraft was ever employed in carrying mail over the Rocky Mountain segments west of Omaha when this portion of the transcontinental route became operational during daylight hours late in 1920. Indeed, the fourth (Omaha to Salt Lake City) and fifth (Salt Lake City to San Francisco) divisions, newly defined in 1920, seemed for many years the exclusive province of one aircraft alone—the tough, dependable DH–4B.

Shortly before the western divisions were opened for daylight mail flights, another kind of experimentation was begun. This had to do with two "feeder" routes into Chicago. These comparatively short runs were intended to feed into the main trunk line between New York and San Francisco, allowing important population centers off the main line to avail themselves of those air mail services that were part and parcel of the coast-to-coast airway.

The first of the experimental secondary routes connected St. Louis with transcontinental air mail service at Chicago. A 270-

mile run, the Chicago–St. Louis service was inaugurated formally on August 16, 1920. The route, which called for one flight in each direction daily except Sunday, involved a roster of four regular and two reserve pilots, six planes, and the creation of a refueling stop at Chanute Field, Rantoul, Illinois. Maywood Field was the Chicago terminus, and the Forest Park landing field at St. Louis served as the air mail activity center at the southern end of the line.

E. Hamilton Lee, one of the most experienced airmen in Post Office Department uniform, completed the southbound flight in 3½ hours on opening day, well ahead of schedule. He flew a Curtiss Jenny with "St. Louis to Chicago" painted in bold white letters on the side of his plane. Pilot Russell G. Jones arrived at Maywood Field at 1:20 P.M. carrying about 9,000 northbound letters (six pouches worth) after a trip of 3 hours and 50 minutes. Both Lee's and Jones's loads of mail reached their respective cities in time for afternoon carrier delivery. Without service by air, this mail would have been in the next morning's delivery, requiring an additional 14 or 15 hours in transit to destination.

On November 29, the Post Office Department undertook flights of mail between Chicago and the Twin Cities area of Minneapolis and St. Paul. Assuming the successful completion of these flights, a second feeder route, this one close to 360 miles in length, was to be operated daily beginning December 1. Again, the route was not intended to function Sundays or holidays. A refueling stop was created at La Crosse, Wisconsin and an emergency field was set up at Lone Rock, in the same state.

The first regular flight from Chicago over the new route was made by William T. Carroll, a young ex-military aviator and a native of Minneapolis. In a twin-engine modification of the DH–4B he delivered close to 175 pounds of mail to Wold-Chamberlain Field by 2:08 P.M. on the 29th. Piloting the same type of experimental De Havilland biplane, E. Hamilton Lee, who had carried the first mail from Chicago to St. Louis in August, carried over 6,000 letters into Chicago from Minneapolis, St. Paul, Madison, and La Crosse on the same day that Carroll was heading in the opposite direction. Lee flew in fog most of the way to Chicago and had to navigate with compass headings.

The usual outpouring of civic pride and celebration greeted their arrivals. Lee would recall in later years that the flurry of excitement surrounding first flights thrilled the pilots. He lists the air mail inaugurations in which he participated as his most memorable experiences in pre-1927 flying. "Generally," Lee said, "air mail pilots did have a sense of pioneering a fast mode of mail transport when flying the earliest routes around the nation."

It was becoming increasingly clear that pilots like Lee and Carroll were plying a dangerous trade and demonstrating extraordinary courage in the face of constant risk. As miles were added to the transcontinental airway in 1920, the cost in life rose right along with an increase in hours flown. Ed Gardner had a close call at Cleveland in September 1919. He crashed while working the New York–Chicago run, but escaped with injuries. Not as fortunate as Gardner were pilots Lyman Doty and C. W. Stoner. Doty lost his life at Catonsville, Maryland late in 1919; while hauling the mail on the Washington–New York route, his plane struck a tree in a forced landing attempt. Stoner lost his life in March 1920, following a battle with fog on the New York-Chicago portion of the transcontinental air mail network.

On September 7, 1920, "Buck" Hulfron led the way over the final 1,484 route miles from Omaha to San Francisco. By flying 380 pounds of mail over this stretch in a special pathfinding flight, Hulfron brought the long-standing transcontinental dream of the air mail service one step closer to fruition. His flight had taken him by way of North Platte (Nebraska), Cheyenne, Salt Lake City, and Reno and confirmed that the fourth and fifth divisions of the transcontinental route were finally operational. Hulfron's success served as a switch that activated Air Mail Superintendent L. B. Lent's plan for the inaugural departures of a permanent service the very next day.

In addition to having secured satisfactory aircraft and prepared main, secondary, and emergency landing fields, Lent and his aides had wrestled with countless other nagging problems in anticipation of the big day. Confronted was the matter of carrying full mail loads at altitudes of more than 12,000 feet over the western mountain ranges. There was the question of emergency measures in the mountainous regions...of weather conditions to be measured, understood, and allowed for...of pilot apparel and pilot comfort and protection in all weather conditions in all seasons...and there was the intricate and complex chore of working up the schedules, schedules that would take into account time zones, train departures, weather, and all the possible variables that a 3,000-mile route would entail.

One might expect that the first flights on the much-heralded transcontinental route, like those on the smallest feeder route, would have occasioned long speeches, martial music, and waving crowds. But on September 8, 1920, the crowd was surprisingly modest; the pomp and circumstance consisted of little more than a brief handshake between postal officials and pilot. Such was the scene at Hazelhurst Field on Long Island as the first scheduled transcontinental flight of mail was ready to go.

Actually, two flights were readied as the "Columbia" was officially opened. Randolph G. Page took the first DH–4B aloft shortly after 6:00 A.M. with approximately 400 pounds of mail aboard. A second DH–4B left right after Page; piloted by William

"Big Bill" Hopson, it carried a load of mail about equal to Page's. Plans called for Page's mail to fly all the way to the West Coast, its progress being contingent upon the distance that could be covered on daylight flights. Hopson's mail, on the other hand, was to connect with particular trains, thereby alternating between train and plane but moving day *and* night toward its destination.

En route to Reno with Page's mail, which had moved steadily westward, a second relief pilot, John P. Woodward was slightly shaken up after a forced landing near Lovelock, about one-hundred miles east of Reno. Deteriorating weather conditions had led to the set-down and, subsequently, to a slightly damaged aircraft. Pilot Edison E. Mouton, who had just joined the air mail service two days earlier as an ex-Lafayette Escadrille veteran and who had been standing by in Reno, rushed to Lovelock. At 8:15 the next morning, having repaired the plane, he took off in place of the injured Woodward and carried the mail that day to its final destination, reaching Marina Flying Field in San Francisco at 2:20 P.M. on September 11, 1920. His six pouches of mail weighed in at 430 pounds.

In just under nine years of government flying, senior pilot of the air mail service E. Hamilton Lee spent 4,220 hours aloft and covered 382,426 route miles. Shown in his official mail pilot's uniform, Lee flew both feeder-route inaugurals in 1920, pioneering the Chicago–St. Louis run on August 16th (see photo at right), and the Minneapolis–Chicago leg on November 29th. "Ham" Lee retired from United Airlines in 1949, with more air time logged than any other flyer. He continues to praise the DH-4 mail plane—"It could fight winds and weather and carry heavier loads."

As mail loads increased in volume, and more equipment was pressed into service on the early route divisions, a high level of teamwork developed between pilots, mechanics, and mail handlers. Here, mail is hastily off-loaded from a DH-4—note pilot's name on plane—at a busy air mail field. At this stage of the system's growth, train departures for off-route cities and towns influenced schedules and pressured the pilots to get the mail through on time.

At the Western terminus of this first cross-country flight, the welcome was in keeping with the historic moment. Not only was the mayor of San Francisco on hand to greet Pilot Mouton, along with Colonel John Jordan, head of the Salt Lake City–San Francisco division of the air mail service, but in true California style, the movie cameras were in position to record the drama.

The first trip "across" had consumed almost 76 hours, of which 34 hours involved actual flying time. Americans, though perhaps they little realized it, had suddenly been brought much closer together.

Jack Knight—air mail legend

Until the initiation of flights on the transcontinental airway, the story of United States Air Mail reflects a picture of steady, inexorable growth. The historic moment and the mood within the flying fraternity continued to coincide in a way that boded well for the air mail service.

An evident romanticism about the acrobatic mode of flying, which attached itself to so much of World War I aerial combat, now seemed in peacetime to be transforming itself into the concept of planned, scheduled straight-and-level flight over long distances and challenging routes. Transoceanic flights and altitude records, which were clues to the change in emphasis that was taking place, became sensational, front page news in these post-war years.

However bright the future of air mail appeared in 1920, with close to 520 individuals employed on the transcontinental route during peak periods, the moment when Senator Warren G. Harding was elected to the presidency caused these feelings of optimism to dramatically reverse. Without much warning a new political reality became a fact of life throughout the land, and it was unhesitatingly interpreted as a mortal threat to the entire air mail enterprise.

For better or worse, the air mail service under Burleson and Praeger had been closely identified with the Wilson administration, and many Americans viewed it as a pet project of one political faction. Air Mail seemed, therefore, a natural whipping boy for the incoming Congress, whose majority belonged to the other party. Retrenchments and eliminations were a foregone conclusion anyhow, since the new legislators were about to confront a disorganized budget, imbalanced by many carry-over expenses of the war period. Further, the service had been noticeably slow in gaining broad public acceptance because at the outset it served very few cities; its constituency was simply too small to exert pressure on Congress to continue the appropriations upon which it depended.

Recognition of the precarious state of air mail service pressed lame-duck administrators and supporters into a hastily devised ploy to demonstrate its worth one last time. As noted, the first Air Mail Superintendent's plan for the growth of air mail called for faster planes, heavier loads, and longer routes. Ben Lipsner also sought to obtain increased flying time over those longer routes, which, were it to be done most effectively, required keeping the airways active during the hours of darkness. Post Office Department thinking turned in this very direction early in 1921. Well before the airway lighting problem had been fully solved, it was arranged to send four mail loads across the country by air to publicize the dramatic speed that air mail could obtain by incorporating stretches flown at night.

The date chosen for this great test was Tuesday, February 22, 1921. Plans called for two departures from each coast on that morning, and the hope was that at least one flight in each direction would get through in spite of anticipated weather trouble. DH–4Bs were to be used in both directions.

The two westbound flights that took off from Hazelhurst Field on Long Island at about 6 A.M. (ET) experienced a nasty weather system stretching from Pennsylvania through the Midwest. E. G. Leonhardt, pilot of the first plane out of New York, encountered gale-force winds shortly after leaving Bellefonte and was forced down in the vicinity of Du Bois, Pennsylvania. Westbound pilot Ernest M. Allison fared better, getting his mail through to Cleveland, where Wesley L. Smith served as the relay pilot and was able to carry on as far as Maywood Field in Chicago. The snowfall was so heavy at that location, however, that no further progress was possible. The weather had won out as far as the westbound flights were concerned.

Now, the successful outcome of the entire experiment hinged on the performance of the eastbound pilots. Departing San Francisco's Marina Flying Field shortly after 4 A.M. (PT) were W. F. Lewis, who had been flying the mail for four months, and Farr Nutter, an experienced air mail pilot.

Once the spacious, fertile valley east of San Francisco had been past, Lewis and Nutter successfully cleared the 10,000-foot-high Sierra Nevada Mountains in early morning darkness and were able to land at Reno without incident.

Lewis, in the lead plane, moved on quickly, squeezing through passes of the Humboldt and Stillwater mountains en route to Elko, Nevada, 235 miles to the east. Nutter turned over his mail in Reno to J. L. Eaton, who zoomed off over the brown terrain in the first light of morning, hot on the trail of Lewis. Upon arrival at Elko at 9:24 A.M., Eaton's relief at being safely through a challenging part of his journey was replaced with shock and dismay. Upon climbing out of his cockpit, he was informed that Captain Lewis had just crashed and been killed while taking off from that very field. At an undetermined altitude, Lewis had lost control of his craft when it went into a tailspin during a steep and rapid climb toward eastern skies.

At 9:31 A.M., Eaton took off toward the Humboldt Range and Salt Lake City. He knew full well that, as far as the eastbound mail was concerned, his flight alone bore full responsibility for the outcome of the test initiated by Burleson and Praeger. This awareness competed in his mind with other routine concerns about terrain, weather, and the rhythm of his engine sounds. On winter flights through inaccessible mountain areas the air mail pilot always had to deal with the question of rescue should his plane go down. The question was generally precipitated by an imagined emergency caused by accumulated moisture freezing and blocking that crucial tube through which fuel was fed to a straining engine. The morning sun and scenic splendors he barely noted, but luck was with him. He glided easily to a graceful landing at Salt Lake City close to 11:30 A.M. (MT).

Eaton's relay pilot turned out to be a James P. Murray, who had lugged the mail from Chicago to Salt Lake City during the first scheduled transcontinental carry of mail the previous September. He soon was on his way to Cheyenne, some 4 hours and 400 miles away—dodging the Wasatch Mountains, the 13,500-foot King's Peak, and the Rocky Mountains of Wyoming.

A few months later Murray's adventure in pine-covered terrain would become a memorable contribution to air mail lore. Clouds bearing a late spring snow squall had opened before him to reveal a white wall of mountainside that his plane was unable to leap over. He pancaked down on a remote slope midst a carpet of trees. He then struggled on foot through the raging storm, unsure of his direction, until—almost twenty-four hours later—he reached the settlement of Arlington.

"Just as I was getting into town," reported the flier, "a cowboy rode up and said he'd run across my broken path in the snow, as he was riding over from Elk Mountain. Thinking I was in trouble, he had galloped after me, for paralleling my trail for miles he had found the fresh tracks of a mountain bear."

Murray brought the mail into Cheyenne just before dark on February 22. With his limited range of instruments—a compass, altimeter, tachometer, and oil, water, and fuel gauges—he had successfully navigated over and around some of the world's most difficult topography.

By this time the failure of the westbound flights out of New York was known all along the line, as was the death of Captain Lewis at Elko. The pilots assigned to the remaining eastbound shuttle flight realized the load they bore on their shoulders. If they failed, it was not unreasonable to think that Congress would eliminate partially or even totally the appropriations for air mail in the ensuing year. Continuation of mail flights on the transcontinental route depended at that moment on the uninterrupted movement of these few sacks toward New York City.

Just two minutes after Murray had come in from Salt Lake City, pilot F. R. Yager was rolling toward takeoff. Another concern pushed Yager into the air as quickly as possible: there remained very little daylight. Fortunately, weather conditions were ideal for night flying, and Yager was able to follow rail and river to his destination at North Platte, Nebraska.

Waiting for Yager was James H. "Jack" Knight, a pilot in his mid-twenties. His task: To carry the mail to Omaha (247 miles away) and, at the same time, to achieve the first scheduled air mail flight entirely at night on the transcontinental route. As Yager arrived, Knight's plane #188 was warmed up and ready to

go. But while the mail was being transferred to his plane, a crack in the tail skid was discovered. The eager pilot's takeoff was delayed an excruciatingly long three hours for repairs.

For Knight, the wait may have been a blessing in disguise. It provided a rest he would badly need. For not only had he ferried a mail plane to Cheyenne and back earlier that day, but unknown to him, his flying stint this night would extend well beyond its expected limit.

Finally, at 10:44 P.M., Knight was off, after receiving a send-off by a crowd of interested spectators alerted by radio newscaster to the progress of the flights across the country. As he rose to about 2,500 feet and sped on toward Omaha through broken clouds, he attempted to follow the frozen Platte River. Various groups of private citizens had banded together along the route to light bonfires and oil drums to help guide him. These signs of encouragement warmed him inwardly against the bitter cold of the Nebraska winter, which seemed as formidable a hurdle to him as had mountain peaks to fellow pilots earlier that day. He touched down in Omaha at 1:10 in the early morning of the 23rd.

At Omaha, Superintendent of the Air Mail William I. Votaw and a crowd of well-wishers greeted Knight, and their comments seemed to be telling him that with his landing the great air mail experiment had come to an end. Confused, Knight queried Votaw, who replied that no more flying would take place because Knight's relief pilot, Wesley Smith, had been snowbound in Chicago and unable to get through that night.

Without hesitation Jack Knight informed Votaw that he had a pilot to carry on. "We can't let the transcontinental effort end here. I'll fly her on through!" Having already flown almost 600 miles since noon of the day before, Knight volunteered to fly another 425 unlighted miles through the night to Chicago. What is more, when Votaw asked him, Knight, who had joined the Air Mail Service in June 1919, confessed that he was proposing to fly a route that he had never traversed before even in daylight. Tired as he was, Knight summoned sufficient energy to deal with the superintendent's strongly worded objections, and finally obtained a go-ahead.

After some food, warmth, and a quick study of a pair of Iowa and Illinois road maps, Knight was ready to go. He felt fairly secure about his own stamina and ability to stay with the route; what posed a potentially serious problem was the weather he would confront. The massive storm that had stalled the westbound flights now had spread its effect to large areas west of Chicago. There appeared no way that Knight could avoid meeting the brunt of that vicious storm system. Yet, at 2:00 A.M., his DH–4 was climbing into the darkness again.

Knight intended to set down as often as possible at emergency fields, Des Moines being the first planned landing point. Flying in and out of a gradually thickening cloud cover, he began to contend with a 25 mph cross wind that blew in a northwesterly direction. Fortunately, he occasionally spotted the tracks of the Rock Island Railroad, and these helped him find a reasonably direct path to Des Moines. When he located the airfield, however, it was partly obscured by ground mist and seemed to be under a heavy blanket of snow. He chose to continue on toward his next stopping point at Iowa City, 120 miles to the east.

The cold was now insidiously penetrating Knight's fur-lined coveralls. Further, swirling around him were particles of wind-driven snow; he had met the blizzard less than 30 minutes past Des Moines. The twisting play of the snowflakes rushing toward him, then sweeping past his wings, produced wild, dancing patterns that almost hypnotized him. He was discovering a tiredness that he had never known before. On several occasions, when he had descended through the clouds to get his bearings, he was startled by land forms or trees uncomfortably close to his wheels. Repeatedly slapping his face and limbs to remain alert, on he flew.

After what seemed an eternity, he found Iowa City and its airfield. He made several passes over the field, thus attracting the attention of a night watchman, who then activated some flares that helped him make a safe landing. Knight had used up most of his fuel on the trip from Omaha. As the air mail ground crew had signed out by that time, believing Knight's flight cancelled, he and the watchman refueled the plane. Then he rested. His best judgment told him to delay his departure before confronting the 200-mile trip to Chicago. The first light of dawn was only about an hour away and the weather on ahead was still reported to be "atrocious" for flying.

At 6:30 A.M., with a final wave to the watchman and a small group of huddled figures, Knight was Chicago-bound. Desperately tired, he was relieved to finally move out of the sleet and snow belt. But a long stretch of Mississippi Valley fog followed, which intensified his already difficult navigational problem.

His course corrections proved sound. Nearing the end of this 10-hour ordeal, he sighted rising smoke dead ahead and confirmed the fact that he was right on course for Chicago.

Jack Knight knew when he reached Maywood's Checkerboard Field, at 8:40 A.M., that he had made history. He had just completed the first transport of United States mail by air entirely at night and covered 680 miles in so doing. He was greeted by a joyful crowd who had followed his progress by radio. Some had even gone to the airfield in their formal evening wear. Also on hand were a handful of reporters and photographers, whose work helped to announce the name and fame of Jack Knight to a grateful nation. Overnight, he became known as the "hero of the air mail."

James Herbert "Jack" Knight (left) joined the U.S. Air Mail Service as a pilot on June 25, 1919, and remained on active duty with the Post Office until June 30, 1927. A rare commercial cover, believed to have been carried on his epic 1921 flight, is shown above a 1929 Boeing Air Transport cover that he flew and signed.

Pilot J. D. Webster missed the festivities. He was given the six pouches of mail, then departed just before 9:00 A.M. for Cleveland. Ernest M. Allison flew most of this mail on the final leg into Hazelhurst Field on Long Island, encountering strong headwinds and snow en route, and arrived there at 4:50 P.M. (ET). It was still Wednesday afternoon, February 23. Eastern Superintendent of the Air Mail, J. E. Whitbeck, happily received the San Francisco mail from Allison and telegraphed the good news of the long journey's successful conclusion to Washington officials.

Seven air mail pilots had flown the mail 2,666 miles in 33 hours and 20 minutes. (The actual flying time amounted to almost 26 hours.) The 33⅓ hours were less than half the time required for the fastest previous mail to travel from coast to coast and represented a remarkable improvement over the 108 hours needed by train.

Otto Praeger was understandably thrilled. Among his public comments about Jack Knight's achievement were these:

The all-night flight from Cheyenne, Wyoming to Chicago, a distance of 830 miles, of San Francisco mail bound for New York by the regular equipment of the Air Mail Service, is the most momentous step in civil aviation. The Postmaster General some time ago, directed that the air mail enter upon regular night operations, and the flight by a pilot never over the ground before, in black night, through snow flurries and fog drifts, with three night landings [actually Knight made only two landings *at night*] for refueling and exchange of mail, is a demonstration of the entire feasibility of commercial night flying. It will mean the speedy revolutionizing of the letter transportation methods and practices throughout the world.

The feat by Knight and his fellow airmen was so convincing and so widely acclaimed by the American public that President Harding actually prevailed upon Congress to authorize *increased* appropriations for the development of the Air Mail Service. This proved to be an unparalleled advance in the growth of commercial aviation in the United States.

Jack Knight retired from flying in 1937—after flying over 417,000 route-miles for the U.S. Air Mail Service and serving with Boeing Air Transport and United Airlines. He died in 1948

Odd rules and quaint regulations

Early in 1920, the United States Air Mail Service issued a set of rules and instructions for pilots to follow in the regular operation of their aircraft. Though the rules sound almost ludicrous in contemporary terms, they were taken quite seriously by Post Office Department pilots, and others, who realized that deviation from carefully established procedures could be a rather serious matter on the transcontinental air mail route.

Don't take the machine into the air unless you are satisfied that it will fly.
Never leave the ground with the motor leaking.
Don't turn sharply when taxiing. Instead of turning short, have someone lift the tail around.
Never get out of the machine with the motor running unless the pilot relieving you can reach the engine controls.
Pilots should carry hankies in a handy position to wipe off goggles.

Riding on the steps, wings or tail of a machine is prohibited.
In case the engine fails on take-off, land straight ahead regardless of obstacles.
No machine must taxi faster than a man can walk.
Do not trust altitude instruments.
If you see another machine near you, get out of its way.
Before you begin a landing glide, see that no machines are under you.
Hedge-hopping will not be tolerated.
No spins on back or tail slides will be indulged in as they unnecessarily strain the machine.
Pilots will not wear spurs while flying.
If emergency occurs while flying, land as soon as you can.

One other rule established a priority system that delighted the schedule-bound air mail pilot:

Pilots landing with mail should have the right of way over all others.

Lighting the way for private carriers

Shortly after Jack Knight's epic flight, Will Hays replaced Albert S. Burleson as Postmaster General, and Colonel E. H. Shaughnessy became his second assistant. These men inherited an aerial arm of some four-hundred-fifty individuals engaged in moving and processing two million pounds of letters and parcels per year. Fifty-five pilots were completing 87 percent of their scheduled flights as the third full year of air mail came to a close.

As the Harding forces moved into office, it was generally agreed that the Post Office's major task, as far as its aerial division was concerned, was to build a profitable operation that the government could some day turn over to private interests. The way forward, Shaughnessy insisted, involved reorganization of the existing air mail apparatus, relinquishment of unnecessary routes, and perhaps most important of all, proceeding with the construction of lighted airways to insure safe, round-the-clock operation. The period between June 1 and July 1, 1921, was the time-frame for implementing a number of the Hays-Shaughnessy schemes toward these ends.

On June 1 the original pioneer route between Washington and New York was abandoned. A Post Office Department statement released at the time sought to reassure the public, claiming that the route had outlived its usefulness. It said in part: "There is no further necessity for our continuing the New York–Washington route as an experimental one because we have better opportunities for conducting experimental work on the New York–San Francisco route." Postmaster General Hays added that the action of halting operations on the pioneer route "is in no way to be construed as a lessening of interest in nor a curtailment of air mail development." Then on June 30, the feeder routes into Chicago from St. Louis and Minneapolis were also cancelled, with personnel and equipment being shifted over to the single remaining route in the United States—the transcontinental. The Post Office Department released its connections with air mail facilities, space, and landing privileges at College Park, Bustleton, Newark, St. Louis, Minneapolis, and La Crosse.

Reorganization of the air mail structure affected the remaining cross-country route. Here, the streamlining involved a reduction of the divisions to three. An Eastern Division, with a service center at Hempstead, New York, embraced the mail run from New York to Chicago. The Central Division was established to operate the service between Chicago and Rock Springs, and the Western Division covered the balance of the airway leading into San Francisco. The Central Division maintained a service depot at Omaha, and San Francisco repair facilities supported the Western Division's flight activity. At the same time there was a reduction in total employees on the transcontinental route from more than 500 to 382. Of the latter figure, 39 were pilots.

While consolidating the route system, Colonel Shaughnessy also cancelled the department's program for testing aircraft. The modifications completed on the still inexpensive DH–4Bs assured that mail pilots were flying a sturdy, safe, and reasonably swift machine. On July 1, 1921, the DH–4 became standard equipment in the service of flown mail in the United States.

In 1922, following the untimely death of Colonel Shaughnessy, another former military man, Colonel Paul Henderson, took over as head of the air mail service. Henderson's appointment proved fortuitous. With a business background and particular expertise in advanced planning, he was ideally suited to guide air mail fortunes in the closing years of the government era. Henderson's vision of great air lines operating between the nation's major cities led him to further plans for a profitable system that private contractors would be eager to take over when the time came. A 'round-the-clock air mail schedule was the direction in which the Post Office had to move to best compete with trains and maximize profit. As Henderson knew, the key to that was safe night flying over well-lighted airways.

Colonel Henderson had good reason to turn to the Army for assistance. A pair of young lieutenants at McCook Field near Dayton, Ohio—the Army Air Corps' research center—had been hard at work on the same problem for a number of months. Lieutenant Donald L. Bruner, in particular, had in 1921 persuaded the Army to develop and operate experimentally the world's first lighted airway between McCook Field and Columbus, Ohio, approximately 80 miles away. Bruner's work with Lieutenant Harold R. Harris involved aircraft landing lamps as well as ground navigational aids such as beacons, building markers, field floodlights, and so on. This support from the Army, along with excellent cooperation from manufacturers of lighting equipment and lamps, led to rapid development of a lighting plan for the air mail system.

Overseeing the lighting research from the Post Office side were Carl F. Egge, General Superintendent of the Air Mail, and an illuminating engineer by the name of J. V. Magee. The Egge-Magee plan for lighting a portion of the Central Division of the transcontinental route, approved in April 1923, called for a ground navigation support system utilizing small acetylene gas beacons, visible for about 10 miles, installed at 3-mile intervals. At each emergency landing field, 25 miles apart, a rotating beacon on a 50-foot-high tower would sweep the horizon 6 times every minute. At the regular landing fields there were, in addition to mounted beacon lights of twice the size and visibility range as those at the emergency fields, high-intensity lamps set behind lenses that dispersed light across the landing field, so that there was minimum interference with the pilot's vision during his approach and landing. These mounted 36-inch arc searchlights produced just under 500 million candlepower and were located at the landing fields in Chicago, Iowa City, Omaha, North Platte, and Cheyenne—that portion of the Central Division selected to serve as the lighting-test segment of the New York–San Francisco route.

Besides the lights mentioned, there were to be white boundary lights every 150 to 300 feet around the regular landing fields. All hangars, sheds, and service buildings were to be floodlighted, and other high-rise obstacles in the vicinity of the fields were to have red lights showing. Planes to be used in the test flights over the lighted airway were specially equipped with luminous instrument dials, navigation lights (red on the left wing; green on the right; white on the tail), and two landing lights near the lower-wing tips.

The new lighting system was ready for testing by August 1923. Between the 21st and 24th, air mail was flown around the clock, not in the "advancing" way that utilized trains after dark. Night flying continued as Jack Knight had done it, but the pilots now had the use of a clearly illuminated pathway between Chicago and Cheyenne.

Five years after the test was undertaken, Superintendent Carl Egge wrote about its outcome: "It was a stirring time when on August 21st, the carefully laid plans were put to a test, and for four days mail planes, for the first time in history, roared through the darkness of night on schedule-time over a long stretch of country . . . the test was a supreme success."

So encouraging was the test, in fact, that it was decided to extend the lighted airway in both directions as appropriations became available. Also planned was the establishment of transcontinental air mail service on the through basis at the earliest feasible moment. One eastbound load of mail during the test had arrived in New York only 26 hours and 14 minutes after it had departed San Francisco.

Largely as a result of Jack Knight's memorable flight, and air mail service efforts on the lighted airway, the service was twice awarded the Collier Trophy for the years 1922 and 1923, a trophy presented annually "for the greatest achievement in aviation in America."

In anticipation of the through service from coast to coast, the Post Office Department issued a second series of three air mail stamps in August 1923. In values of 8 cents, 16 cents and 24 cents, the stamps reflected a planned rate of 8 cents for transport of mail by air within one of three newly announced postal zones of the transcontinental air mail route. If a letter moved by air within two zones, for example, the rate became 16 cents; within all three zones, the rate was 24 cents. One of the new stamp designs featured a DH–4 air mail plane, a fitting tribute to the workhorse of the air mail service during the government years.

By July 1, 1924, a thirty-day test of night flying on the transcontinental route was put into motion. Congressional appropriations had made possible extensions of the lighted airway from Cleveland to Rock Springs, Wyoming, and a field at Rawlins, Wyoming, had been added to the system. In anticipation of the test, more planes were equipped for night operation.

The inaugural flights on the transcontinental experimental day-and-night (or "through") schedules took place as planned. The westbound flights arrived on July 2, well ahead of schedule. Eastbound flights arrived in New York, also on July 2, just six minutes behind schedule. Weather along the full length of the route had been entirely favorable for the first flights, and there were no surprises or untoward incidents to mar the performance of all branches of the air mail service. Twenty-one different pilots took part in the flights of July 1 and 2. The two senior pilots of the air mail service, E. Hamilton Lee and Wesley L. Smith, flew the first legs out of Hazelhurst Field on Long Island, and Claire K. Vance started the mail moving from the west with his successful flight from San Francisco to Reno on July 1. Jack Knight, the "hero of the air mail" from the 1921 test, again flew at night. This time the bonfires that had once lighted his way had been replaced by the sky-piercing beams of powerful beacons.

The test proved so successful that the through service, envisioned by Colonel Paul Henderson and followed to its inception by third assistant Postmaster General W. Irving Glover, was continued as a permanent service.

"Having proved the feasibility of continuous transport (of mail) by air over long distance without regard to darkness or ordinary adverse weather conditions, the Post Office Department then was ready to step out and permit private initiative to take over the new transportation system it had developed." Such were the sentiments of a gratified General Superintendent of the Air Mail, Carl Egge, as the government era of the air mail neared its end.

The elation and satisfaction that was felt after each new success, however, would never quite eclipse the memory of sacrifice, sheer hard work, and close calls, which had been companions of progress during the route-building years. This record of costly achievement had been indelibly written into a nation's history by a handful of dedicated men, who perfected the service.

Pilot Lester Bishop's experience in the waning days of his term of duty with the air mail service offers fitting illustration of the way this fraternal bond operated in both routine situations and moments of critical need. During a winter flight over the forbidding terrain west of Rock Springs in the extreme southwest corner of Wyoming, Bishop encountered a blinding snowstorm that forced him to land on a broad area of flatland known as Granger's Bench. Once down, he kept his engine idling, believing that he would be able to lift off again when the storm passed. After a couple of hours of continued snowfall, he gradually realized that a takeoff would be impossible. He killed his engine, carefully drained the radiator, and made a decision. He would try to hike out in the direction of Lyman, some twenty miles away.

After he had traveled through waist-deep snow too far to return to his plane, he realized that his remaining energy would never get him to safety; yet he kept moving, he had no choice. Suddenly, he heard the familiar roar of a Liberty V–12 approaching at low level. Another mail plane had been sent out to search for the overdue pilot. Fortunately, Bob Ellis had spotted the abandoned craft, sighted a trail in the fresh snow, and located Bishop, then barely visible. Moments later, after Ellis made a difficult landing on a wind-swept patch of ridge, Bishop found himself crammed into the mail pit of a DH–4 enroute to Rock Springs.

The powerful beacon lights were important to the extension of air mail service across the country. Below: Photo of beacon tower in Sherman Hill, Wyoming.

Opposite: The Henderson-Egge team applied itself to the urgent problem of night flying. Lighting-equipment producers came forward with new devices, such as this illuminated wind-direction unit that could be seen from the air. Landing lights of 250,000-candlepower intensity were added to 17 planes. Field lights and beacons were in place on part of the Central Division by 1932.

Three new U.S. airmails were issued in 1923 for long-haul air mail use. Supporting a three-zone rate scheme, the stamps pictured two DH-4 views and the air mail service insignia.

Air Mail Service pilots wore their wings proudly. "Most of us are in it," said one, "because we see the mail service as providing the best opportunity to advance the cause of commercial aviation." Among the select fraternity of government airmen were Frank Yager (above left), whose plane was once slammed down by a tornado near Chappell, Nebraska, and Wesley L. Smith (lower left), who trail-blazed on the transcontinental.

They were all rugged, hard working men, who often paid highest price for their achievements. Maurice Graham (back to camera on right), CAM 4 pilot of a later era, would lose his life flying mail in 1930.

With the transcontinental airway reorganized on a three-division basis, and with almost of half-million dollars worth of lighting equipment in place by late 1923, the hard daily test of the entire system was about to begin in earnest. Pilots and planes were changed six times on the coast-to-coast run, and the average hop for each pilot along the route was close to 380 miles. Major relay stops on the airway were located at Cleveland, Chicago, Omaha, Cheyenne, Salt Lake City, and Reno, with a sprinkling of backup and emergency fields in between. Nowhere could the pace, mood, and vitality of the burgeoning air mail enterprise be more truly felt, than at one of these transfer points.

The Omaha air mail facility, located at Fort Crook Army reservation, was about 12 miles from the center of the city and included the Central Division's headquarters and main service depot. In 1924, Omaha's hangar was demolished by cyclonic winds and replaced by a new hangar (below), proving that pilots were not always alone in being subject to the vagaries of the weather. A dispatch board in the division office tracked every pilot and plane to the minute.

The proficiency and safety of pilots in the air was contingent upon a dedicated and skilled band of air mail employees on the ground. Pictured here at Omaha's Fort Crook air mail depot are some unsung heroes of the Service and their work milieu, which seemed always to reflect precision and order.

Mechanics like these often worked in below-zero temperatures until hangars were equipped with heating systems. A system of checks and counter-checks by pilot, mechanic, and chief mechanic helped insure optimum readiness of each mail plane. A chief and two assistants were always on duty at Omaha. Overhauls, and scheduled replacement of parts and engines, were important parts of a repair depot's work. Engine changes occurred after 100 hours' service, and aircraft were fully overhauled after 750 hours in the air.

5

Contracts and private carriers

Air mail to McGrath   When air mail contracts were finally awarded under terms of the Kelly Bill, they were not the first the United States Post Office had granted ... they were just the first on the "Outside." (The "Outside," to Alaskans, being anything beyond their own borders.) Actually, there was a pioneer air mail contract granted in Alaska almost a year before the Kelly Bill. It was an experiment of sorts, and it involved a pioneer airman by the name of Carl Ben Eielson.

Eielson was not exactly a bush pilot. He was more of an explorer, one who sought his way along untried aerial trails. Noel Wien, Sam White, now they were bush pilots! Eielson, you might say, was pre-bush. He was showing folks in Alaska for the first time what an airplane looked like. Whatever it took to make a bush pilot, though, Carl Ben Eielson had a lot of it. He had the courage to blaze a trail. He also wanted to find a way to make it pay.

Eielson, from North Dakota, went to Fairbanks in 1922. Like Charles A. Lindbergh, he had earned his wings in the Army Air Service and then purchased a surplus Jenny to take back home after he got out of the service. He flew his plane all over North Dakota. Then one day that plane got tangled up in a telephone wire and was demolished. That slight indisposition—to be without a set of wings—allowed Eielson time to finish college. He became a teacher. Later he went to Alaska, not to fly, but to teach.

Yet the undeveloped land beckoned and so did the thought of flying over that land. Before you knew it, there was Eielson exploring Fairbanks and its environs from the air—in his new OX5 Jenny. Thanks to the support of some friendly people in Fairbanks, backing to buy the plane was found, and with it the opportunity to see if flying could pay its way on the "Inside."

During the summer of 1923, after he had been in Alaska about a year, Eielson was giving exhibitions and taking people for rides in his Jenny. But that was small potatoes. What he wanted was a sound aerial project, and he applied himself to it. Soon it paid off. The project at hand was a contract to fly air mail.

In the early days of 1924, Eielson began to fly mail under contract for the Post Office Department. The contract called for ten bimonthly flights of mail to McGrath from Fairbanks, a distance of about 300 miles one way. For hauling this mail, he was to be paid two dollars a mile. In addition, the Post Office Department shipped him a Liberty-powered DH–4 airplane for his mail work, with U.S. MAIL boldly lettered on the side of the fuselage. When Ben received the plane it had a set of wheels, but before long it had a pair of skis, made by Charles Schiek, a Fairbanks carpenter. Ben's contract was only good for the winter months, and wheels were out of fashion in winter.

Pulling his ship out onto the local ballfield from its makeshift

135

hangar, where wood stoves were set up to keep it as warm as possible, Alaska's first flying postman took to the air with a load of mail—some 500 pounds of it—and flew down to McGrath. The date was February 2, 1924. Due to an impromptu inaugural celebration offered by the grateful citizens of McGrath, Eielson got a rather late start back to Fairbanks. He also lost his way a couple of times during that journey, and night had fallen by the time he arrived. Some bonfires had been lighted to guide him into his landing, but he misjudged the distances and went careening into some trees at the edge of the field. The DH–4 flipped over on its back. After making sure that he was okay, his Fairbanks greeters carried Eielson on their shoulders like a conquering hero to the tent-like hangar, where, in warmth and flickering light, he received an engraved golf watch for becoming Alaska's first official air mail pilot. It was morning before the plane was towed to the hangar.

Air mail usage in the states had proven the durability of the DH–4. It was a rugged plane. The trouble was it had a fairly fast landing speed, and on Alaska's frozen, rutted surface, even with a 300-pound pair of skis, that often meant crunch. Finally, toward late spring, after his plane had been wrecked often enough, Eielson had need of a new plane to complete the remaining two flights on his contract. The Post Office Department decided, in its infinite wisdom, that the experiment in Alaska had gone on about long enough. So the historic contract was terminated prematurely, and Ben was asked to ship back whatever remained of his battered plane.

Regular air mail service arrived in Alaska in 1938, when a regular route from Juneau to Fairbanks via White Horse, Yukon Territory, was established. Prior to that, mail had been flown officially on many occasions, often under the same kind of limited authorization that Eielson had received. Not always in those instances where a contract was involved, however, was a DH–4 sent along with Post Office Department approval. In fact, you might say the Eielson was given preferred treatment in that regard. Collectors bemoan the fact that no example of his first air mail to McGrath is known today. A good many would love to give that cover, whenever it does turn up, the central place in their collection. For it was flown by a man who owned a rare kind of courage.

Before his canvas-draped hangar, and beside a resting team of sled dogs, Ben Eielson prepares his ski-equipped DH-4 for its first mail run to McGrath.

ALASKA'S MAIL SERVICE
YESTERDAY AND TODAY

29. First Flight Air Mail from Alaska, U.S.A.
F. A. M. Route 16.
Fairbanks, Alaska.

Below: Captain S.E. Robbins has just landed his twin-engine transport at Fairbanks, Alaska, with inaugural mail from Juneau and points south. FAM 16's opening saved a day's time for mail between Seattle and Fairbanks.

Franked by the stamps of two nations, and signed by two postmasters, this cover's globe-circling journey is traced by ten backstamps. It began its journey with Alaska's first regular southbound mail from Fairbanks on May 8, 1938, with Pacific Alaska Airways the carrier. A required stop at White Horse, in Canada's Yukon, necessitated the FAM designation for Route 16. A 7¢ U.S. airmail was issued on January 3, 1959—the day Alaska attained statehood.

A pivotal year In a letter sent to Thomas A. Edison, his close friend at Menlo Park, industrialist Henry Ford chose not to discuss automobiles, but rather aviation. He told Edison that "the pioneering in plane building and operation is in the past. It now remains for men of business to take hold of this opportunity."

These sentiments had been voiced right along by Otto Praeger, Paul Henderson and Irving Glover. The men who had undertaken the imposing task of building a transcontinental air mail service had always visualized it as being carried on by private interests, albeit at the request of and regulated by the Post Office Department. Now that the coast-to-coast route was a reality and now that air mail revenues, surprisingly, were quite close to the level of operational costs—which was the case when the 1924 figures were tabulated—it was high time for air mail to enter a new phase of growth. The moment had arrived to turn over the job of transporting the mail to private carriers.

Air mail's pioneer years had been "laboratory" years, of experimenting, testing, and dreaming. This was especially true in terms of the "hardware"—the airplane. Then followed the "formative" years, the government era of air mail, the period drawing speedily to a close. Prototypes of planes, routes, and schedules were assembled, put to work, then revamped, and then tried out again until satisfactory models emerged. It was also a time of outlay, a time when expenditures soared and it seemed that air mail could never turn the corner on its costs. Now, as Henry Ford had correctly divined, the tide was changing. The system was prepared for serious commercial development, and because it was an American system, this meant that the door opening to the future was opening as much to let the government out as to let private enterprise in.

This great transition was greatly speeded along in 1925. A number of events that year directly paved the way for the "Contract Era" of American air mail and for the true birth of a commercial aviation industry in the United States. Passenger traffic return was hardly an enticement for investment capital in 1925; but passenger revenues, undergirded by a steady, substantial income from hauling mail under contract to the government—this was another story. Overnight the Henry Fords suddenly felt their pulses quicken; they were ready to move the mail.

What led President Calvin Coolidge to sign an air mail act early in 1925 was not simply that a group of entrepreneurs had pressed for it. There was a considerable groundswell already in evidence throughout the United States favoring the issuance of mail-carrier contracts to private concerns. American railroads had long sought to have the government remove itself as a competitor from all transportation forms that attracted private initiatives. Secondly, as small as it was, the infant aircraft manufacturing industry, then relying primarily on a trickle of military-related contracts, was outspokenly in accord with actions that would put private air carriers into business. Their interest was, quite obviously, a new market for their products. Finally, the American public, informed by General "Billy" Mitchell and a group of round-the-world Army pilots about the United States lag in aviation, wanted to see faster development of commercial aviation, believing that progress in the civilian sector guaranteed progress in the military/defense sector as well. The prevailing mood disapproved of direct subsidy of aviation programs but could justify the indirect kind (such as might be obtained with all mail contracts). After all, payments to railroad and steamship operators for hauling mail had been made in the United States for a long time.

On February 2, 1925 legislation, introduced more than a year before by Representative Clyde M. Kelly of Braddock, Pennsylvania, was speedily passed. Known ever after as the Kelly Bill, this legislation was "an act to encourage commercial aviation and to authorize the Postmaster General to contract for air mail service." Essentially the bill authorized the Post Office Department to license individuals or companies to carry official United States mail through the air, granting the carrier service four fifths of the revenue derived from the postage, with the government claiming the remaining fifth. Ultimately this plan, providing financial "life-blood" to the commercial operators of air mail routes, would place these fragile operations (for the most part) under the control of the postmaster general, who could by law extend, consolidate, or eliminate routes that in his judgment were not in the public interest.

The first bid requests under the Kelly Bill were announced on July 15 after Second Assistant Postmaster General Paul Henderson had enumerated the specific contractual details called for in the bill itself. Mention of a few of these details will indicate the general tenor of the plan. In the first place it was made clear that local postmasters were to petition for contract mail service, spelling out the need for such service in their area, the availability of aviation facilities, the schedule that could be maintained, the potential air mail volume, and so on. Secondly, it was implied that for the time being the Post Office Department would continue its service on the main transcontinental route. At the outset, the contracts to be let to private carriers were intended to foster the development of feeder routes connecting with the main line. The aim was to press for an expanded service in the country, not to duplicate service that was currently being offered.

Other details were as follows:

Contracts could be terminated by either party with 45 days notice, but the Post Office Department termination must be for cause.

Contractors...could carry packages or passengers, at rates initiated by the contractors. However, contractors would have to give preference on all trips to the air mail offered for transport.

Special postage rates for this contract air mail service would be 10 cents for each ounce or fraction thereof on routes 1,000 miles or less; 15 cents on routes between 1,000 and 1,500 miles; 20 cents on routes over 1,500 miles. Direct air mileage would be the control figure in each case.

Monthly payments for this service would be four fifths of the special air mail postage on letters actually carried and would be made upon certification by postmasters.

Pilots and other employees handling mails of such contractors would subscribe to the usual government oath of office.

Delay to mail carried by contractors, brought about wholly by act of God, would not be chargeable to the contractor.

Another proviso specified that no contractor or his employee would open any mail bag or other mail-carrying receptacle offered to him for transport.

The year 1925 would have been a banner year for commercial aviation if it held nothing other than the passage of the Kelly Bill. But other significant developments did occur. On April 13, the Ford Motor Company of Dearborn, Michigan, began to operate a daily air transport service between Dearborn and Chicago. The established schedule called for one flight in each direction each weekday, with the Chicago flight departing for Dearborn at 8 A.M. and the westbound flight leaving Dearborn at 3:15 P.M. Parts and materials moving from one Ford plant to another were carried at first, but then executives and technicians began to travel between company locations. A short time after the service began, it was expanded to include Cleveland, Ohio trips, and by the end of 1925 three trips between Detroit (Dearborn) and Chicago were scheduled daily in addition to two Cleveland trips.

Ford Air Transport, although not serving the general public, was the first permanent aerial passenger/freight line in the United States. It used the Stout all-metal 2–AT transport powered by a single 400 hp Liberty engine. The 2–AT was designed by a Ford acquaintance, William "Bill" Stout, whose manufacturing operation was located adjacent to Dearborn's airport. Pleased with the operation of his little airline, Henry Ford bought up the Stout Company on July 25, 1925. Ford retained the services of Stout until Stout's effort to produce a tri-motored, all-metal version of his 2–AT ended in failure. At that juncture, Ford put together a design team of John Lee, Harold Hicks, Otto Koppen, William Mayo, James McDonnell(later the founder of McDonnell Aircraft), and Tom Towle. Handed the tri-motor transport project, this talented group proceeded to develop an all-metal 3-engine plane for Henry Ford, which became known

139

as the Ford *Tin Goose* and which turned out to be one of the all-time "stars" of commercial aviation in the United States.

A third occurrence of note involved the Post Office Department's inauguration of regular overnight service in both directions on the New York–Chicago portion of the transcontinental route. Beginning on July 1, 1925, this service demanded a roster of sixteen top pilots; it also occasioned some important changes along that segment of the coast-to-coast airway.

The New York–Chicago stretch was the most challenging of the entire transcontinental system. Not only did this portion support the heaviest traffic loads, but it was in many respects the most hazardous real estate that the air mail pilots traversed. The problem was not that the Allegheny Mountains of Pennsylvania were so high—they are about 2,600 feet at their highest point—but that they presented such topographical confusion that safe emergency landings in their vicinity were simply not possible. When night service in this area was planned, a new and carefully worked out beacon system became a top priority.

Landing fields were another important consideration, with the new night schedule precipitating three major changes in this area. Bellefonte, some 225 miles from New York, was reactivated as an operating field. Secondly, five new emergency landing fields with special lighting schemes had to be carved out in the vicinity of the trouble spots in Pennsylvania. And finally, the eastern terminus was transferred from east of New York City (Hazelhurst) to a location in New Jersey, west of the metropolitan New York area. Known as Hadley Field, the new terminus was a seventy-seven acre field near New Brunswick. Choice of this location reduced the leg by some fifty miles and permitted the pilots to avoid the fog and smoke conditions that were often troublesome in the New York City area. Fast mail trains stopping at New Brunswick made an ideal shuttle for air mail into New York's General Post Office.

Postmaster General Harry S. New and a crowd of more than 15,000 people gathered at Hadley Field on the evening of Wednesday, July 1, 1925, to witness the inaugural night flights on the New York–Chicago route. Pulled in from the night run between Chicago and Cheyenne, veteran pilot Dean C. Smith took off at 8:45 P.M. (DST) with 87 pounds of mail. He was followed two hours later by J. D. Hill, carrying in his DH–4 more than three times the load that Smith had taken. Because Smith encountered some generator trouble en route to Cleveland, his mail was slightly delayed getting into the hands of his relay, Art Smith. Nevertheless, both westbound loads arrived in Chicago in time to be processed and put in morning deliveries in that city.

At Maywood Field in Chicago, Second Assistant Postmaster General Paul Henderson, and Air Mail Superintendent Carl Egge, led a ceremonial send-off for the eastbound mail on the evening of July 1. Pilot Shirley J. Short was first to depart for

The Chicago air mail field cancellation displays a date indicating that this cover traveled on the first flight of overnight mail between New York and Chicago. Franking includes the extra 2¢ required for this service.

Shown here are key figures in the formation of Western Air Express. Harris Hanshue, founder and first president, hands the mail to his chief pilot and operations manager, Fred Kelly. WAE chose the Douglas M-2 for CAM 4, liking its ceiling and range.

Cleveland that evening, leaving at 7:48 P.M. George I. Meyers followed in his DH–4 at 9:40 P.M. The Chicago mail made excellent time, reaching Hadley Field in relays at 2 A.M. and 4:37 A.M. respectively.

All of the pilots that night, even those who arrived well after midnight, were greeted in Cleveland by large crowds, drawn by a large civic celebration surrounding the opening of the new Cleveland Municipal Airport. Because of the festivities in that city, no one had time to apply an official cachet to the overnight mail originating there; nor was the cachet applied to all of the mail in New York and Chicago. The 3-line cachet was found on all mail out of Bellefonte, (Pennsylvania) and Bryan (Ohio) and read: AIR MAIL/First Overnight Flight/New York to Chicago (or Chicago to New York). The rate for postage on this overnight service was 10 cents per ounce.

While the excitement of overnight mail was receiving its share of headlines in the east, an unnoticed event occurred in the Far West that was another clue as to what was happening in aviation circles. On July 13, a small company called Western Air Express (W.A.E.) was born. Incorporated at Sacramento, California on that day, W.A.E. was headed by a Las Vegas, Nevada visionary by the name of Harris "Pop" Hanshue, who had looked to the day when airlines would carry people across the vast western reaches. To a man such as Hanshue, passage of the Kelly Bill was a signal to get moving. Lining up two key supporters in Los Angeles, Hanshue proceeded to secure financial backing, enlist personnel (mostly pilots), assess equipment, and do all the things necessary to organize an airline.

In going to Los Angeles, Hanshue knew he was riding a horse that could obtain full civic backing and have a good shot at one of the first contract routes once the bids were opened. It had continued to rankle southern Californians that the western terminus of the transcontinental air mail system was located in San Francisco. Hanshue and his backers placed their money on the possibility of a Los Angeles–Las Vegas–Salt Lake City connection with the "main line" of the air mail service. This was not unlike many other aviation ventures that constellated in 1925.

A final aspect that truly identified 1925 as the key year of transformation of commercial aviation and air mail practices in the United States related to the award of the first contract routes under the impetus of February's important legislation. The bids were invited in July, they were opened on September 15, and the successful bids on five routes were announced publicly on November 7. Under the law, contractors named were granted reasonable time to make their routes operational. The cheer that went up when Harris Hanshue in Los Angeles, his vice president Corliss Mosely, and their four pilots learned that the route from Salt Lake City to Los Angeles had been awarded to Western Air Express could almost be heard in Las Vegas.

141

First flights and Ford

One of Eastern Air Transport's pilots, Captain E. H. "Pete" Parker, was once asked about the kind of passenger service that was offered in the cabin during the early years of commercial passenger transport.

"Well," he replied, "the co-pilot would walk back and collect the tickets, because hostesses didn't come along until later. Sometimes he'd discover a stowaway without a ticket and we'd throw him out at the end of the runway. About the only thing else the co-pilot did was to show the passengers the cotton ear plugs and the little vials of ammonia for air sickness.

"One day," he recalled, "we found a lady who had the ammonia vials stuffed in her ears. She was smelling the cotton with a curious look on her face."

Airmen relate countless amusing anecdotes about the early days of commercial aviation when the public and planes were first brought together. But the stories are usually masks for the seriousness with which the era was greeted. Note the remarks of Postmaster General New, as he announced the first contract air mail routes on November 7, 1925.

The awarding of contracts this day for the carrying of the mail by air transport over five routes in widely separated sections of the country marks an epoch in the history of the American post office. Upon the result of the enterprise this day entered upon depends the future of aerial transport in the United States. Because of the importance of the subject and because it is the first time the [P.O.] Department has had this problem before it, the Postmaster General has been particularly careful and has exhausted every means to investigate and critically scrutinize every bid offered and every bidder that has submitted a tender. In the exercise of this care I have had in mind the protection of aviation, as well as the obvious necessary protection of the postal service....I have required that every bidder should satisfy this Department that it has immediately available the means necessary to the successful performance of its contract.

Though seventeen proposals to operate contract air mail routes were received by the postmaster general, only five were successful and granted route numbers. In the beginning of private-carrier service, the route numbers were applied on a chronological basis, being assigned as a contract was awarded and always stenciled on the fuselage or tail fin of the contractor's aircraft. Much later the chronological system became irrelevant as route cancellations and consolidations occurred. The successful bidders for the first five routes were as follows (CAM meaning contract air mail, the word *route* understood):

CAM 1 *Boston–New York* via Hartford awarded to: Colonial Air Transport, Inc., Naugatuck, Connecticut

CAM 2 *Chicago–St. Louis* via Peoria and Springfield awarded to: Robertson Aircraft Corporation, St. Louis, Missouri
CAM 3 *Chicago–Dallas* and *Fort Worth* awarded to: National Air Transport, Inc., Chicago, Illinois
CAM 4 *Salt Lake City–Los Angeles* awarded to: Western Air Express, Inc., Los Angeles, California
CAM 5 *Elko* (Nevada)–*Pasco* (Washington) awarded to: Walter T. Varney, San Francisco, California

All of the above contractors had their routes operational by mid-1926, and by that time they were joined by four other successful contractors, making ten routes on which service had begun, one contractor being granted contracts on two adjoining routes. Route numbers bore no relationship to the dates on which services started up. Among the ten CAM routes inaugurated by July 1, in fact, CAM 1 was the last to get itself going. Interestingly enough, the first firm to carry air mail for the government was not one of the five announced by Postmaster General New in November of 1925.

On January 27, 1926, before any United States mail was carried over a CAM route, a bulletin was sent out by the Post Office Department. It read:

Postmasters and others connected with the Postal Service are notified that the department is about to issue a new 10¢ air mail stamp in connection with the Postmaster General's Order No. 3817 dated January 19th, 1926 as published in the Postal Bulletin of January 26. This stamp intended primarily for use in the air mail service, will be valid for all purposes for which postage stamps of the regular issue are used.

This new airmail, printed in a blue ink and issued in one value only, was an attractive oversized stamp featuring a map of the United States with two biplanes resembling DH–4Bs at either end of the country. The plane pictured to the left over the West Coast is heading east, and the plane to the right is heading in a westerly direction. The Kelly Bill of 1925 had specified a rate of 10 cents an ounce on contract routes, marking the new issue as a response to that directive.

After forming his company airline in 1925, Henry Ford purchased the Stout Metal Airplane Company of Dearborn, including its entire output of five 2-AT single-engined monoplanes. It was a 2-AT named Maiden Dearborn IV that would fly the very first mail for Ford on February 15, 1926. Here, the famed plane is shown during a tune-up of its Liberty 400 engine and as it warms up for its historic CAM 6 inaugural flight. An important Stout feature was a thick, internally-braced wing that eliminated struts.

What was revealing about the final paragraph of the bulletin was its list of "first sale" locations. The new stamp was to be placed on sale on February 13 in Detroit and Dearborn in Michigan, in Chicago, Illinois and in Cleveland, Ohio in addition to Washington, D.C. This ended the guessing game in regard to which CAM route would be placed in operation first. It was now obvious that Henry Ford's airline—Ford Air Transport—would lead the way into the fabulous new CAM era of air mail.

The Ford Motor Company of Detroit signed a contract with the Postmaster General on January 7, 1926, to operate two CAM routes. Ford thus joined the other contractors of record and was the first company to hold a contract on more than one route. It is not surprising that Ford was able to move into operational readiness more quickly than the other carriers, having had its internal airline already operative for the better part of 1925. February 15 was the date set for the first flights on CAM 6 (Detroit–Cleveland) and CAM 7 (Chicago–Detroit), and the new stamp arrived just in time to frank and decorate the first CAM mail in history.

In preparation for the Ford flights and for other inaugural flights on CAM routes, the Post Office Department designed and produced special large double-circle cachets. The inner circle contained the city name, time, and date (where and when the postal item originated) and the outer circle made clear that the card or cover being stamped was being carried on a "first flight" inaugurating a CAM service. The bottom portion of the large outside circle repeated the names of cities on the route (or routes) being joined by the service. The familiar double-circle design was used for over a year as CAM routes were opened up in a steady stream. Mail that displayed these or other "first flight" designations was sought by an aviation-adoring public through the late twenties and thirties and forms the core of many aerophilatelic collections today. Literally thousands of first flight covers exist, and they are still produced with distincitve cachets whenever an airline inaugurates a new route or extends one, celebrates an anniversary, alters its type of service over an existing route, or initiates the use of a new aircraft on a particular

Bearing the large, familiar double-circle cachet applied to almost all CAM inaugural covers until mid-1927, this specimen is signed by pilot Lawrence G. Fritz, and was carried on his epoch-making flight to Cleveland. The cover bears the proper franking for the date, but not the 10¢ "map" airmail issued just two days earlier.

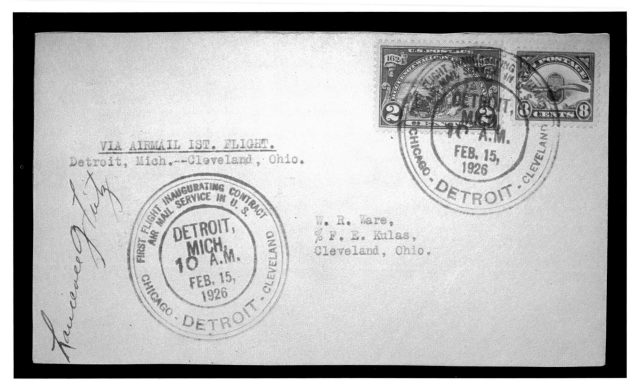

route. A collection of first flight covers can not only document the history of air mail and postal rates, but the collection itself can become a veritable catalog of aviation history.

A large motor parade took place in Detroit on the morning of February 15, 1926, as officials from the Post Office Department joined local civic and Ford dignitaries in a procession to the Dearborn airport. Among those present for the inauguration of contract air mail were Henry Ford, his son Edsel, Second Assistant Postmaster General in charge of air mail, W. Irving Glover, and Detroit Postmaster Charles C. Kellogg. A ceremonial bag of mail was handed to Henry Ford by Glover and in turn given to the waiting CAM pilot Lawrence G. Fritz. At exactly 10:40 A.M., Fritz began his takeoff run with almost 72 pounds of mail aboard bound for Cleveland. He was flying a Ford Air Transport single-engine Stout 2–AT.

Ford plans had originally called for Fritz to make the second CAM flight of the day instead of the first. However, the flight of D. E. Burford on CAM 7 from Chicago into Dearborn was delayed while he awaited the arrival of a tardy Post Office Department mail plane coming into Chicago on the transcontinental run. Burford finally left Chicago for Detroit at 1:37 P.M., thereby making the second CAM flight in history.

Fritz reached Cleveland's Municipal Airport approximately twenty minutes ahead of schedule and turned his mail over to Assistant Postmaster Frank A. Donda. On his return flight Fritz felt impelled to perform a duty that lengthened his flight by a few minutes. The following entry from the "Interrupted Flight" section of the American Air Mail Catalogue provides a clue to the mission:

February 12, BRYAN, OHIO—USG—10:10 P.M. Chicago–New York. Pilot Art Smith killed. Plane crashed into tree and was destroyed by fire. Mail carried 82 lbs. But 6 pieces addressed to Europe and a few loose pieces are known to have been salvaged.

A close friend of the deceased airman, and aware that Art Smith's body was at rest in his home at that time, Larry Fritz elected to take a slight detour from his assigned route and fly over the late pilot's house. In a parting salute, he dropped a small wreath from the cockpit. The bond between these two men had been a close one, and the whole episode was a poignant reminder that Post Office Department pilots were still paying their dues on the great transcontinental airway.

Among the Ford Air Transport pilots, there was one flying that inaugural day who would, within a short three months, become the first aviator to perish on the CAM routes. Ross Kirkpatrick, pilot of the first westbound mail on CAM 7, would crash on the very route he was helping Burford inaugurate. That accident took place at Argo, Illinois on May 18. Kirkpatrick's plane was demolished, but his mail was recovered intact.

One major ingredient was missing as commercial aviation got rolling in the United States. The game plan was now revealed, with air mail contracts intended to provide the financial springboard, and the players beginning to divide into competitive teams. But the truth was that on February 15, 1926, the game itself had very few rules (other than postal rules) and no referees. With commercial aviation about to mushroom, the government was increasingly aware that some degree of federal regulatory control would be necessary. Secretary of Commerce Herbert Hoover took the lead by recommending to President Coolidge that he appoint a top-level advisory board to study thoroughly every phase of aviation in the United States, commercial as well as military. The dual approach became critical at this time in history because Hoover's approach ran head on into Billy Mitchell's stated view that aviation development ought to proceed with the military dictating the requirements almost entirely. General Mitchell was keenly aware of the then-current European lead in all phases of aviation.

An advisory board was named. It made its report to President Coolidge and to Congress, and, in a politically effective way, it evoked an Air Commerce Act that was passed on May 20, 1926. Described by the National Advisory Council for Aeronautics as "the legislative cornerstone for the development of commercial aviation in the United States," the act became just that.

A Bureau of Aeronautics was created in the Commerce Department, and William P. McCracken, Jr., an attorney and Army Air Service veteran, was named Assistant Secretary of Commerce for Aeronautics. This was the key result of the Air Commerce Act: the establishment of a rule-making body with the discretionary enforcement powers of a referee. Under the Bureau of Aeronautics came licensing of pilots, air traffic procedures, control of the airway lighting program, weather service, mapping, research of engines and aircraft, enforcement of standards for all aviation equipment, and statistical information compilation and dissemination.

If 1925 had been the year of transition, the opening of the CAM routes and the passage of the Air Commerce Act confirmed that commercial aviation had truly taken off by 1926. As Lieutenant J. Parker Van Zandt of the Army Air Service had put it in January of that year: "There is a revolutionary fact abroad in the land; aircraft have gone to work. And the nation is waking to find itself fast wedded to a new handmaid of progress—the United States Transcontinental Air Mail Service." People were now coming to see how important a factor the air mail experiment had been, and would continue to be, in the growth and prosperity of a young, sprawling, and vital nation.

145

CAMs blanket the nation

In ceremonies held at Chicago's O'Hare Airport, a new United States commemorative postage stamp was introduced for the first time in March 1976. The 13-cent stamp, celebrating the fiftieth anniversary of commercial aviation in the United States, featured in its design two aircraft that transported mail over the new contract mail routes in 1926, the Ford 2–AT transport and the Laird Swallow biplane. Present for the occasion were a number of aviation pioneers, United States airline officials, representatives of various aviation-related organizations and the United States Postal Service, several distinguished aerophilatelists, and invited guests. The Postmaster General of the United States and the President of the Air Transport Association were the principal speakers.

The audience that day relived the years of amazing growth that commercial aviation and air mail experienced together. Since 1953, the audience was told, the volume of airline reservations, air cargo, and air mail in the United States had increased more than tenfold! Not long after contract mail was introduced, the carriers transported close to 16 million pieces of mail in the course of one year; now the figure, according to the Postmaster General, was over 16 billion. Eight out of every ten intercity first class letters moved by air in 1975, and the United States, with about six percent of the world's population, claimed more than 60 percent of the world's air mail. At the time of the anniversary in 1976, American commercial aviation boasted a fleet of 2,200 aircraft and was carrying out 13,000 flights each day. As the pioneers recalled—"It wasn't always so!"

What was true about the early years of contract mail flights is that the growth came remarkably fast. Post Office Department figures for the closing years of the 1920s seem to bear out this dynamic trend.

AIR MAIL CARRIED ON PRIVATE CONTRACT ROUTES

Year	Pounds Flown	Cost
1926	3,000	$ 89,754
1927	473,102	1,363,228
1928	1,861,800	4,042,777
1929	5,635,680	11,169,015

In contrast to the 1927 contract figures, government operated routes (meaning essentially the transcontinental) in 1926 had carried 354,000 pounds at a cost of $2,782,000. The CAM routes almost cut the per pound costs in half in their first full year of existence. By 1931, the private carriers would lower their own handling cost to less than $1.98, a reduction from $2.90 per pound in 1926.

Two events that occurred in 1926 within about ten days of each other served to demonstrate that Post Office Department officials were hardly oblivious to the increases in air mail volume that were certain to emerge out of the new contract carrier system. One event involved the method of reimbursing private contractors; the other involved aircraft.

In a report to the President dated November 1925 Postmaster General New had proposed a Kelly Bill amendment regarding the basis of payments for contract service. The existing system involved a pay-out to the contractors of four fifths of the air mail postage on all flown mail. In order to calculate that payment, each piece of mail had to be handled separately and a figure entered on a postmaster's record. The proposal suggested paying contractors at a fixed rate per pound. The accounting requirements under the existing procedure tended to slow up and make awkward the handling of air mail and therefore fostered a resistance to the use of it in every local post office. Open to opportunities for carelessness and error, it was an unsatisfactory, if not intolerable, situation, about to be made worse by the expected increase in air mail flow. This state of affairs led Representative Kelly of Pennsylvania to propose a major amendment to his air mail act of 1925, which passed into law as HR 11841 on June 3, 1926. It read in part:

> Existing contracts may be amended by the written consent of the contractor and the Postmaster General to provide for a fixed rate per pound.

A difficult situation had been speedily dealt with by Congress.

The second indication that the Post Office Department anticipated additional volume had to do with official realization that the time to retire the DH–4 was at hand. The system was in danger of choking itself as the loads began to exceed the capacity of the DH–4. An improved aircraft was eased into the system just in the nick of time. Produced by the Douglas Aircraft Co., it was known as the M–4.

Initial deliveries of Donald Douglas' plane were made as early as May 26, 1926. The full order to Douglas, involving one M–1 and a few M–3s in addition to the M–4s, amounted to 51 airplanes. The M–4 could haul 1,000 pounds of mail (almost twice the DH–4 load limit) and fly it at an altitude of 17,500 feet. And though faster than the DeHavillands being replaced, the Douglas planes had a comfortably slow landing speed in the neighborhood of 52 mph.

These new planes had an effect on the transcontinental route. Now it was possible and advisable to bypass certain stops on the cross-country route. Wherever possible these stops were then promptly eliminated. Such time-honored names like Rawlins, Bryan, and Bellefonte were totally phased out. North Platte, Rock Springs, and Iowa City were released as regular service stops for eastbound flights. The Douglas M–4s were brought in service from Salt Lake City to New York City, while DH–4s continued to operate from Salt Lake on to the West Coast. No further construction of DH–4s at the Chicago repair facility started after July 1, 1926. It would not be long before a good share of the newly purchased M–4s would be sold to contract air mail carriers as part of the government's withdrawal from the business of transporting air mail. That withdrawal, however, would have to await the award of contracts on the transcontinental itself.

While these events were taking place on the government side, the first wave of air mail route contractors were busy getting their own houses in order. As the government had learned back in 1918 and all through the early 1920s, this was no mean task. It seems that higher levels of organization and integration are achieved only after periods of chaos, regression, sacrifice (perhaps), and disorganization. Although the government era of air mail taught many hard lessons about transporting written communications by air on a regular schedule over long distances, the new era was not about to sidestep its own unique growing pains.

In a generally exuberant atmosphere, moderated by a strange blend of confusion and challenge, small companies, many operating on fragile shoestrings, began to break in some difficult routes with a variety of aircraft and a diversity of pilot experience. How they got on about their task is an inspiring chapter of aviation history and helps to explain the fascination that grows in aerophilatelists as they study the artifacts that were spawned in this period.

The halcyon year of 1926 saw eleven CAM routes wing into action. The first route placed into service after the Ford inaugurals in February was CAM 10 between Jacksonville and Miami. This April 1 opening was followed on April 6, 1926, by a CAM 5 opening between Elko, Nevada and Pasco in Washington State. The initial contractor on CAM 5 was Walter T. Varney. Because the route between Elko and Pasco involved some of the highest and roughest terrain in the country, there were not many bidders. In fact, there were not any except Walter T. Varney. Lecturing in Seattle shortly before CAM 5 began operations, General Billy Mitchell, when asked about the route's chances for success, responded: "If they knew what they were trying to do, they wouldn't even start it." But start it "they" did, and that start, according to Varney pilot Leon Cuddeback, had some interesting moments:

When the Post Office Department proposed civilian contract airmail in 1925, Varney was interested and was in a position to bid on Contract Air Mail route #5. . . .

Among Varney's operations was a sales agency for new Swallow aircraft, which were manufactured at Wichita, Kan-

sas. We operated some of those planes with underpowered OX-5 and OXX-6 engines. But for the airmail service, we needed aircraft with greater carrying capacity and higher performance, so we had the factory redesign the Swallow with a different, high-lift wing for high altitude takeoffs and landings.

We got some used 150-horsepower Curtiss K-6 engines from St. Louis and had them shipped to San Francisco, where they were reconditioned and overhauled. All six Swallows were delivered from Wichita without engines. In early 1926, the first one was shipped to Elko, and I was there with our three mechanics to assemble the airplane and install the engine. Then I test flew it to prove that it could fly high enough to get over the mountains in the area.

The rest of the airplanes, in crates, and the rest of the engines were shipped to Boise, where we assembled them in an open field provided by the Boise City Council.

There were no maps or charts of the area at that time, so Walter Varney drove over the route in an auto and traced a map on a postcard. It was rather simple from Pasco to Boise because the route followed the highway and a railroad, but from Boise to Elko there was just a dirt road with very few landmarks.

Meanwhile, at Boise we found that our disassembled aircraft had not had the parts matched up first at the factory and that very few parts fitted together. We had to ream every hole to make a bolt fit, and Chris DeVelschow, our chief mechanic, proved himself an artist with a sledgehammer.

The day before the service was to begin on CAM 5, Cuddeback received word of a severe setback to his initial plans. Two of his pilots, sent to Pasco to arrange the inaugural flight from that terminus, had crashed on landing there, both breaking their noses. He had to revise assignments, and rush off at once to fill in for the injured men.

I arrived [in Pasco] without incident at night, and there was a lot of talk that night about a big celebration the next day because of the inaugural flight.

The Army Reserve from Vancouver and Spokane, Washington, had sent planes down for the event, and newspaper reporters came from Spokane, Portland, Seattle and surrounding areas. I wasn't particularly interested in any celebrating, so I got my airplane all ready to go and then went to the hotel and went to bed.

The takeoff was scheduled for 6 A.M.—just about daylight—and the mail arrived from Portland, Spokane and Seattle by railroad sometime during the night. I got up at 4 A.M., had some coffee and went to the airport, and quite a crowd had gathered there.

Appropriate for the occasion, an authentic mail stagecoach drove up and handed over the mail, which I signed for. There were 9,285 pieces of mail in six sacks, weighing just over 200

Shown here is a letter carried by Leon Cuddeback from Pasco, Washington, to Elko, Nevada, during the CAM 5 inaugurals in April, 1926. Badly stained, and therefore less coveted by collectors, this cover nevertheless has many desirable features. Beneath the 10¢ U.S. "map" airmail is a two-line cachet that spells out the main purpose of the first contract routes: to connect with the government-operated transcontinental service.

pounds, destined for Boise and points east. We put the mail in the Swallow's mail pit, and I was all set to go. But when we tried to start the airplane, the engine balked. We cranked, and it balked, and we cranked. I was almost ready to set fire to the darn thing to see if it would burn up, but it finally got going.

I was 23 minutes late getting off, but the 244-mile flight went fine. The weather was clear at Pasco, and the flight was uneventful, even over the Blue Mountains. They were only about 4,500 feet high and were not a very high range.

I flew at an altitude of about 500 feet over the mountains to LaGrande and flew at 2,000 feet over the flatlands from there on. The flight took less than three hours, and I arrived at Boise at 10:10 A.M. local time [9:10 A.M. Pasco time].

I didn't expect much of a reception, but there was a huge crowd at Boise when I touched down. It seemed like everybody was there—dignitaries from Washington, D.C., the state, the city, postal officials and a number of school bands. I dropped off the mail for Boise and picked up the mail from Boise to other points and had it all loaded aboard another Swallow that I was to use for the Boise to Elko leg.

But again the K–6 engine wouldn't start. So I had them fuel up the original airplane I arrived in, Varney airplane number 3.

In those days, three or four hours of flight time were supposed to be the maximum put on an engine at one time. After that it needed an overnight overhaul.

I took off again in number 3 from Boise at 10:55A.M., and all went well at first. I faithfully followed that little map Walter Varney had drawn on the postcard as I was afraid that if I lost my way for five minutes I probably would never find it again.

About half way to Elko I ran into a mean thunderstorm, with

heavy rain and quite a bit of turbulence. It was rough, with some hail, and it forced me to stay down very close to the road, right down on the ground. Fortunately, I was over a valley with no hills to cross, so I was able to get low under the storm clouds.

I got into Elko at about 12:27 P.M., Pasco and Elko time [1:27 P.M. Boise time], and again there was a big crowd to greet me, with more bands and officials. I briefed Rose on the thunderstorms and advised him to go around them to the southwest, and he took off. Rose got blown far off course and landed in the desert, and it was days until we heard that he was all right.

I didn't have much else to do as Walter Varney was at Elko to meet me, and he took charge of things. And his father, Thomas H. B. Varney, sent me a telegram from Los Angeles, which read: "Congratulations on the first successful commercial airmail delivery."

There was a lot of celebrating, too, at Elko, but I was tired and my cares were over, so I relaxed. I went to the hotel and went to bed.

It had been a long day for all of us, and we had proved a lot of people wrong. We had been told we were trying to do the impossible, but we didn't know better, and we went ahead and did it.

The CAM 5 inaugural was reminiscent of Potomac Park, Washington on May 15, 1918, when another plane wouldn't start and another pilot, named Boyle, lost his way. Cuddeback's successful flights in Swallow #3 were highly gratifying to Walter Varney. Pilot Franklin Rose, who was forced down in Jordan Valley, Oregon by the same storms that Cuddeback en-

148

Pilot Franklin Rose met with misfortune flying the inaugural mail out of Elko on CAM 5. Driven 60 miles off his course to Boise by severe storms, Rose was forced down in Jordan Valley, Oregon. Moving with his mail on foot and horseback, he was eventually reported safe, though his mail was two days late. A piece of this mail, (right), is considered a "crash" cover as well as a first flight. The U.S. "map" series of airmails was issued between February 13, 1926, and January 25, 1927, to meet prevailing rates, which finally settled at 10¢ per half-ounce on February 1, 1927, when the zone system was discontinued.

countered, hiked with his mail bag for ten miles until he found a working farm. There, he borrowed a horse and rode to the nearest phone thirty miles away. His mail required two days until it was processed in Boise and three until the backstamps were rendered at Pasco.

After the first day's flights were part of the record, Walter Varney asked for permission to suspend service in order to make equipment adjustments. CAM 5 resumed operation again on June 1.

On the fiftieth anniversary of CAM 5 in 1976, Leon Cuddeback at age seventy-seven traveled to Boise's airport and was honored by having a United Air Lines (a successor of the Varney Company) 727 jet transport named in his honor. Cuddeback was undoubtedly delighted also with the commercial aviation commemorative postage stamp introduced at O'Hare a few weeks before the Boise celebration. Right there on the stamp, with the Ford transport, was his Swallow biplane.

Harris Hanshue's Western Air Express was one of four CAM routes to get underway in 1926. On April 17, inaugural flights were carried out in both directions between Los Angeles and Salt Lake City, with Maury Graham flying the eastbound trip and Jimmy James doing westbound honors. As routine as these trips seemed at the time, they were of consequence. By virtue of later airline mergers, the modern day giant, TWA, traces its origins to the Western Air Express mail flights of April 17, 1926.

When Western Air Express was awarded the contract for its route on November 7, 1925, it had several matters of business to attend to before it was ready to fly the mail. Planes and pilots headed the list. Western Air Express eventually settled on Doug-

Walter Varney's chief pilot on opening day of CAM 5 was Leon D. Cuddeback, whom Varney had taught to fly in 1921. Cuddeback recalls having little sense of "trail blazing" in his tiny Swallow biplane when he was a young mail pilot (lower photo). On the 50th anniversary Cuddeback, age 77, was reminded, in a celebration at Boise, that United Airlines traces its birth to his flight of April, 1926. Varney Air Lines was acquired by United in its formative years.

Opposite: 9,285 pieces of mail were driven to plane-side in an authentic mail stagecoach as part of the Pasco festivities on the morning of April 6, 1926.

las M–2s, predecessors of the M–4s that joined the Post Office Department routes in 1926. Having a payload about equal to the M–4s and a slightly lower ceiling, the M–2 could still cover 600 miles without refueling. This was important for the mountain stretches between Los Angeles and Salt Lake City. They also had the ability to get airborne quickly, desirable in the event of a forced landing where the takeoff run was restricted. Hanshue ordered six M–2s for his airline.

Western's operations manager and chief pilot was Fred Kelly, and he and Western Vice President Corliss Mosely then found the pilots. Mosely, a World War I aviator himself, eventually

hired three other flyers, two of whom, Graham and James, flew the inaugural flights on CAM 4. The fourth pilot was Al De-Garmo, who had tried unsuccessfully to get a passenger service going between Los Angeles and San Francisco in 1923. The four Western Air Express pilots garnered a title early; they were known as "the four horsemen."

What these pilots did to prepare for their mail flights sounds very much akin to Walter Varney's automobile trip over his CAM 5 route. As Al DeGarmo tells it, "We took a couple of Dodge panel trucks and loaded them with rolls of canvas two feet wide. We then spent two weeks driving over the L.A. to Salt Lake pathway, camping out at night and cooking for ourselves. When we found a level place where we thought we'd be able to manage a forced landing, we would unroll enough canvas to help us spot it from the air. We'd make a "V" with the canvas to tell us which way to land." DeGarmo also reported the use of another letter: "T" meant "try a landing here if necessary, but chances are you won't fly out." Thirty-eight times those canvas markers came in handy, as weather and mechanical problems caused that many emergencies.

A spacious second cockpit led Western Air Express to experiment with passenger carries. Although by far its greatest revenues were obtained through its mail contract, Hanshue's airline did carry just over 400 fare-paying passengers in 1927. One of the first passengers Al DeGarmo took along on his route jumped the gun on Western's eligibility to carry anyone. In order not to get the airline in trouble, the passenger paid the air mail rate for his weight and "mailed himself" on the flight. The passenger's name: Will Rogers.

Western Air Express received a special Guggenheim grant in 1928 that allowed it to give up its mail income for a time to see if an American airline could yet sustain itself with passenger fees alone. The answer was no. Western Air Express promptly returned to air mail duty.

CAM 9 was inaugurated on June 7, 1926. It was the most disastrous debut along the early CAM routes, so disastrous in fact that one pilot lost his life and the inaugural contractor lost his contract. Service was suspended at once and not resumed until October under another contractor. Only two of six flights succeeded in reaching their destinations. Undoubtedly more mail reached the terminal points by train than by plane. The reason for CAM 9's debacle: one of the worst wind-driven dust storms to ever hit the area blew down out of the northwest just as these first flights were getting under way.

Because of the number of pilots involved, and the correspondingly high number of mail batches, the CAM 9 picture has remained confused for many years. Only in June 1976 did the issue resolve itself. At that time, the eminent aerophilatelist Dr. Perham C. Nahl of the American Air Mail Society published in the Society's *Airpost Journal* a definitive study answering most of the remaining questions about the CAM 9 inaugural day. Through his article, Dr. Nahl provided a memorable example of philatelic detective work, and an exciting demonstration of how the mails and their markings can be employed to reconstruct and confirm historical events.

152   Charles Dickinson, the contract holder on CAM 9, the route between Chicago and Minneapolis, had a winged emblem applied to each of his planes just below the cockpit. Above the spread wings were the words CELERITY–CERTAINTY–SECURITY and

above those words, U. S. AIR MAIL. While an early United States air mail inaugural was never less swift nor less certain nor less secure, this was not the fault of Dickinson or his pilots. They gave their best effort, and in retrospect, it seems remarkable that even two men, Nimmo Black and William Brock, were able to get through.

The following is a brief review of how the day of June 7, 1926, went for six courageous CAM pilots, beginning first with four pilots who attempted to carry mail from Chicago to the Twin Cities area, thereby meeting the violent wind head on:

Pilot Daniel Kiser—departed Checkerboard Field (Maywood, Ill.) at 6:16 A.M., made a stop at his hometown of Milwaukee, departed for La Crosse and was reported down at Rio, Wisconsin, 15 miles southeast of Portage. Kiser was forced to land when the fabric of one wing began to tear in the relentless wind.

Pilot Emil (Nimmo) Black—departed Checkerboard Field eight minutes after Kiser, but he flew direct to La Crosse in the roughest weather he had ever encountered. After a 3½ hour delay, Black flew on arriving at Wold-Chamberlain Field, Minneapolis by 6 P.M., almost eight hours behind schedule. He was the only westbound flyer to reach Minneapolis.

Pilot Henry Keller—departed Chicago's Checkerboard Field (Maywood) at noon to retrieve Kiser's mail. After landing near Rio and helping Kiser to patch his plane, he departed for La Crosse, being forced down just short of that city by a broken gas line. Since it was too dark to repair his plane, he spent the night where he was, but not before sending the Kiser/Keller mail on to La Crosse by automobile. This mail departed for Minneapolis by train the same evening.

Pilot E. M. "Matty" Laird—Since the New York–Chicago over-night Air Mail was six hours late reaching Chicago, Laird was delayed until 1:03 P.M., when he left Checkerboard Field for La Crosse. Arriving at 6:05 P.M., he was too late to proceed on to Twin Cities, so his La Crosse mail was processed and his Twin Cities mail was placed aboard the same train as the Kiser/Keller mail.

The final two pilots who were to attempt the eastbound flights would not depart Wold-Chamberlain until midafternoon. They had battled the storm that morning to reach Minneapolis to prepare for their inaugural departures in the opposite direction. A cabin plane that started to follow Pilot Brock westbound to Minneapolis on his positioning flight had this report: "The pilot became so 'sea sick' that he had a hard time handling his controls long enough to get back to Chicago. One of the passengers was knocked out when an 'air bump' jolted his head against the roof, and the other received a bad bruise over the eye when he put his head out and was hit by a hailstone." The eastbound flights were reported this way:

Chief Pilot William S. "Billy" Brock—took off for La Crosse, Milwaukee and Chicago at 3:00 P.M. Using the gale to good advantage, Brock was ahead of schedule at each stop and reached Chicago at 7:10 P.M. He later said, "It was the first trip and I wanted to make it a fast one."

Pilot Elmer Lee Partridge—Flying a cabin plane of his own manufacture, this veteran pilot crashed to his death at Mendota, Minnesota nine miles south of his take-off point. He was intending to fly directly to Chicago with the overflow of inaugural mail that Brock had been unable to carry. It is reported that he lost control in a blinding dust storm and wind that boiled up from the high bluff near Mendota. Partridge, the man who had lured E. Hamilton Lee into the Air Mail Service,

was the sole CAM 9 pilot who had not fought this storm from an open cockpit. His mail, undamaged, was forwarded by train.

The covers Elmer Lee Partridge carried for nine miles are listed in the "Interrupted Flight" section of the *American Air Mail Catalogue*. It is ironic to note that two entries below the Partridge accident listing in the *Catalogue* is notice of a crash that took place on October 1, 1926. The very day that service was resumed on CAM 9—now operating under its new contractor, Northwest Airways—one of the pilots crashed on takeoff. This time, however, the pilot lived to fly again, and the jinx on CAM 9 was dealt a severe setback.

Fred Kelly receives another mail bag during ceremonies at Las Vegas, on April 17, 1926. Losing the toss of a coin, Kelly was not a pilot of record as CAM 4 got underway; Maurice Graham and Jimmy James were.

Some famous air mail carriers

Douglas M-2   The biplane which established a perfect safety record for Western Air Express in its first year of operations. Used on contract route No. 4 between Los Angeles and Salt Lake City, the M-2 was later joined on the air mail routes by M-3s and M-4s.

Speed: 120 mph (cruising)
Range: 600 miles
Payload: 1,000 pounds of mail
Engine: Liberty 400 hp

Curtiss Carrier Pigeon   Produced in 1926 by Curtiss for National Air Transport, the Carrier Pigeon was first used on the Chicago-Dallas route in September 1927. It had a top speed of 130 mph and, along with the Douglas M-2, was one of the first mail planes with a 1000-pound load capacity. A later model with a 600 hp Curtiss engine was able to carry 3300 pounds of mail at 150 mph.

Speed: 105 mph (cruising)
Range: 525 miles
Payload: 1,000 pounds
Engine: Liberty 400 hp

Ford 4-AT Tri-motor   Affectionately known as the "Tin Goose," the Ford Tri-motor first flew on June 11, 1926 and eventually served hard duty with more than 100 airlines around the world; 78 aircraft of the 4-AT design were built prior to the introduction of the 5-AT in 1929. It was produced with wheel, float and ski landing gear.

Speed: 107 mph (cruising)
Range: 570 miles
Payload: 1,725 pounds; 13-15 passengers
Engines: 3 Wright J4 Whirlwinds 200 hp (first 14 planes)
        (4-AT-E) Wright J6 Whirlwinds 300 hp ea.

Sikorsky S-42-B   Equipped with automatic mixture control and Hamilton Standard constant speed propellers, the S-42-B was the pioneer of transpacific route surveys flown by Pan American. One Sikorsky S-42-B, named the "Samoa Clipper" and piloted by Captain Edwin C. Musick, was lost near Pago-Pago while attempting to return to base during an in-flight emergency.

Speed: 170 mph (cruising)
Range: 1,200 miles (at cruising speed)
Payload: 9,495 pounds, 32 passengers (day), 14 passengers (night)
Engines: 4 Pratt & Whitney Hornets 750 hp

Pitcairn Mailwing Produced by Harold Pitcairn at Willow Grove, Pennsylvania, the Mailwing first saw air mail duty in May 1928 on CAM 19 between New York and Atlanta. The PA-6M version was selected by the Department of Commerce to be the testbed for the first U.S. electronic navigational system.

Speed: 128 mph (high), 110 mph (cruising)
Range: 500 miles
Payload: 500-600 pounds
Engine: Wright J5-9 220 hp

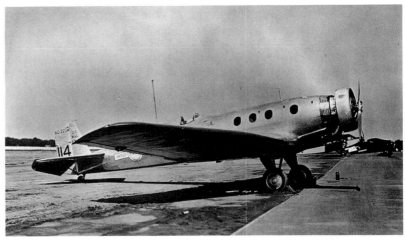

Boeing Monomail Forerunner of the later Boeing 247, the Monomail was a new departure for its day with its smooth-skin, all-metal cantilever low-wing design and was the first commercial aircraft in the United States fitted with retractable landing gear. The Monomail made its first flight in 1930, and one model 221 was in brief mail/passenger service with Boeing Air Transport.

Speed: 137 mph (cruising)
Range: 540 miles
Payload: 750 pounds; 5 passengers
Engine: Pratt & Whitney Hornet B radial 575 hp

Boeing 314 Largest of the Pan American flying-boat Clippers—Boeing 314—initiated the first regular transatlantic mail and passenger service just prior to the outbreak of World War II. Maximum take-off weight for this trans-ocean giant was 82,500 pounds, with flight crew and cargo sharing the plane's upper deck.

Speed: 193 mph (high)
Range: 3,500 miles
Payload: 10 crew, 74 passengers
Engines: 4 Wright GR-2600 Double Cyclones, 1,200 hp ea.

Douglas DC-3 Between December of 1935, when its prototype was flown for the first time, and the beginning of World War II, 455 of this type aircraft were produced. Almost 8% of this total were sleeper transports (DSTs) to meet a requirement of American Airlines. By 1938 the DC-3 hauled a staggering 95% of all U.S. airline traffic and was the major carrier of flown mail in the United States. The DC-3 was one of the most successful airplanes ever built and can still be found in service today somewhere in the world.

Speed: 185 mph (cruising)
Range: 1,500 miles
Payload: initially 4 crew, 21 passengers
Engines: 2 Wright SGR-1820-G2 Cyclones 1,000 hp ea.; or
         2 Pratt & Whitney R-1830 Twin Wasps 1,000 hp ea.

Joined to the air mail

He liked to fly. As a young trainee at a Nebraska flying school, Charles Lindbergh wrote in his diary, "I decided that if I could fly for ten years before I was killed in a crash, it would be a worthwhile trade for an ordinary lifetime." What seemed to set him apart from other young men who liked to fly was the intensity of his commitment. It ruled his life and caused him to focus his energies. It was part of a deep-seated need to test his own limits.

Unrelenting intensity helped the tall, serious cadet through his Air Corps training and to the top of his flight class. Only 18 out of 140 young men survived the rigors of that program.

Lindbergh wrote about taking leave of Kelly Field following his graduation in spring 1925. He immediately headed out for some barnstorming, traveling with an OX-5 Standard through Illinois, Missouri, and Iowa. He had done a lot of this kind of flying—the aerial circuses and county fairs, the wing-walking, the breakaway, the plane change. A full day's work there for many a happy-go-lucky pilot. Yet, somehow Lindbergh was a shade more serious about his flying and about his use of time than this roving path could satisfy. He was not one to wait for his life to unfold.

Small wonder, then, that his interest was aroused when Bill Robertson asked him to become chief pilot if Robertson's company got the nod on route #2 of the contract air mail network. Lindbergh knew it was a rare opportunity. The job would mean a fairly good salary and lots of flying. Even more, it offered him a fresh direction and something to match himself against. Flying against a schedule in all kinds of weather could really serve as an aviation laboratory where he and the other pilots would be measured by statistics—where they would continually go up against their own best performance and against each other.

He also looked at CAM 2 in broader terms. Air mail was at that moment in history the cutting edge of commercial aviation in the United States. To be able to fly, and prove at the same time that private enterprise and flying were prepared for a creative marriage, was to Lindbergh an ideal arrangement.

During the interval between his initial conversations concerning the air mail offer and the end of October 1925, when his new job was finally confirmed, Lindbergh barnstormed some more, got involved in a cross-country air race, and instructed a bit. However, when the time grew near for contract awards to be announced in Washington, he managed to be in St. Louis reminding Bill Robertson of his offer. And then word came— Robertson Aircraft Corporation was to be the first contract holder of an air mail route that would provide five round-trips each week between St. Louis and Chicago. "Slim" Lindbergh was designated chief pilot on CAM 2.

He may not have realized it then, but his new connection with the air mail was going to be a tight one. It would never really leave him. He was thinking about it even as he approached the coast of Newfoundland on his flight to enduring fame. "Ours is not a nation built on too much caution. I concluded that this flight over the Atlantic would be no more dangerous than flying mail for a single winter—well, I'd rather fly ten miles over Missouri and Illinois than one mile over this ice pack—or would I? How about that storm northeast of Peoria, last December?"

When he returned home from Paris after the conclusion of his breathtaking flight, he would still be thinking air mail. He inscribed one photograph, "I am proud to have done it for America. My reward will be your continued use of 'air mail.' Charles A Lindbergh." He would be presented by Postmaster General Harry S. New with two copies (one for his mother) of a unique commemorative air mail stamp issued in his honor, the first such commemorative air mail ever issued by the United States Post Office. And he would remark publicly, during the Washington festivities following his triumphant return from France in 1927, "All Europe looks on our air mail service with reverence. There is nothing like it anywhere abroad."

Lindbergh would ask permission to fly the mail once more over his old route in February of 1928. He would carry mail officially on at least twelve occasions. He would fly at least eight inaugural mail flights in the Carribean area, both in Central and South America. The covers carried on his official, courtesy, good-will, and survey flights would be catalogued with other commemorative covers celebrating flights, anniversaries, and events of his life to form an entirely new philatelic category know as "Lindberghiana." In five short years after he first carried mail on CAM 2, Charles Lindbergh would accomplish more to advance the cause of air mail and aviation in the United States than any other individual.

But back in 1926, he was a relatively unknown air mail pilot. His intensity was about to be applied to opening up the nation's fifth contract mail route, the third to get under way that month and just two days ahead of the first Western Air Express runs between Salt Lake City and Los Angeles. His sole aim at that moment in his life was to fly safely and speedily between Chicago and St. Louis.

The Robertson Aircraft Corporation was a family business organization in 1921 and operated from St. Louis Flying Field, later to be known as Lambert Field. With Major William R. Robertson serving as president, Frank Robertson as vice president, and Daniel R. Robertson as secretary and treasurer, the company conducted a flying school and also an airplane sales and service operation, which involved the marketing of reconditioned army training planes, engines, and spare parts. The opportunity to serve as a contractor on one of the new CAM

Charles Lindbergh, in the winter garb of the air mail pilot, stands ready to make another mail run on CAM 2. Within a few short weeks he would depart for San Diego to oversee the building of his Spirit of St. Louis.

feeder lines seemed to fit in admirably with their plans for growth.

Once CAM 2 was theirs, Bill Robertson went out and purchased four military surplus DH–4s for use on the mail runs. These planes had to be converted to mail carriers, and this task Robertson placed in the hands of a pilot he had hired the previous year, Harlan A. "Bud" Gurney. When chief pilot Lindbergh organized his team of mail pilots, Bud Gurney would be his backup pilot. Along with Lindbergh, the regulars, selected by him, were Thomas P. Nelson and Philip R. Love.

Two intermediate stops were established on the new route, one at Springfield, Illinois and one at Peoria. Lindbergh once termed the Peoria landing field a "narrow strip of cow pasture," and the Springfield mail stop he described as a "meadow." Neither field was lighted nor, at the outset, were there any beacons or guiding lights on CAM 2 except at the St. Louis and Chicago fields. Still, the service was to undertake five round-trips each week. The task required transporting St. Louis, Springfield, and Peoria mail to Chicago each afternoon in time to connect with transcontinental night flights to New York. It was a plan intended to have the previous day's midwestern mail included on the first morning delivery in New York City.

On April 10, five days before the inaugural flights on CAM 2 took place, Lindbergh and Love made a final survey of the route, flying north to Chicago in two planes. With Lindbergh was Gregory Brandeweide, Superintendent of Robertson Aircraft. Philip Love had with him two members of the press, Ray Anderson of the *St. Louis Post Dispatch* and V. Y. Dallman of the *Illinois State Register*, published in Springfield. The purpose of the trips was not so much to familiarize the pilots with geography that they knew fairly well, but to conduct final field inspections at Springfield, Peoria, and Chicago, to finalize and coordinate schedules with the Chicago terminus, and to obtain as much advance publicity for the new route as possible. The returning survey flights from Chicago took place on April 11.

As inauguration day on CAM 2 arrived, Gurney had the planes in tip-top condition. Each craft had U. S. AIR MAIL printed in bold white letters on the side of the fuselage. Underneath the larger letters appeared white lettering of a smaller size identifying the planes as belonging to C.A.M. No. 2.

As chief pilot, Lindbergh was given the honor of carrying out the first flight on April 15, a southbound trip from Chicago's Maywood Field. After taking part in appropriate ceremonies at the northern terminus, Lindbergh got under way at 5:51 A.M. He picked up first flight mail in both Peoria and Springfield, and also participated in early morning air mail celebrations in each city. According to him, the "pilots, mechanics, postal clerks and business executives at St. Louis, Springfield, Peoria, (and)

157

Chicago, all felt that we were taking part in an event which pointed the way toward a new and marvelous era.''

Lindbergh's first flight was carried off successfully and involved 87 pounds of mail from Chicago, 23 pounds from Peoria, and 93 pounds from Springfield. Chicago and Peoria mail had the usual contract air mail double-circle cachets, with the Chicago time reading 5:30 A.M. in the center with the date of April 15, 1926. Peoria southbound mail showed a time of 7:00 A.M. with the date. The cachet used at Springfield was more distinctive bearing the words WHERE LINCOLN LIVED in the center of the circles near the date. The Springfield cachet, also decorated with a tiny head-on view of a biplane, showed a time of 7:45 A.M.

Philip Love flew the first northbound flight on CAM 2, departing for Chicago with 144 pounds of mail at approximately 3:45 P.M. Due to the size of the northbound mail reported waiting at Springfield, it was decided that Love would fly the inaugural mail from St. Louis straight through to Chicago and that Lindbergh would turn around and fly a second northbound section, taking aboard the mail at Springfield (timed at 4:30 P.M.) and Peoria (timed at 5:30 P.M.). The heaviest load of CAM 2's opening-day mail was the 385 pounds that Lindbergh took aboard his DH–4 at Springfield while en route back to Chicago. Springfield Postmaster Wiliam H. Conkling had undoubtedly stirred up a good deal of interest in the new air mail service in his city.

Opening day mail loads were especially heavy, but a tapering-off set in immediately. The CAM 2 contractor, as all CAM contractors had to during the introductory phase of the system, faced an up-hill struggle to make ends meet. The Robertson balance sheet was not helped a bit when Lindbergh lost two planes in the fall and force landed a third. The weather began to worsen as the summer ended, which appeared to be the cause of the two crashes. Lindbergh bailed out of his DH–4 near Ottawa, Illinois, on September 16, when he ran out of fuel looking for a pathway out of rain and fog. In this instance, he was aided by local citizens in finding his downed airplane. The recovered mail, unharmed, was sent on to Chicago by train, arriving at 6:00 A.M. on the seventeenth and being backstamped by postal authorities at 8:30 A.M.

Exactly two weeks later Lindbergh experienced an emergency landing in a soft field of new clover near Athens, Illinois. His plane narrowly avoided flipping over when his wheels sank deeply into softened soil. A broken throttle control caused this incident, which was resolved when Herman Dirks, a farmer, drove Lindbergh and his mail into Springfield where it was placed aboard a Chicago and Alton train bound for the Windy City. Weather that day was quite foggy in Chicago, causing Love to cancel an earlier southbound flight out of Maywood at noon. It is possible that Lindbergh had been saved further trouble to the

north by his precarious but safe landing at Athens. The mail on this flight of September 30 has never been listed with crash mail as it was not appreciably delayed.

On November 3, 1926, again on a northbound flight, Lindbergh had to bail out for a second time in weather conditions which paralleled those at Ottawa in September. Rain and mist, coupled with a determined and perhaps ill-advised effort to get the mail through to Chicago, led to the pilot's bailing out at 14,000 feet when his gasoline supply ran out. This mail was recovered from the wreckage at Covell, Illinois the next morning and sent on its way. Eventually twenty-three covers, which had become oil-soaked in the crash, but which were legible, were given special markings at Newark, New Jersey. Two of these

Opposite: Covers flown by or honoring Charles A. Lindbergh are numerous enough to form a philatelic category called "Lindberghiana." Official mail flights, courtesy flights, survey flights, and career history are a few of the sub-categories. The cover signed by General Lindbergh in 1939, was carried by him on his first trip as an air mail pilot in 1926. The very rare, signed, first-day cover below displays a block of the 1927 Lindbergh commemorative airmails.

This cover is unique. Signed by Lindbergh before he died, the cover displays a first-day-of-issue cancel on a block of 1977 commemoratives honoring his solo flight to Paris.

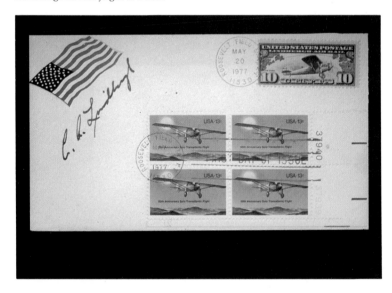

covers are known today and are extremely rare mementos of Lindbergh's career as an air mail pilot.

Losing two planes in less than two months caused a great deal of concern among the Robertson people in St. Louis and the postal and civil aviation officials in Washington. William P. MacCracken, Jr., the first Assistant Secretary of Commerce in charge of aeronautics, reported in later years that he was on the verge of grounding the young air mail pilot but refrained from doing so when Bill Robertson went to bat for him. It was generally agreed that Lindbergh had been overly aggressive in trying to get the mail through; at the same time, it was recognized that an inadequate weather-reporting system on CAM 2 had been a contributing factor to both interrupted flights.

Not always was the air mail task quite as hair-raising as the Ottawa and Covell parachute jumps suggest. Lindbergh reported with pride a 98 percent success record for the first five months of operation on CAM 2. He also reported times of public assistance. "A bright light appears between my right wings. I bank toward it. Yes, it's the 'beacon' that boy put up and wrote to us about. 'Your mail planes fly over my house every day,' he'd said in his letter, 'so I have fixed up an electric light in our yard. Maybe it will help you when the weather is bad this winter. I will keep it lit every night,' " On the occasion recounted by Lindbergh, the homemade beacon did indeed prove of real value to him. By its light he was able to confirm his location during another challenging bout with overcast skies.

When fair weather ruled, air mail duty seemed anything but perilous. In a chapter of his book, *The Spirit of St. Louis*, entitled "The St. Louis–Chicago Mail," Lindbergh reported:

> I welcome the approach of night as twilight fades into brilliant moonlight. The day has been crystal clear and almost cloudless; perfect for flying. It's been almost too perfect for flying the mail, for there's no ability required in holding your course over familiar country with a sharp horizon in every quarter. You simply sit, touching stick and rudder lightly, dreaming of the earth below, of experiences past, of adventures that may come. There's nothing else to do, nothing to match yourself against. There hasn't been even an occasional cloud near enough to burrow through. Skill is no asset. The spirit of conquest is gone from the air. On such an evening you might better be training students. It's an evening for beginners, not for pilots of the mail—no tricks of wind, no false horizons. Its hours were shaped for beauty, not for contests.

> It was on a gentle evening such as this, while plying his route to Chicago, that Lindbergh first conceived the idea of a flight to Paris.

> I wake soon after dawn. There's much to be done. As I fry potatoes and eggs for breakfast, I list items to be covered on this new day of the new life I've entered. For it is a new life; I'll now bend every thought and effort toward one objective—landing at Paris. All else is secondary.

The young pilot thought in terms of transformation—in terms of a new life—but how little he envisioned what his step beyond the air mail would truly mean to himself and to a world still skeptical about the possibilities of flight. How surprised he would be that in testing and extending his own reach and the limits of his art, he would so quickly and so largely contribute new life also to the air mail process. The postmaster general noted a 20 percent increase in the poundage of contract air mail during June 1927 over that carried during May, the month in which "Slim" made it all the way to Paris.

159

Counting the cost

Crash covers commemorate and symbolize, as no other covers do, that part of air mail history that Charles Lindbergh was pointing to—the side of risk, the side of sacrifice—when he wrote in his book, *The Spirit of St. Louis:*

> We pilots of the mail have a tradition to establish. The commerce of the air depends on it. Men have already died for that tradition. Every division of the mail routes has its hallowed points of crash where some pilot on a stormy night, or lost and blinded by fog, laid down his life on the altar of his occupation. Every man who flies the mail senses that altar and, consciously or unconsciously, in his way worships before it, knowing that his own next flight may end in the sacrifice demanded.

Lindbergh, a pilot with two listings in the *American Air Mail Catalogue's* "Interrupted Flight Cover" section, could well point to the hallowed points of crash. There were many, and every air mail pilot knew them well.

A rather prosaic definition of an interrupted flight cover, more commonly known as a crash cover, deals with the fact that such a cover has resulted from a "known important interruption or mishap on scheduled air mail routes." It is, in other words, a relic of a disaster.

There is no better reminder of the costs that air mail pilots paid than a list of the crashes. The names of the few are honored and deserve to be remembered.

Most aerophilatelists are therefore especially proud of the crash covers in their collections. There are several reasons why crash-cover collecting is fascinating. To begin with, most collectors of postal history items insist upon pristine, near-perfect specimens. Crash covers, however, represent a field where condition of the cover, except for the legibility of its markings, is secondary. When crash covers are removed from a downed aircraft, they may display no damage whatsoever. More likely, they will show evidence of fire, grease, water soaking, mold, or dirt. Often they will be stained with oil or other fluids. A reasonable sign that a cover was involved in an air mail interruption is its disturbed condition, and covers are known in shredded condition as a result of impact explosions.

In 1919, postal officials began the practice of adding a rubber-stamp or manuscript notation to the face of an envelopes whose movement through the mails had been slowed by an accident. The variety of postal markings has hardly been uniform over the years, but markings have usually been intended to explain to an addressee why the piece of mail was damaged and/or delayed. In some cases the damaged mail is forwarded in post office envelopes, and mimeographed explanations are sent along with whatever portion of the letter remains.

The first air mail crash covers in which postal markings were

William C. Hopson joined the air mail on April 14, 1920 and remained in harness all through the government era. Spending many years with the Central Division out of Omaha, "Big Bill" helped put the transcontinental route together, and did his share of trail-blazing on the new routes. He won a pilot's incentive contest in 1921, a contest inspired by Otto Praeger. In 1927, within four days of leaving Post Office ranks, Hopson was sharing in National Air Transport's first flights on the "new" New York–Chicago service. His fatal CAM 17 crash at Polk, Pennsylvania, October 18, 1928, is pictured here.

used came from the wreckage of a Post Office Department plane in 1919. In that accident, on May 25 at Cleveland, pilot Frank McCusker was killed in a desperate leap from his plane, which had become enveloped in flames shortly after takeoff. McCusker's death was the first on government routes after they opened up in May of 1918. In this instance, the 258 pounds of salvaged mail were forwarded in official envelopes bearing a mimeographed notation that read: "The enclosed piece of mail matter was damaged in aeroplane accident at Cleveland, Ohio, May 25th. The incident is very much regretted. W. B. Carlisle, Postmaster."

Thankfully, not all of the more than 300 crashes listed in the *American Air Mail Catalogue* indicate a pilot fatality, but all too many do. Of twenty-one accidents recorded in the single year of most crashes—1929—ten involved a pilot's death. Eight of the crashes that year occurred on the transcontinental route, which at that time was operated jointly by Boeing Air transport and National Air Transport. Regarding the question of crashes, it is interesting to note that the ten-year period of 1930 to 1939, entirely in the CAM era, produced almost twice as many crash-cover listings as the earlier era of 1920–29. Though planes were getting safer, a great many more air-mail miles were being flown over a great many more routes. The chances for interruptions to occur multiplied.

The list of crash covers maintained by the American Air Mail Society is a carefully prepared one. The society does not accept as a crash cover a piece of mail involved in private transit or in a minor accident or forced landing where no appreciable damage or delay occurs to the mail. On the other hand, the society does publish a list of the places and dates of reported air mail interruptions and would add those incidents to the crash-cover list if authenticated covers are ever located.

Though they did not occur on regularly scheduled air mail routes and are not listed as crash covers, five United States pioneer flights were interrrupted by crashes or forced landings. Flying the mail at Birmingham, Alabama on October 7, 1912, pilot Joseph Stevenson was killed when his plane fell to the ground shortly after takeoff. The temporary route number in that instance was #624,001.

One of the other pioneer crashes occurred on route #604,003 and involved a young pilot by the name of Harry Jones. Between January 13 and March 9, 1913, Jones was undertaking a leisurely journey from Boston to New York City at the behest of the United States government. On his flight Jones carried some parcels to help government postal officials publicize their new parcel post program, which saw the issuance of a special parcel post stamp series in 1912. Due to severe winter weather in the northeast, Jones was under no pressure of time, and his trip was accomplished in stages. One of his landings took place on the football field at Yale University. On March 9, 1913, Jones, almost at his destination, crashed and wrecked his plane at Mamaroneck, New York, and completed his trip by train and subway. The parcel post pouch that he finally delivered to Postmaster Morgan in New York City contained the first aerial parcel post in United States history.

A random survey of the crashes that have dotted the American scene reflects an honor roll of names of the men who played a major part in the development of air mail in the United States.

Sept. 1, 1920—Morristown, N.J.—government Pilot Max Miller—killed while attempting to land a flaming plane.

Jan. 4, 1921 — San Francisco, Calif. — government Pilot Stanhope Boggs—forced to land in a city street because of fog, and his plane caught fire.

Dec. 15, 1922—Porcupine Ridge, Utah—government Pilot Henry C. Boonstra—crashed plane into mountain ridge at 9,400 feet, but miraculously was uninjured.

Oct. 1, 1925—Bellefonte, Pa.—government Pilot Charles H. Ames killed—plane crashed into mountain (along "Hell Stretch") and was not discovered for ten days.

Sept. 16, 1926—Ottawa, Illinois—CAM Pilot Charles A. Lindbergh—forced to bail out due to weather conditions. Mail recovered.

Sept. 3, 1930—Mercer, Pa.—CAM Pilot Charles W. Haas—in making emergency landing crashed into barn.

Four of the first five crashes in 1934 involved men who have a USAAC designation beside their names. All four were U.S. Army Air Corps pilots. Their involvement with the mail relates to the first use of army pilots for mail duty since Army Signal Corps pilots under Reuben Fleet and Benjamin Lipsner inaugurated United States air mail in 1918.

Military pilots were pressed into service in February 1934 when President Franklin D. Roosevelt abruptly cancelled all air mail contracts. Roosevelt and Postmaster General James A. Farley had been subject to mounting pressure from aviation groups and private citizens, who felt that Walter Folger Brown, the previous postmaster general, had not handled air mail contracts fairly in his efforts to promote bigness among a few airline companies. There were also feelings that some degree of collusion existed between these larger airlines, and that many overpayments had been made by the government on air mail contracts. Roosevelt decided on a drastic action, cancelling all contracts pending renegotiation and rebidding. This decision had far-reaching repercussions that the president did not anticipate.

Flying an unusual assortment of Boeing fighters, Douglas observation planes, Curtiss strike-attack aircraft, and Martin and Keystone bombers—all outmoded and hardly designed for the transport of mail—the army pilots went to work with the mail on February 19, 1934, but were able to operate only 11,106 route miles, as against the 27,062 miles in the contract system. Flying in rather severe winter weather, five died in crashes and six others were critically injured in the first week alone. Before the carnage was over and new contracts were awarded, the Army Air Corps had lost twelve pilots and endured sixty-six forced landings. The entire fiasco put a damper on commercial aviation growth in the United States for several years and opened the Roosevelt administration to severe public condemnation. Fur-thermore, it clearly showed how budget limitations had seri-ously affected the quality of training which the army could offer its pilots. The reorganized CAM system, now 28,924 miles in length, was in operation by May 31.

The moratorium on CAM flights did, however, have some positive residual benefits. It focused public attention on the antiquated state of military aircraft in the United States. It also demonstrated once again that the transport of air mail was a highly specialized activity that required skilled aviators flying planes designed with specific performance factors in mind.

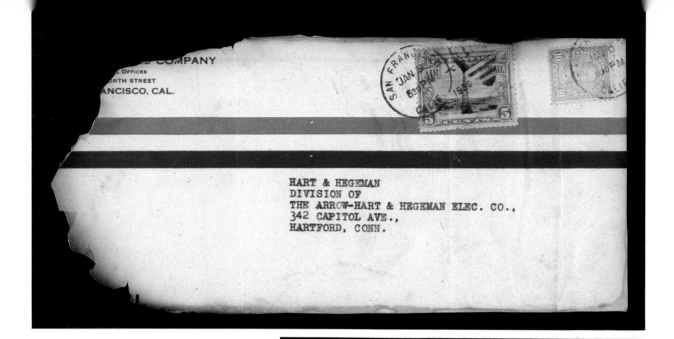

Boeing Air Transport pilot Charles ("Chuck") Kenwood came down on a Nebraska farm on January 10, 1930, while attempting an emergency landing in a winter storm. Documenting this tragic event, where Kenwood lost his life in the ensuing fire, are a badly-burned cover salvaged from the wreck and a mimeographed note from postal inspectors explaining the delay and the condition of the mail. A three-line cachet reading, "Damaged by Plane/fire Sidney Nebr/ JAN 10, 1930," marked some of the mail recovered from this crash, the first of seventeen in 1930.

POST OFFICE DEPARTMENT.
Office of Inspector.
Omaha, Nebraska.

The enclosed piece of mail, addressed to or sent by you, was damaged in an air plane wreck near Sidney, Nebr., on the evening of January 10, 1930.

V. C. Batie,
W. M. Coble, Post Office Inspectors.

The same day Kenwood died, Western Air Express pilot Maurice Graham froze to death while hiking away from his crash in rugged country near Cedar City, Utah, on January 10th. Graham's body and the wreckage of his plane were not found until June 24th.

A slightly damaged, but seriously delayed, special delivery cover from Maurice Graham's accident. Covers were given a two-line cachet—"Delay due to wrecked mail plane/January 10, 1930."—and returned to the sender on June 28th. This processing step is indicated by the cancellation at the bottom of the cover.

163

A distinctive experience   Futurists in 1910 could never have foreseen the pattern of Canadian air mail development. The form followed in that sprawling land was unique. Because of the independent character of its air mail process, Canadian aerophilately remains fascinating and virtually unknown beyond that country's borders.

Canada was the ninth country in the world to experience heavier-than-air flight, just after Germany and just before Austria. Yet Canadian air mail experiments did not begin until 1918, whereas more than ninety pioneer flights in the United States had been completed by 1916. Canada undertook regular government-sponsored flights in 1926, the United States in 1918. United States air mail stamps appeared early—in 1918. Canada did not issue her first until 1928.

This is not to imply that Canadian enthusiasm for the air age lagged. Few countries in the world responded with more fervor over the airplane or offered greater opportunities for air transport development than did Canada. When J. A. D. McCurdy returned to Nova Scotia from Hammondsport, New York and took his A.E.A. *Silver Dart* into the air for the first time over the frozen surface of Bras d'Or at Baddeck, a thrill of excitement swept across the Dominion. The town commissioners noted officially "an event of historic importance"—not just Canada's first flight, but the Empire's first! "It now became obvious that the whole country had become flying-machine crazy," reported one Canadian newswriter. In Baddeck, one-hundred forty-five signatures were recorded to attest to McCurdy's flight, including those of Mr. and Mrs. Glenn H. Curtiss.

The key to understanding Canadian air mail history is to see how it is inextricably related to Canada's commercial and social development. Candian air mail services were essentially local in nature and based on the needs of particular communities or industries.

Canada's air mail story is composed of three major eras, with some international ramifications and some chronological overlapping. Unofficial mail-carrying flights have been a secondary dimension of each epoch.

Period 1 Air Force Captain Brian Peck undertook his nation's first authorized mail flight to initiate pioneer air mail service in Canada. Peck's trail-blazing flight involved 150 pieces of mail, which he transported from Montreal to Toronto on June 24, 1918. His demonstration flight, made in a Canuck JN–4 CAN (the Canadian version of the famed Curtiss Jenny, which had carried the first regular air mail in the United States just a month earlier), was conceived by the Aerial League of the British Empire branch in Montreal and given official backing both by

6

Intercontinental trail-blazing

Dr. R. F. Coulter, the Canadian Postmaster General, and Mr. J. E. Leonard, Postmaster of Montreal. The aim of the flight was basically to promote aviation and air mail interest.

Peck's mail displayed an inverted triangular cachet reading Via/Aerial Mail/Montreal/23/6/18, all under the words IN-AUGURAL SERVICE. This cachet was stamped on the letters in red ink. Newspapers were notified of the flight in advance and one headline on the twenty-second read First Royal Mail by Air Tomorrow.

Bad weather prohibited flying on June 23, but the next day Captain Peck and a Corporal E. W. Mathers departed on their historic journey from the Montreal Polo Club grounds at 10:12 A.M. In addition to the mail, they carried along a case of whisky for an Ontario (dry at that time) wedding reception. Peck reported that a low ceiling made it necessary to fly under telegraph wires and around squalls before the first refueling stop at Kingston. A second stop occurred at Deseronto, followed by the final hop into Leaside. Arrival time was set at 4:55 P.M. After the cancellation of the previous day, Toronto officials had given up on the flight and were caught napping when Peck landed. The mail itself reached Toronto Postmaster William Lemon at 6:07 P.M., and Toronto Mayor Church had a number of official letters in his hands at 6:30 P.M. He later replied to one letter sent to him by Mayor Martin of Montreal, saying, "I rejoice to think that on this terrible war [a reference to World War I] has been the establishment of such complete accord between Montreal and Toronto.

166

Katherine Stinson (far right in photo) seems to be pointing to Edmonton, as her special Curtiss biplane warms up at Calgary. Her transport of mail between the two cities, on July 9, 1918, was Canada's second authorized pioneer air mail flight. Just a month earlier, on June 2nd, she completed a flight with official U.S. mail from Chicago to New York.

When a February, 1925, crash doomed Canada's first mail-carrying aviation company, its successor was promptly formed. The new company, known as Northern Air Service, Ltd., issued its own stamp and began mail flights to the Rouyn gold field using an old Curtiss HS2L flying boat. Bill Broatch, pilot-president of Northern, signed and flew this cover on June 27, 1925. Canada's multi-faceted aviation history is documented by her stamps. The 50¢ green of Newfoundland depicts the start of Alcock and Brown's successful transocean flight in 1919. Newfoundland's first airmail, an overprint of a 3¢ Caribou stamp, was issued for an unsuccessful transatlantic attempt in 1919 and is a truly great philatelic classic.

After having been the first woman to carry official United States air mail from Chicago to New York between May 23 and June 2, Katherine Stinson, the noted American aviatrix, made an exhibition tour of the Canadian prairie provinces in July and carried out that country's second pioneer mail flight. After a week at the famed Calgary Exhibition, Stinson was enlisted to fly a sack of mail to Edmonton. All 259 letters were stamped: "Aeroplane Mail Service, July 9, 1918—Calgary, Alberta."

Flying a special Curtiss machine, built to her specifications and powered by a 90 hp Curtiss OX–2 engine, Stinson left Calgary at 1:30 P.M., but encountered trouble and was forced to land only seven miles from her takeoff point. After a four-and-one-half-hour delay, she was under way again above the Canadian Pacific tracks. A wild welcome greeted her landing at the Edmonton Fair Grounds at 8:30 P.M. She had traveled at close to 85 mph in her contribution to Canadian air mail history.

Other early pioneer flights in Canada included a series of experimental military mail carries between Toronto and Ottawa in 1918 and a memorable effort by Captain E. C. Hoy in traversing the Canadian Rockies (Vancouver to Calgary) with mail in 1919. A mention of 1919 would not be complete without noting Alcock and Brown's flight from St. John's, Newfoundland to Clifden, Ireland on June 14. Special air post stamps were issued by the government of Newfoundland to mark official mail carried on several Atlantic flight attempts in 1919. These stamps and covers are extremely valuable today because of their rarity and must be seen as part of the early Canadian air mail story even

though Newfoundland did not join the Canadian Confederation until 1949.

Period 2 Canada's second phase of air mail development centered around semi-official flights. Spanning the years 1924 to 1932, this period in many respects remains the most interesting and most distinctly Canadian air mail era. Several Canadian companies were granted the privilege of issuing their own stamps during this time, but they were considered semi-official because they were not viable unless used in conjunction with regular Canadian postage. The discovery of gold, oil, and other resources in the sparsely settled areas of northern Canada brought about a need for small, independent aviation companies to operate as a part of the supply and communications network serving these regions. Air mail duty proved to be a welcome sideline for these service air lines as many of them were in precarious financial positions. The companies had colorful names, they produced interesting stamps, and they became an important part of Canadian economic growth.

The first of the commercial aviation companies that carried mail came about as an outgrowth of a forest fire spotting service that, while effective in reducing fire losses, proved too expensive a service for the lumber companies that had hired it. The firm then reorganized itself under the name of Laurentide Air Services, Ltd., with a Canadian shipbuilding magnate supplying the funds, and a man by the name of Harry Wiltshire managing the business. The tiny airline initially served as a taxi and aerial photographic service but became an air mail communications link with the Rouyn goldfield's main base at Hailybury on Lake Temiskoming.

Because air strips did not exist at this time, the planes landed on the water in the summer and exchanged pontoons for skis in the winter. The flyers who flew the Laurentide planes were dubbed "bush pilots," as were the Alaskan aviators, who also worked above rough and forbidding terrain in all kinds of weather. To make ends meet, Laurentide Air Services obtained permission from the Canadian Postal Service to print its own stamps and charge a fee for carrying mail to interior areas. The plan called for the company's adhesive to be applied to the back of the letter with ordinary Canadian postage on the front. The air fee charged by this carrier was 25 cents. The green stamp issued by the company was attractive, showing a plane in flight before a rising sun. A very limited first issue had the stamps sold in booklets of two, rouletted (perforated with large holes). The same design was printed in larger quantities using red ink. Altogether about 9,000 Laurentide semi-official stamps were issued.

The first flight of mail under the surcharge scheme developed by the Canadian Post Office and Laurentide took place on September 11, 1924, and went from Haileybury, Ontario, to Rouyn, Quebec. This air mail arrangement was the basic model for fourteen more to come. Unfortunately, Pilot Jack Caldwell crashed Laurentide's De Havilland 9A in February 1925, and that caused the company to go out of business. It proved the trail blazer, however, for Canada's second period of air mail.

By May 18, 1925, one of Laurentide's pilots, Bill Broatch, had been able to purchase an old Curtiss HS2L flying boat and flew off on his first trip to Haileybury, later taking up where his former company had left off. His firm, Northern Air Services, Ltd., had its own semi-official air mail issue printed by the time flights commenced on June 27, and completed over 200 successful ones (carrying at least 1,000 pounds of mail) before dissolving.

Then, late in 1925, as a furious gold rush was occurring in the Red Lake, Ontario area some 500 to 600 miles west of the Quebec goldfields, a bush pilot took two Canucks to Rolling Portage and began service flights to Red Lake under the name of Jack V. Elliot Air Service. A succession of four companies followed, utilizing the names Elliot and Fairchild together or separately.

And so it went. Wherever there was a need, an air service would spring up, making an air mail tie with the Canadian Post Office Department a part of its life. Eventually private air mail stamps became obsolete as the government extended its own system of contract air mail throughout the country, legislating government franking only on all letters. The government awarded contracts to some of the companies that had already been at work in the second era of Canadian air mail, for these air lines continued to thrive—but minus their attractive and appealing semi-official airmails.

Period 3 The third stage of Canadian air mail history produced the unusual situation of having a government offer two different air mail services to different segments of its populace at the same time.

The first type of service, known as AMS—Air Mail Service—involved the carrying of air mail over an AMS route at a premium rate specified by the national Post Office Department. The citizen had the choice on an AMS route of marking his letter to go air mail and paying the premium for that service, or choosing not to pay the premium and having his letter go by ordinary means on the ground.

On ASS service—Air State Service—however, the citizen, because of the isolated location of his address, could receive and send mail at the first class rate only. Weather and conditions permitting, letters on ASS routes would always receive air mail service, but there was no guarantee of this. The type of delivery would depend on prevailing conditions.

The inaugural flights of Canadian contract AMS were undertaken between March 27 and April 12, 1926, by Patricia Airways Ltd. Captain Roy Maxwell was the pilot of record on these official flights, and he carried the mail on a permanent route between Toronto, Sudbury, Pogomasing, Sioux Lookout, and Red Lake, all in Ontario. Western Canada Airways flew the first authorized ASS flight on October 4, 1927, which went from Lac du Bouney to Wadhope and back. Both towns are located in Manitoba.

There is one instance when regular Canadian air mail rates can be paid on an ASS route, and that is the first day that a new route goes into service. The air mail premium in that instance is optional. If one chooses to pay the premium, however, the additional amount is not for the air mail service, but it goes for a commemorative first-flight cachet that is rubber stamped on the letter. When a new ASS route opens up, if the citizen chooses to disregard the philatelic addition, he or she merely pays the first class rate as usual.

Because of the nature of Canadian geography, many exciting unofficial flights have taken place. These normally occur when a plane is traveling to an extremely remote outpost and is able to take mail along. Needless to say, some of the unofficial flights have been among the most challenging from an aeronautical standpoint, and their mail among the most interesting for an aerophilatelist to research.

1918-1939

The European initiative The efforts of the British, French, and Germans to establish international aerial networks in the period between the World Wars were truly heroic. The evolution of these aerial connections saw passengers and mail fly together from the outset; and the emergence of civil air transport in Europe was almost immediately and inevitably international in scope. In contrast, international flights basically concerned North American countries only when the range of aircraft permitted men to fly across oceans.

Unlike the other visionaries and aerial route builders who were either preoccupied with overland systems or betting on the long-range heavier-than-air flying boat to conquer the larger oceans, many Germans still advocated the use of lighter-than-air dirigibles for long-distance transport and were determined to demonstrate anew the often, and widely, doubted capabilities of airships. One Zeppelin in particular—the *Graf Zeppelin* (LZ-127)—performed with unusual distinction in this period between the Great Wars and her feats remain a most glamorous and captivating chapter of the air mail story. This awesome giant of the skies carried written communications over tremendous distances to exotic places in quantities that still excite the imagination.

1918-1936 France

Aéropostale conquers the ocean In many respects the French air mail and commercial aviation growth parallels the British experience. France's fledgling aviation services, following World War I, initiated both mail and passenger operations on shaky financial bases, struggled to make a go of it on the overcrowded European routes, and then looked farther afield for commercial transport possibilities. It was this move to other continents that allowed the French, like the British, to make their greatest contribution to the building of a worldwide aerial communications network, for wherever French air transport companies ventured, they always carried the mail.

The French in the early 1920s had three relatively small companies vying for the business on the London–Paris route. One of these, the Farman Company (later called Lignes Aériennes Farman), had established an irregular Paris–Brussels run as early as March 22, 1919. Other small French air transport companies developed simultaneously. Formed in 1920, Compagnie Franco-Roumaine de Navigation Aerienne (C.F.R.N.A.), for example, opened a service from Paris to Strasbourg in April 1920, and in October of the same year a service to Prague by way of Innsbruck. C.F.R.N.A. extended this latter route to Warsaw in 1921 and also inaugurated a Balkan section in 1922, initially linking Paris with Belgrade and Bucharest and later to Constantinople. During most of this year of route formation, C.F.R.N.A.'s chief reliance was on the Potez 9, a single-engine biplane that carried four passengers in an enclosed cabin at a speed of 112 mph.

Eventually, on August, 30, 1933, a major amalgamation brought together various small French airlines and Air France was born. This only occurred after the pioneering work of Lignes Aériennes Latécoère, the first French airline to reach out to West Africa and South America. This company's record belongs in the same class with the celebrated contributions of Britain's Imperial Airways and Germany's Deutsche Luft Hansa and Deutsche Zeppelin Reederei. Perhaps because an intimate record of the life and work of the Latécoère pilots has been so artistically preserved in the writings of pilot/poet Antoine de Saint-Exupéry, their experiences have somehow seemed representative of the challenges, struggles, and courage of air mail pilots the world over.

Lignes Aériennes Latécoère, later to be known as Aéropostale, was founded by munitions and aircraft manufacturer Pierre Latécoère. Based in Toulouse in southern France, this firm early on sought opportunities beyond the bounds of commercial aerial development such as was occurring in northern and western Europe. In December 1918, the Latécoère enterprise was making proving flights along the Mediterranean to Barcelona, which proved to be the first modest steps of an airway that moved down the coast of Spain to Alicante and Malaga en route to North Africa. On September 1, 1919, using Breguet 14 aircraft, the Latécoère organization inaugurated a regular service from France to Casablanca, Morocco, the first aerial service joining the two continents of Europe and Africa. This route was extended to Dakar on June 1, 1925, by which time the company's name had been changed to Compagnie Générale d'Enterprises Aéronautiques (C.G.E.A.). Also, since Latécoère flying boats had been introduced on its North African route, its perimeters had been widened to accommodate direct trans-Mediterranean flights to Oran and Algiers from Alicante. During this period, Latécoère's essential purpose was to transport mail and parcels; only occasionally were passengers carried. C.G.E.A. eventually flew more than five million letters per year between France and North Africa.

Once the Toulouse–Dakar linkup was firm, air mail service to a string of cities along Africa's Atlantic coast was maintained with surprising regularity. Throughout, the elements of weather and terrain had to be dealt with. In flying to Dakar, the pilots often cut inland from the shoreline to save time, but this proved extremely dangerous if bad storms or engine trouble forced the

169

plane down. That corner of the Sahara Desert, an intensely hot area, made flying uncomfortable even at higher altitudes. Emergency landing space was, of course, plentiful, but it so happened that much of the region was inhabited by fiercely antagonistic Moorish tribes. If a downed pilot was not rescued quickly, either heat or a Bedouin was likely to exact a terrible toll. Famed airmail pilot Jean Mermoz experienced two miserable weeks in captivity after he force-landed during his fourth desert flight in May 1926. His company finally succeeded in rescuing him from his Bedouin captors by payment of a heavy ransom. He was luckier than others; some never returned.

The next big challenge faced by Latécoère's air line, now known as Aéropostale, was the very one that he had envisioned many years earlier—the establishment of a regular aerial service across both the South Atlantic and the imposing barrier of the Andes to any desired location in South America. When Latécoère first dreamed his dream, it required a full two months to receive a reply to a letter posted from Paris to Santiago, Chile, or Buenos Aires. He was sure that mail sent by air could reduce this time to a single week. His planes and pilots would be the ones to accomplish this miracle.

The South Atlantic had first been crossed by airplane in March 1922 by Captains Gago Coutinho and Sacadura Cabral of the Portuguese Navy. Now Aéropostale was poised to attempt a regular mail service between France and South America. Initially the ocean crossings would be made by a shuttle utilizing obsolete French destroyers between St. Louis, Senegal on the West Coast of Africa and Natal, Brazil, the easternmost point of South America. Later, when possible, long-range aircraft would cross the ocean, making it an aerial service all the way from Paris to Buenos Aires.

In preparation for this long and demanding route, Aéropostale opened in 1927 an aerial service along the Atlantic coast of South America from Natal in the north to Buenos Aires in Argentina. On March 1 of the following year the full run from France to South America was inaugurated. Transit time for mail from Toulouse to Buenos Aires was suddenly reduced to eight days, with five of those days spent aboard the converted destroyers. Also in 1928, a subsidiary company of Aéropostale, Aeroposta Argentina, extended its service well south of Buenos Aires to the oil center of Comodoro Rivadavia—another 590 route miles along the eastern coast of South America. In July 1929, Aéropostale flights were finally able to traverse the Andes, and a regular air mail service between Buenos Aires and Santiago, Chile was begun.

Just as Alan Cobham had surveyed most of the Indian and African route segments for Britain's Imperial Airways, so Jean Mermoz had been assigned by Aéropostale operations manager

Air labels, like postage stamps, provide clues to aviation history. SCADTA labels are relics of a 1921 Colombian airline. Joining inland Bogota (Girardot) with coastal Barranquilla and using Junkers W-34s with floats, the Sociedad Colombo-Alemana de Transportes Aereos had strong German ties.

Two French stamps, one from 1937 and one from 1970, honor air mail pioneer Jean Mermoz. French airmail of 1936 salutes the 100th South Atlantic air mail crossing.

This historic cover was flown on a first attempt to carry mail eastward across the South Atlantic in June 1930. Flying an Aéropostale Latécoère 28, pilot Jean Mermoz and his mail had to be rescued at sea 500 miles short of their goal, the Senegal coast.

Didier Daurat to blaze the French routes to and within South America. On May 12, 1930, this remarkable aviator made the first direct flight with mail across the stretch of ocean until then traveled by the destroyers. Flying a Latécoère 28 floatplane named *Comte de la Vaulx*, Mermoz required 21 hours to reach Natal after taking off from St. Louis, Senegal. Two hundred and eighty-five pounds of mail were carried on this historic survey flight. After more trials with new equipment, Mermoz was able to reduce the flying time to 14½ hours in 1933, preparatory to the initiation of semi-regular mail flights across the South Atlantic in May 1934.

In the same year, a Blériot 5190 flying boat, the *Santos–Dumont*, was tested for service on the South Atlantic route. This craft demonstrated that the time for Toulouse–Buenos Aires mail could be reduced to 3 days and 20 hours, a performance standard far exceeding expectations. The craft went into service early in 1935 and made 22 ocean crossings under the banner of Air France.

Jean Mermoz had logged more than 8,200 hours in the air and achieved 23 crossings of the South Atlantic by the end of 1936. Tragically, he and his crew were lost at sea during a westbound crossing in a Latécoère 300 flying boat on December 7, 1936.

An article in the *London Sunday Times* of October 8, 1939, reviewing Antoine de Saint-Exupéry's book entitled *Wind, Sand and Stars*, talked about Jean Mermoz and the gallant band of French pilots who opened the airlanes in and to South America. Its author Sean O'Casey wrote:

> Mermoz had been forced down, with his mechanic, at an altitude of 12,000 feet on a tableland at whose edges the mountain dropped down sheer. For two mortal days they hunted a way off. But they were trapped. Everywhere the same sheer drop. So they played their last card: themselves still in it, they sent the aeroplane rolling and bouncing down an incline over the rocky ground till it reached the precipice, went off into the air and dropped. In falling, the plane picked enough speed to respond to the controls. Mermoz was able to tilt its nose in the direction of a peak, sweep over it, and, while the water spurted through all the pipes burst by the night frost, the ship disabled after only seven minutes' flight, he saw beneath him the Chilean plain, shining like the promised land.
>
> And the next day he was at it again.
>
> So go they, these airmen on their missions, flying fair and flying foul; tossed like a whirling leaf in a desperate wind, plunging through the clinging snow on the side of a mountain, trying to get somewhere, their plane a shattered thing behind them; or up to their chin in the sand, waiting for the dawn to come that they may stagger on with burning throats and blazing eyes to where they may or may not find a drop of water to cool the tip of their tongue, and, if they're lucky, find all humanity in the shape of a single helper; or lapping about in the green sea, waiting for a wave to sink them; and, after it all, sitting safe in a cafe, drinking hot coffee, trying to think out all that has been put behind them.

A fine tribute to a rare group of airmen who made the world much smaller because they dared to achieve the impossible over some of air mail's most fearful routes…the very routes that claimed the lives of 121 French airmen in less than a decade of operation.

171

Spanning the empire
When the railroad systems of France and Belgium became increasingly disrupted as a result of military action during World War I, planes were pressed into service to carry important individuals from front to front and from city to city. Planes also proved an effective means of moving confidential messages from one place to another. Wireless systems and codes were speedy, but they offered no guarantees of secrecy. Between January and September 1919, British Communications Squadron (No. 2) stationed at Buc near Paris flew mail three times a day from Paris to Hendon airfield, London. This same unit also carried diplomats and negotiators back and forth from London to the peace conference at Versailles in its DH–4A converted bombers.

The British Air Ministry in 1919, however, was looking beyond the period of military occupation and duty on the Continent. In February, the Air Ministry formed for the first time a Civil Department under a Controller-General, and an Air Navigation Act came into being in Britain on May 1 to regulate the course of civil aviation. A branch of the Civil Aviation Department was authorized to survey and propose a route system throughout the entire empire, initially only a theoretical planning exercise in the realm of long-distance international air transport and control.

Spurred to action, however, by the occasional arrivals to and departures from London of French and Belgian transport planes belonging to newly formed civil air lines in those countries, a pioneering British passenger and parcel service began daily operations on the manageable run between London and Paris. Known as Aircraft Transport and Travel, Ltd. (A.T.&T.), the service was provided by Britain's sole active commercial air line, which until that moment in its brief existence had been undertaking only domestic courier flights.

A.T.&T., Ltd., directed by General Sefton Brancker, made commercial aviation history when it began operations on the London–Paris route on August 25, 1919. Pilot Lieutenant E. H. Lawford in a DH–4A flew the first regularly (daily) scheduled *international* commercial airline flight anywhere in the world. (The first regularly scheduled *domestic* passenger service by airplane had already taken place in Germany when Deutsche Luft-Reederei inaugurated a Berlin–Weimar daily public run on February 5, 1919.) Flying from Hounslow Airdrome to Le Bourget near Paris in 2½ hours, Lawford had with him one passenger and a small load of newspapers, leather, grouse, and Devonshire cream. Although several airlines had formed in the world after the St. Petersburg–Tampa Airboat Line had begun the process in the United States in 1914, A.T.&T. was the first to meet all the criteria of regular, civil, daily, passenger, international, and sustained operation.

"Much doubt had been expressed," recalled pioneer aviator Claude Graham-White, "as to whether a London–Paris aeroplane service could be conducted reliably, having regard to the difficult weather conditions on this route. But the pioneer British services soon dispelled these fears. On the first week of the Airco (A.T.&T.) service extremely trying weather was encountered; while matters were made more difficult owing to the fact that the organization of the route left much to be desired. There was, it is true, some sort of a pioneer meteorological service; but there was no wireless telephone, then, upon which pilots could rely. Even so, however, our British airmen put up a magnificent show. Only one flight on that pioneer week had to be cancelled; while Lieut. Shaw, on one trip from Paris to London, came through weather of such an abnormally bad kind that on his Channel crossing, he had to do battle with winds reaching the hurricane force of approximately 100 miles-an-hour."

At the outset, A.T.&T., Ltd., carried only passengers in addition to urgent parcels, but in November the British Postal Service made arrangements for first class mail to be flown between London and Paris. The normal charge for this service was 2 shillings 6 pence for each letter.

As might be expected, the entry of two more British carriers—Handley Page Transport and Instone—on the London–Paris route by mid-1920, in addition to the French carriers then active, generated an over-capacity situation that quickly led to the financial downfall of an under-capitalized A.T.&T. In April 1922, Daimler Air Hire, Ltd. replaced A.T.&T. on the lucrative run to Paris, but it remained clear that there simply was not enough business to allow three British air lines to survive on this route. In an effort to improve the revenue picture, the companies decided on a course of action. They agreed that after October 1, 1922, Handley Page would be the exclusive operator on the London–Paris run; Daimler would be the sole British air line between London and Amsterdam; and Instone obtained exclusive right to the London–Brussels route.

When the new monopoly scheme failed to bring much bottom-line improvement in the profit and loss statements of the carriers, it became time for Secretary of State for Air, Sir Samuel Hoare, to order a careful study of the problems of future air line development in Britain. The committee making the study, under Sir Herbert Hambling's leadership, put forth a recommendation that all existing British air lines, including one serving the Channel Islands, be amalgamated into a single operation. Subsequently, on March 31, 1924, a subsidized air line known as Imperial Airways, Ltd. was incorporated. Britain thus became the first major power to sponsor a unified national air line. With courage and vision, Sefton Brancker, then Director of Civil

Two stars of the Imperial fleet. Above: The famed City of Glasgow that began "Silver Wing" service to Paris May 1, 1927 and carried the first England-India mails in 1929. It accommodated 18 passengers, had a bar, and was later reworked for Middle Eastern mail routes. Also serving mail routes to India and South Africa, after June 1931, were Imperial's Handley Page H.P. 42's (below), the world's first 4-engined transports.

Aviation in the United Kingdom, and Sir Samuel Hoare proposed that Imperial's goal was to become truly imperial—that the new line could well grow beyond its European services to forge linkups with India and beyond.

Until late in 1926, Imperial Airways concentrated on its European operations. Her pilots sported handsome new uniforms. New types of aircraft were tried out, including Handley Page W9s and Armstrong Whitworth Argosies. A deluxe service to Paris, called the Silver Wing, was announced and inaugurated. It was initially flown in 1927 by an Argosy G–EBLF—the *City of Glasgow*—and was the first named aerial service in the world. Everything possible was done by Imperial to improve its competitive position against the more highly subsidized national air lines of continental Europe. Money was still being lost, however, and this factor hastened the airline's move to broaden its mission.

Imperial's herculean task of spanning the globe with new air trails and ground facilities began in earnest in 1927 when the company assumed charge of a Royal Air Force desert air mail route that had been carried on by the British military since June 1921. Stretching from Cairo to Baghdad and Basra, this route opened officially on January 7, 1927, and advertised an air mail fee of 3 pence an ounce. The Cairo–Baghdad segment proved to be only step one in an ambitious reach toward Australia.

A fair idea of what desert flight was like when Imperial took over its first mid-Eastern route has been provided by Wing-Commander Hill, one of the hardy Royal Air Force pilots who had worked the route. He describes a mail flight from Baghdad:

Ramadi is 65 miles from Baghdad, and it feels like a gate through which the pilot passes out to new and exciting adventures. Beyond is the open desert with all its mysterious fascination; and few who behold it thus for the first time can fail to experience the slight catch of the breath that comes with the sudden view of the sea from a high place. It seems to be a land with no ending; and it has an unreal atmospheric quality comparable with the sky. Perhaps this is why people call it the 'Blue.'

The mail aircraft had to fill up with petrol at Ramadi, because the trip from Baghdad to Ziza was just beyond the endurance of a Vernon [aircraft].

We sleep [at Ramadi] outside at the foot of one of the wireless masts, and disengage ourselves as best we can from the attentions of the twin-engined sandfly, who also use Ramadi as an aerodrome. We hope a night breeze will spring up, because the sandfly is very lightly loaded, and he cannot land on you in a wind. A hot whisky before turning in is also a help; for during the first half of the night you do not notice the sandfly, and during the second half he becomes laterally unstable and cannot bite you.

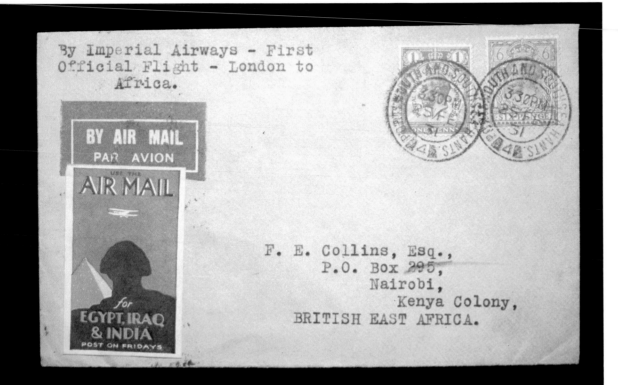

We get up at 3:30 A.M., and those of us who are not too exhausted with dodging sandflies and scorpions snatch a hasty breakfast, for we have a long day ahead.... On leaving Ramadi we climb very slowly, with throttles wide open.

As it is summer we probably set out from Ramadi in a shirt, khaki shorts and stockings, with a mackintosh on top just to keep out the early morning chill. If we are sensible we are wearing tinted goggles, for the glare of the desert and the perpetual watching of the track tend to fatigue the retina. We now feel that it is time to discard the mackintosh and open the throats of our shirts, as although the top plane [wing] is still keeping the cockpit in shadow, the air feels as if it came out of an oven and gently roasts your hand if you put it outside.

This trip was accomplished once a fortnight in fair weather or foul, in intense heat and sometimes in bitter cold, as a part of the Squadron's normal duties. The mail itself was practically never late.

Such was the setting of the first of three major aerial trunk lines undertaken by Imperial as it attempted to join together the remote areas of an empire. Not before March 30, 1929, would the route be pushed westerly to London and eastward to Karachi and Delhi, thereby making the dream of an England-to-India service a reality. The well-remembered, silver-winged *City of Glasgow* flew the first leg of this longer route by carrying mail (no passengers, initially) from Croydon Airfield, London, to Basel, Switzerland. The mail eventually reached Karachi on April 6. The first westbound delivery, which departed Karachi on April 1, finally was carried into London aboard the same *City of Glasgow* on the 14th. Approximately 12,000 pounds of mail were transported over this route during the first three months of the service.

In July 1929, when passengers were received as far as Cairo, the trip was by air to Basel, by train to Genoa, and then by Calcutta flying boats to Cairo by way of Naples, Corfu, Athens, Suda Bay, Tobruk, and Alexandria. By December 1934, mails on this route were carried beyond India to Australia, with passengers being accommodated in April of the following year.

A second major priority of Imperial Airways was to establish an all-African route, intended ultimately to reach Cape Town. As in the Middle East, an experimental mail and passenger service conducted by the military in Africa became the entry point for commercial route development. In 1927, the Royal Air Force operated an irregularly scheduled service between Cairo and Khartoum in the Sudan. After a number of survey flights, various formal studies of the particularities of the African situation, and a necessary build-up of Imperial's equipment base, a regular passenger and mail service incorporated the military route and more. Using Argosies from Alexandria to Khartoum and Calcuttas from Khartoum to Mwanza, on Lake Victoria,

Opposite: *This cover, cancelled February 28, 1931 at Portsmouth, appears to have been aboard Imperial's first East African air mail flight. Carried to Alexandria and to Khartoum by Argosies, the cover finally reached Kisumu on the 10th of March and Nairobi on the 11th. Without the backstamps, its course remains in doubt. The mid-East air label is appropriate for the first leg. Mounting tape stains on the back detract from the cover's appearance.*

In a two year period between July 1, 1920 and June 7, 1922 an experimental air mail service carried 4,400 pounds of mail between Kinshasa and Stanleyville in the Congo. The 2-franc blue stamp, with its Blériot plane over a river, was part of Africa's first airmail set issued by the Belgian Congo to frank mail on this pioneer African route. The lower stamp, a 30¢ red of China featuring a Curtiss Jenny over the Great Wall of China, is part of a re-issue of a 1921 set that confirmed world-wide commercial use of the airplane.

Right: *An otherwise undistinguished cover made interesting by the boxed cachet which indicates that the cover initiated its journey to London over the British military desert air mail route that preceded the first mid-East Imperial route of 1927. Franking on the back of the cover includes three stamps of Iraq's first postal issue and a 1923 Baghdad cancellation.*

Imperial initiated on February 28, 1931, a semi-regular aerial service from London. At the time this route was inaugurated, passengers were carried only as far as Khartoum. It took almost another year to extend it all the way to Cape Town. When the entire route from London to Cape Town was brought into service in January 1932, the three-engined De Havilland DH 66 Hercules was utilized by Imperial between Nairobi and Cape Town.

The challenges that faced Imperial Airways in its African venture were formidable. Extremes in temperatures, variations in altitude, seasonal turbulence and rains—all contributed operating problems. The completion of the company's African system-building occurred in 1939, the year in which Imperial's giant flying boats began service on the company's third major international route, the transatlantic.

The founders of Imperial had always visualized a service from Britain to Canada and the United States. This venture, of course, involved long-range flying boats, the evolution of which took place finally in the mid and late thirties. With land-mass stepping-stones all along the way to Australia and South Africa, the matter of aircraft range was far less critical on these routes; range on the transatlantic route, however, was a matter of prime importance, and represented a single leap of gigantic dimensions.

Imperial Airways finally finished preparations for its transatlantic passenger and mail flights in 1939, about two months after Pan American's *Yankee Clipper* (a Boeing 314) had inaugurated regular service over the North Atlantic and one month before Prime Minister Neville Chamberlain announced the state of war in Europe. Imperial's first transatlantic service was experimental and involved sixteen flights (eight round-trips) before the war intervened. The inaugural one took place on August 5, 1939, when Captain (J. C.) Kelly Rogers flew *Caribou*, a short S30C flying boat, to New York via Foynes (Ireland), Botwood (Newfoundland), and Montreal.

The name of one particular pilot in Britain became a household word. Alan J. Cobham will always remain associated with the development of the first two of Imperial's three major trunk lines. Sefton Brancker, Britain's Director of Civil Aviation, was flown by Cobham from London to Rangoon, Burma, and back as the general studied the possible routes to India. This formidable journey of 17,000 miles, made in a DH–50 biplane powered by a 230 hp Siddeley Puma engine, began on November 20, 1924.

Not quite a year later on November 16, 1925, Cobham took off on a survey flight of a route to Cape Town and South Africa. This remarkable and historic trip was again made in Cobham's DH–50, now called DH–50J because a new 385 hp Jaguar engine had been installed. Traveling with Cobham this time were his expert mechanic, A. B. Elliott, and a skilled photographer, B. W. G. Emmott. They returned to London on March 13, 1926, having

175

flown by way of Egypt and East Africa both going and coming. Within three months time, Cobham's DH–50J, now fitted out with floats, was off again on a 13,000 mile survey assignment; Cobham and Elliott were intending to travel all the way to Melbourne, Australia. Regrettably, Elliott was killed early on this trip, struck by a Bedouin's bullet as the plane flew low over the desert between Baghdad and Basra. On his return journey Cobham displayed split-second timing as he set his floatplane down in the Thames on October 1, 1926, precisely when he had predicted he would. A tremendous ovation greeted him and he was knighted shortly afterward for his signficant contributions to civil aviation in Britain.

Two other events took place in the mid-1930s that were milestones in Britain's air mail development. On April 12, 1933, the first regular commercial air mail was finally flown within Britain itself. The Great Western Railway was the carrier on a route between South Wales (Cardiff and Newport) and Devon and Plymouth. In initiating this inland air mail, Great Western was exercising a certification granted to it by the government four years earlier, and the company charged the same 3-penny fee for air mail that it charged for mail carried by rail. As part of this service, semi-official stamps were approved by the British General Post Office and issued by the carrier. The first regular air mail within Great Britain that required no surcharge came about the next year when Captain Edmund E. Fresson's Highland Airways carried non-surcharged air mail between Inverness and Kirkwall.

The adoption of the Empire Air Mail Scheme (E.A.M.S.) in 1934 was the event that finally brought the British air mail venture a full measure of support from the government. The E.A.M.S.'s basic thrust required the government to underwrite the aerial carriage of all first class mail between various points in the empire, thereby eliciting a volume of mail that would help support the operations of Imperial Airways around the globe. Up to this time the extraordinarily high surcharges for air mail severely limited the amount flown on Imperial routes. So successful was the E.A.M.S. that passenger capacities of some of the Short Class "C" flying boats were reduced to enable another half ton of mail to be carried.

Without the trial-and-error efforts of an Imperial Airways, the great network of air routes we know today would have emerged over a much extended period of time and the then growing contacts between distant peoples would have been immeasurably slowed.

Pictured together at the Khartoum field are two Argosies of Imperial Airways' East Africa service. The near craft (G-EBOZ) is the City of Wellington, the third Argosy Type I delivered to Imperial in 1927. An Argosy II (G-AAEJ), the City of Coventry, is the far plane. Joining Imperial in 1929, the Coventry was powered by three 420 hp Jaguar IVA engines with Townsend cowlings.

The fabulous career of LZ-127 Transport-minded people of many nations were increasingly alert to the commercial possibilities of transoceanic flight in the 1920s. Only one nation and one carrier, however, were eager and ready to initiate such service. That nation was Germany; the company so disposed was Luftschiffbau Zeppelin, then under the leadership of Ferdinand von Zeppelin's nephew, Baron Gemmingen, and Dr. Hugo Eckener. Even today the transatlantic (and transpacific) ventures of this firm in the closing years of the decade seem quite extraordinary.

The Zeppelin's rise to a starring role in worldwide aerial transport came after an improbable, uphill victory over adverse circumstances encountered in post-World-War-I Germany. After the Inter-Allied Commission of Control stripped the company of its remaining fleet of three airships, sending two ships to France and one to Italy, its future seemed bleak indeed. In their darkest hour the directors came up with a plan, which at first appeared merely to postpone the hour of their company's demise, but which ultimately proved to be the thin thread of a life by which their firm would survive. The Zeppelin directors, in a mood of desperation, offered to construct for the American Military Commission an airship that could be placed in service with the United States Navy. Their intent was to settle a reparations debt with a completed airship rather than with an $800,000 financial payment. Since none of the captive airships had been allocated to them, the Americans immediately responded with interest to the proposal.

Final approval from the Allies reached the company only after considerable wrangling among the nations involved over the size of the airship to be constructed. The contract specified that the range and airworthiness of the new LZ-126 would have to be proven by a transatlantic delivery flight. That flight finally became a reality in October 1924. Under the command of Hugo Eckener, the great silver ship made a 77-hour crossing of the Atlantic, arriving at the United States Naval Air Station, Lakehurst, New Jersey, on October 16. LZ-126 immediately acquired the name *Los Angeles* as she officially joined the U.S. Navy.

Successful completion and delivery of the *Los Angeles*, an airship that would transport the first air mail from mainland United States to Bermuda and Puerto Rico in 1925, signaled another reversal in Luftschiffbau Zeppelin fortunes. Free of the hampering restrictions imposed by the Inter-Allied Commission of Control and with an impressive construction achievement to her credit, the company set forth at once to build an even larger airship. LZ-127 was to be 775 feet in length and, hopefully, would obtain an 80 mph speed with her five 530 hp Maybach engines. It is fitting both that Hugo Eckener chose to name the new airship *Graf Zeppelin* and that she was christened by Coun-

tess von Brandenstein-Zeppelin, daughter of the late Count Ferdinand von Zeppelin, when she was completed in July 1928. Once the primary test flights of September 1928 were over, Eckener immediately prepared the *Graf Zeppelin* for its first transatlantic flight.

To aviation-interested people of both hemispheres, 1927 and 1928 proved to be years of marvelous achievement as new heroes made epic flights and became household words. The epoch began on May 20, 1927, as Charles A. Lindbergh, a former air mail pilot, took off from Roosevelt Field, Long Island, on his solo flight across the Atlantic. Other transatlantic flights followed in an unending succession. Soon the LZ-127 joined that parade.

She left Friedrichshafen on the morning of October 11, 1928, carrying 20 passengers and 37 crew members, including Captains von Schiller and Flemming as watch officers and Captain Lehmann as commander. Eckener was in overall charge of the flight, which had on board 55,714 pieces of mail.

On the third day of the trip, which had so far progressed over the Rhine valley, the Mediterranean (via the Côte d'Azur to Gibraltar) and finally, out over the Atlantic, difficulties arose in mid-ocean. The LZ-127 had entered the frontal edge of a low-pressure area, and the accompanying squall, of the kind that had so often plagued Zeppelins from the earliest days of LZ–2, shook the airship violently.

As air currents slammed into the front its nose sharply rose, and a counter-maneuver of the elevator man to lift the tail in order to level the ship came too late. It was quickly found that the linen fabric on one of the stabilizer fins was torn, causing the airship to drift. Eckener stopped all engines and asked for volunteers to go outside on the fin to repair the damage. Among those asking to go on the precarious mission was Eckener's son, Airship Engineer and Helmsman Knut Eckener. Chief Helmsman Ludwig Marx and Engineer-Helmsman Albert Sammit also stepped forward to assist Chief Rigger Ludwig Knorr. The men climbed over the exposed guides to the trailing shreds, and Knorr sewed blankets to the undamaged covering. While the exposed men were contending with the storm over a white-capped sea, they were aware of a battle against time. From the driving rain the dirigible's linen covering had become heavy with moisture, forcing the airship closer and closer to the water below. With the engines immobile, extra lift needed to keep the ship afloat was absent. The *Graf Zeppelin's* altimeter showed a descent to almost 300 feet.

Faced with a critical decision, Eckener was heard to ask American Lieutenant Commander Charles E. Rosendahl, a passenger, whether he felt aid from the United States Navy might possibly be in the area to answer a radio distress signal. He realized that if

177

This cover traveled on the final, Los Angeles to Lakehurst, leg of the LZ-127's remarkable round-the-world flight of August 1929. The cover is signed by Hugo Eckener, American Lt. Cmdr. C.E. Rosendahl and the crew. Two popular Graf Zeppelin stamps are shown: low value of a 3-value U.S. 1930 series and a beautiful Liechtenstein Europa commemorative of 1979 recalling a Graf Zeppelin visit of 1931.

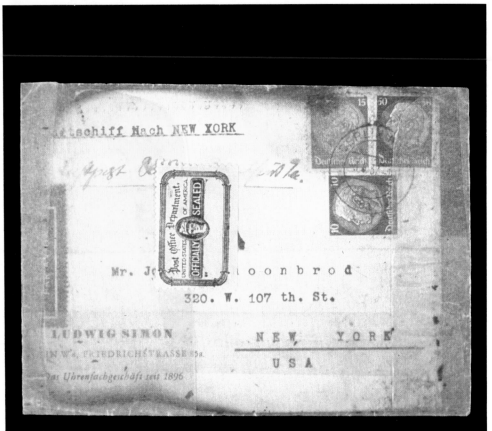

When the German airship Hindenburg (LZ-129) exploded suddenly in the early evening of May 6, 1937, at Lakehurst, N.J., her flames closed the fascinating era of dirigibles. Mail remainders from this tragic event are prized souvenirs today. Seared around the edges by the intense heat, this crash card was enclosed in a glassine envelope and officially sealed by the U.S. Post Office for delivery to the addressee. Very few letters were salvaged from the wreckage of LZ-129, and they obtain high prices whenever they appear in auctions.

the engines were started abruptly, the men on the tail fin would most likely be thrown from their perches. On the other hand, if he did not fire the engines soon, the ship and its passengers would certainly fall into the sea. Miraculously, by the time Eckener ordered "Set the telegraphs for engines three and four at full speed ahead," the volunteer repair crew, realizing their proximity to the sea, had hastily finished their work and made their way back to the interior of the airship.

After more than 111 hours in the air and before an excited crowd of over 20,000 people, the airship finally reached Lakehurst at 5:38 P.M. on October 15, having covered a distance of 6,200 miles. Due to the jury-rigged repair on the tail surface, the final part of the journey was conducted at half speed. Without that repair, and the extraordinary courage of the repair crew, the great dirigible would have met disaster in mid-Atlantic.

Once in the United States, the crew received a ticker-tape parade in New York City and an invitation by President and Mrs. Hoover to attend a banquet at the White House. Unlike the earlier transatlantic flight of the LZ-126, the *Los Angeles*, which principally involved just two nations, this epic voyage of the *Graf Zeppelin* held universal appeal, and it seemed to the general public all over the globe to herald the approach of a new era of air travel. Heavier-than-air craft were still considered unreliable, uncomfortable, and impractical. Thanks to this flight, the next few years would foster a mood in which popularity would swing back and forth between dirigibles and airplanes.

By October 29, the stabilizer fin was repaired and the *Graf Zeppelin* was prepared to complete the return-trip portion of her first transatlantic voyage. Twenty-five passengers boarded, each paying a $3,000 fare to the Thomas Cook Agency. There were no less than 48 sacks of mail (holding more than 100,000 specially cacheted cards and letters) and 331 parcels stored in the baggage

July 12, 1929 was the date for the maiden flight of this giant German 12-engined flying boat called the Dornier 10 (or "DO-X"). Mail from domestic and transatlantic flights of this plane in the early 1930s is highly prized. Baggage labels, like the oval one below, are highly developed collateral area of specialization for aerophilatelists.

rooms as the Zeppelin set sail at 1:55 in the morning of October 29 from Lakehurst. She landed at Friedrichshafen at 7:00 A.M. on November 1, 1928, following an uneventful trip. The crew, met by a cheering crowd of 30,000 people, who alternated their singing of the German and American national anthems, then flew on to Berlin where they were again received by President.

In his welcoming address, President von Hindenburg said, "In this great airship, in its glorious flight through storm and fog, over continents and seas, the Fatherland saw a super German achievement. You have in the best sense of the word completed a national exploit!"

After the regular flights over the Atlantic and Mediterranean had become widely publicized, Eckener announced in the summer of 1929 that the *Graf Zeppelin* would attempt a world flight. All available seats were booked immediately, and the passenger list resembled an international *Who's Who*. The LZ-127 began her globe-circling trip, departing eastbound from Lakehurst at 12:40 A.M. on August 8, 1929. For the next 21 days, 7 hours, and 34 minutes, the *Graf Zeppelin* moved around the world, touching base at Friedrichshafen, Tokyo, and Los Angeles, before finally landing once again at Lakehurst on August 29. The world's circumnavigation was achieved at an average speed of 70.7 mph and covered a total of 21,200 miles. During the journey, 300 hours and 20 minutes were spent in the air; more than 43,000 pieces of mail were handled on the flight.

In 1932, a regular passenger service was established between Europe and South America, the *Graf Zeppelin* having made its first flight there between May 18 and June 6, 1930. The 1930 voyage took the airship to Seville, Pernambuco, Rio de Janeiro, and north to Lakehurst before she finally returned to Friedrichshafen. In 1931, three round-trip flights between Paraguay and Lake Constance were made.

The *Graf Zeppelin* recorded as many as thirteen South American passenger flights from the new intercontinental airship harbor at Frankfurt-am-Main in 1936, and the following year—the anticipated final year of her active service—she made two South American flights. During her second return flight from Brazil, Captain von Schiller received news of the *Hindenburg* disaster, and Eckener cancelled all further flights. The *Graf Zeppelin* remained in the hangar at Frankfurt until she was dismantled on May 6, 1940, her aluminum to be used by the Luftwaffe.

In nine years of service, the *Graf Zeppelin* set record after record. She flew 650 flights, 147 of them across the Atlantic Ocean (140 on the south route; 7 on the northern). She was the only airship ever built to fly over a million miles, which she did in 16,000 hours of flight, carrying 18,000 passengers. And always aboard were the mails, to chronicle her flights and delight collectors of later years.

180

The Graf Zeppelin departed Lakehurst on its 1929 globe circling flight on August 8 and reached U.S. West Coast on August 25. This photo shows the ship moored at Mines Field, outside of Los Angeles, where 12,000 letters were taken aboard.

FAMs begin to cross the ocean

The steady flow of air traffic over the Atlantic in 1927 strongly hinted that the time was fast approaching when mail links would be forged from continent to continent. The dramatically increased range of aircraft had suddenly placed regularly scheduled ocean crossings almost entirely within the realm of imminent possibility. However, just as domestic air mail within the United States and Europe had begun with short, manageable routes, so was it necessary to seek oceans other than the Atlantic and the Pacific to serve as the proving grounds for foreign over-water carries of mail. Small wonder that the Caribbean and Gulf of Mexico areas, laced with islands that comprised a convenient bridge to South America, were the waters toward which United States postal and commercial interests turned in the late 1920s. These were the oceans that spawned the first important FAM—Foreign Air Mail—contracts in United States postal history.

The inauspicious beginnings of Pan American Airways occurred in this very area and at the very moment in time when a pioneer mail route was about to be revived between Key West, Florida and Havana. The story of Pan American's birth as a world carrier is very much the story of the reactivation of that old route and the earliest wide-scale Foreign Air Mail activity by the United States Post Office Department.

In 1926 Juan Terry Trippe—a recent graduate of Yale University and an aviation executive who had directed Colonial Air Transport's entry into the contract era on CAM 1 between New York and Boston—and several Yale flying-club friends formed a holding company known as the Aviation Corporation of the Americas. This young firm, with an imposing name, briefly operated a seasonal air service between New York and Atlantic City. However, spurred on by Trippe's seemingly boundless energy, the company sought out greater challenges.

When Trippe learned that the Post Office Department was asking for bids on a United States mail contract for the route between Key West, Florida and Havana in the spring of 1927, the Aviation Corporation of the Americas hastened to enter a proposal. Two competing companies had also entered bids on the contract. The first, Florida Airways, formed by World War I aces Eddie Rickenbacker and Reed Chambers, eventually lost out because they could not come up with sufficient backing after two of their three aircraft had accidents. The stronger competitor, called Pan American Airways, Inc., was founded by Major Henry "Hap" Arnold, Major Carl Spaatz, and Jack Jouett. Since Pan American had already secured a contract of sorts from Cuba's government to carry her mail from Havana to Key West, Trippe and an associate, John Hambleton, sought to exact an exclusive flying permit from Cuba's dictator, Gerardo Machado, specifying that no other airline could land in or fly from Cuban territory. When this "exclusive" was unexpectedly granted, the other bidder was taken over by the Aviation Corporation of the Americas, their contract having become worthless. Trippe then made Pan American a subsidiary of Aviation Corporation and assumed the principal office of the new acquisition.

Trippe, looking beyond the period of mail hauling to passenger transport, believed that the Fokker tri-motored F–VII, introduced to America by Anthony Fokker in 1925, was the ideal aircraft for his budding airline and ordered three. Unfortunately, on the date of the mail contract deadline, October 19, 1927, not one Fokker had landed at Key West because the new field being constructed there was not quite ready to receive the large F–VII. Pan American's manager at Key West, J. E. Whitbeck, was more than a little apprehensive. The sacks with mail for Havana were already in Key West, and his superiors in Washington were unable to get an extension of time for the inaugural mail flight to Havana.

Then without notice, a small single-engine Fairchild FC–2 floatplane of West Indian Aerial Express (WIAE) came into the bay at Key West to refuel. The pilot, A. A. "Cy" Caldwell, had only recently been employed by Captain Basil L. Rowe, who owned and operated WIAE, an inter-island carrier based in the Dominican Republic. Whitbeck immediately saw an opportunity to effect his mail delivery. With telephoned permission of Pan American officials, he importuned Caldwell to carry the mail to Havana, explaining his urgent need to meet a contractual deadline. Hurriedly, Caldwell was in touch with Basil Rowe, who agreed to "loan" his pilot to Pan Am for a charter price of $175.00.

The small Fairchild named *La Niña* was soon taking off from Key West with seven sacks of mail containing over 30,000 letters. Caldwell covered the 90-mile flight without incident in just over an hour. After a four-hour delay with Cuban customs, who were expecting a Fokker tri-motor and not an FC–2 in their harbor, Cy Caldwell completed Pan American Airway's inaugural air mail delivery to Havana and then flew back to Key West without mail aboard. On October 28, Juan Trippe's fledgling airline, having received their new Fokkers in Key West, began operating a daily air mail schedule to Havana from their completed base at Meacham Field.

An FAM route number did not appear in Pan American's cachet for its first Cuban-bound mail, but it did commemorate a "First Flight Under New Contract." The FAM 4 route number was originally utilized by Inglis M. Uppercu's Aeromarine Airways, which completed several mail flights between Key West and Havana as early as 1920. However, this early service was short-lived and mail carries were abandoned. Nevertheless, Aeromarine holds a key place in aerophilatelic history by being

W.E. "Bill" Boeing (right) and pilot Eddie Hubbard pictured on return from a 1919 trial mail flight in a Boeing C-700 carrying 60 letters from Vancouver to Seattle. On October 15, 1920 Hubbard opened FAM route 2 between Seattle and Victoria, British Columbia. The route operated almost daily for 7 years. In April of 1923 a hydroplane mail service (FAM 3) was established briefly between New Orleans and Pilottown, Louisiana to carry mail to ships leaving for South America. Pilot Riddick and his mail plane are shown in this photo.

Barnstormer and businessman Basil D. Rowe teamed up in 1927 with pilot friend Captain Cy Caldwell to form a tiny Santa Domingo-based airline called West Indian Aerial Express. Needing the help of W.I.A.E. to save its foreign mail contract on October 19, 1927, Miami-based Pan American Airways rented the services of Caldwell. The W.I.A.E. Fairchild FC-2 seaplane La Nina (opposite) and its mail, made the 90-mile flight as required.

one of the first two American-based airlines to operate internationally and to be awarded an FAM contract route number. When the FAM Act was passed in March of 1928, Pan American was then issued the historic FAM 4 designation on the run between Key West and Havana.

Pan Am's first Fokker F–VII, diplomatically and appreciatively named the *General Machado*, began operations at 8:25 A.M. on October 28, 1927 with pilot Hugh Wells, formerly of CAM 1, at the controls and Edwin C. Musick as navigator. This first regular round-trip air mail flight carried 772 pounds of mail on the 1 hour and 20 minute outbound leg to Havana. On January 16 of the following year. Pan American carried its first passengers to Havana, and yet another nine months later, the airline relocated its base from Key West to Miami. On January 2, 1929, the rapidly expanding airline was awarded FAM 7, a route from Miami to Nassau. Pan American also was awarded FAM 5 and FAM 6 early in 1929 as well. The former, a route from Miami to Cristobal via Cuba and Central America, commenced operating on February 4, 1929. The latter route, with service leaving Miami three times a week to San Juan via Cuba and Santo Domingo, was awarded on July 13, 1928 and started operations on January 9, 1929. The landing rights to these islands were

*This cover, signed by Cy Caldwell, traveled with him on his
initial flight of FAM 4, the flight that inaugurated a new FAM era.*

taken over by Trippe when he absorbed W.I.A.E. as another step
in his company's growth. Basil Rowe, who had so helpfully
served Pan American on October 19, 1927, then joined the air
line as a senior flyer and officer and was to play a major role in
the company's continued success.

As the sphere of influence with the Post Office Department
grew, especially in the eyes of Postmaster General Walter Folger
Brown, who was interested in establishing air mail service to
Latin America as rapidly as possible, and in developing the
nation's airlines, so did Trippe's acquisitions. After his takeover
of WIAE, he was able to buy the entire stock of Compañia
Mexicana de Aviación (CMA), which had been founded on
August 24, 1924 in Mexico, and held a ten-year contract with the
Mexican Department of Communications and Public Works for
exclusive flying rights throughout Mexico. On January 23, 1929,
the Lincoln Standard LS–5 biplanes and Fairchild F–1s of CMA
became the property of Pan Am as well as their routes to the oil
fields near Tampico and Merida in the Yucatan.

By July 1929, Pan American serviced both Santiago, Chile
through a route along the West Coast, and Buenos Aires by an
East coast route. Up until the advent of Trippe's airline, the west
coast of South America was the exclusive domain of W. R. Grace
& Company, a powerful shipping conglomerate. By purchasing
a small Peruvian airline, and establishing another in Chile,
Trippe was able to keep the Grace Line from securing landing
rights inland. Trippe, however, needed the assistance of Grace
to operate along the Pacific coast in relative safety. The convenience of radio communications with their ships from shore influenced Trippe to form an alliance with his rival, and on January 25, 1929, he helped form Pan American-Grace Airways,
more commonly known as Panagra. Through this merger,
Trippe was able to obtain a stronger foothold in both Chile and
Peru. Panagra received an authorization to operate FAM 9 on
March 2, 1929, from the Canal Zone to Santiago and Buenos
Aires. When her pilots inaugurated service from Cristobal as far
as Mollendo, Peru, on May 17, another major step in opening up
United States mail connections with most of South America had
been taken.

Pan American had to literally carve out its Latin American
routes. Its pioneering involved not only the establishment of
airfields in jungle and mountainous areas, but the direct negoti-
ation of contracts with foreign governments regarding landing
rights, a task later to be assumed by the United States government. It also had to create area weather services and find a means
of transferring data from station to station. By tackling such
challenges with dispatch, Pan American quickly became the
world's largest airline. By 1931, it claimed 15,000 route miles in
contrast to the 90 with which it had begun in October of 1927.

183

Chaos, then consolidation

The steady and relatively methodical growth of United States foreign air mail routes contrasted sharply with the character and rhythm of air mail expansion at home. To be sure the early years of air mail's contract era saw steady growth, statistics of the period reflecting almost an annual doubling of mail poundage carried. However, this exciting growth in volume came during the formative years of the present airline system and hardly suggests the confusing array of interwoven threads that comprise the early history of domestic air transport in the United States.

By the end of 1926, the first year of contract air mail flights, there were fifteen different operators carrying or about to carry mail for the Post Office Department. By the end of 1928, twenty-one companies held air mail contracts, and the United States had become the world's leader in commercial air traffic. This sudden burst of activity in the air transport field was encouraged, it will be recalled, by the nature of the first air mail contracts. Those contracts called for bids on a handful of short, geographically dispersed feeder routes that connected with the great central route between San Francisco and New York. It was only when the government followed through on its intention to turn over its transcontinental air mail service to private operation, removing itself entirely from the business of air transportation, that the end of a confused beginning of airline growth began to occur.

The call for bids on the transcontinental route, advertised between November 15, 1926, and January 15, 1927, indicated that the Post Office Department had decided to carve the long route into two sections: New York to Chicago and Chicago to San Francisco. Such a move had one pronounced intention—to trigger the kind of bigness in operators that was deemed essential to handle an extended route on a regular basis.

The long western stretch of the transcontinental route, designated CAM 18, was awarded to Boeing Air Transport (BAT) on January 15, 1927. In anticipation of winning the 1,918 mile route, the Boeing Airplane Company of Seattle's W. E. Boeing had hurriedly organized the Boeing Air Transport Company with headquarters in Salt Lake City. Under the leadership of Phil G. Johnson, the new airline also hired Edward Hubbard, contractor and pilot of the earliest official FAM flight in United States history, as its vice president of operations.

Word of the new air mail contracts had instigated a chain of reactions at the parent Boeing Company in Seattle, the most important of which involved reviving the manufacture of its Model 40 biplane. This plane, capable of carrying two passengers and a substantial mail load, had been shown to the Post Office Department in 1925 but had never elicited any purchase contracts. Boeing's attorney, Bill Allen, drew up an agreement

wherein BAT (Boeing Air Transport) was to purchase twenty-five of a Model 40A version from Boeing Airplane Company. To fly and maintain these planes, Hubbard later signed on Post Office pilots and mechanics who had been employed on government routes.

The most noteworthy feature of the Boeing 40A plane was its power plant, the Pratt and Whitney Wasp engine. A 420 hp uncowled radial engine unit, the Wasp was developed by Frederick Rentschler, whose name in the aviation world is as closely linked to the Boeing name as Hugo Eckener's is to von Zeppelin. In 1920, after having worked on 150 hp Hispano-Suiza and 400 hp Liberty engines at the Wright-Martin Engine Company during the war, Rentschler and others bought out a Manhattan firm that made the country's only air-cooled engine. With some difficulty, he soon developed a 500-pound engine capable of turning out 200 hp. This became the famous Wright Whirlwind. Rentschler left this firm, however, when his board refused to back him in developing a more powerful radial engine.

Deciding to establish his own company in direct competition to other engine producers, Rentschler was told by his aircraft designer friend, Chance Vought, that if he could produce a 400 hp engine weighing less than 650 pounds, he, Vought, had a carrier-type aircraft in mind that could win them both contracts. Working out an arrangement with Colonel Edward A. Deeds, formerly of the Aircraft Production Board in Washington, Rentschler and his brother formed Pratt & Whitney Aircraft, and Deeds took the helm as the Hartford-based company's first chairman. Within six months of its initial conception, on December 29, 1925, P & W's first radial engine was ready for testing.

William Boeing and Rentschler had known each other from the early days when Boeing aircraft used engines manufactured by Wright-Martin or Wright Aeronautical, the very companies with which Rentschler had been associated. Because of their close friendship, Boeing stayed with Rentschler's engines when Rentschler established Pratt & Whitney Aircraft. In 1928 they decided to combine their companies into a single holding company for diverse aviation enterprises, which became United Aircraft and Transport Company early in 1929. Boeing Air Transport and Pratt & Whitney Aircraft were the principal shareholders. Also becoming part of this corporation were Chance Vought, the Hamilton Aero Manufacturing Company, and Standard Steel Propeller, the latter two designing the variable-pitch Hamilton-Standard propellers. A few small manufacturers like Sikorsky Aviation Company, Northrop, and later Stearman were eventually included in the amalgamation as was Stout Airlines on June 30, 1929.

Returning to the early formation of Boeing Air Transport, it can be seen that by having a monopoly on the only radial engine available commercially, Boeing was able to gain extra revenue by replacing unneeded water-filled radiators with mail cargo space. His airline was additionally successful because he accommodated his aircraft designs for passengers as well as mail. At first passengers were a less welcome addition to the carriers' loads, since they earned more money per pound carrying mail than with passengers filling comparable space. However, passengers would soon become the prime revenue source for commercial airlines and the Boeing Model 80—successor to the famed Model 40—was one key factor in this transition.

The government relinquished operations between Chicago and San Francisco at midnight of June 30, 1927, and BAT commenced service under contract the next day. Nine Post Office Department pilots effected the final government flights over the route, including veteran Jack Knight, and the very next day several BAT pilots inaugurated the long route in four sections. The pilot roster of Boeing clearly had a Post Office Department flavor, listing such stalwarts as Ernie Allison, Ira Biffle, H. A. Collison, and Frank Yager.

As of July 1, 1927, other changes relating to the air mail service had been or were about to be made. The complicated rate-based-on-zone system that was born when the contract routes were set up was abandoned, and a flat rate of ten cents per half ounce for air mail between any two points in the country came into being—a valuable step in increasing usage of air mail. Also, the lighted airway and ground radio systems were removed from Post Office Department supervision, both networks being transferred to control and operation by the Department of Commerce.

Less than three months after responsibility for the western portion of the great transcontinental route was contractually assigned to BAT, the Post Office Department announced the award of the busy New York-to-Chicago route. On April 2, 1927, this route, CAM 17, was placed under contract to National Air Transport (NAT), the firm that had been successfully operating the prestigious Chicago–Dallas route, CAM 3, since May 12 of the previous year. The award to NAT was granted only after the Post Office Department had rescinded its award of CAM 17 to Charles A. Levine's North American Airways, Levine having obtained the contract through means that appeared morally, if not legally, questionable.

Clement Melville Keys, a former financial editor of *The Wall Street Journal* and an investment banker of great note, was the guiding light of NAT. Key's chairman was Howard E. Coffin and his general manager was Colonel Paul Henderson, the former second assistant postmaster general who had so effectively led the struggle to light the airways for night mail. When NAT flew its inaugural flights on CAM 17 on September 1, 1927, it used the same Curtiss Carrier Pigeons that were busy carrying the mail on its route between Dallas and Chicago. Eventually, NAT acquired 18 Douglas M–4s when they were released by the Post Office, and these versatile planes replaced the Carrier Pigeons over the Allegheny route between Chicago and New York. Frank Burnside, Harry Chandler, William C. Hobson, Leo J. McGinn, Shirley Short, and Warren D. Williams were the men who inaugurated CAM 17 for NAT.

All through the early years of commercial aviation formation in the United States the emphasis among pioneer airlines had been upon mail. However, the revenue figures of one major airline clearly show an expected trend as early air mail contracts eased their holder's growing pains. In 1926, mail pay made up 95 percent of the revenues received by those companies that later were joined together by Frederick Rentschler to form United Air Lines. By 1935, this line's passenger revenues exceeded those provided by mail contracts for the first time, and by 1950 only 8 percent of United's revenues related to the carriage of mail. These figures fail to describe, of course, the setback in passenger revenues caused by the Great Depression, a period when the fortunate holders of air mail contracts were again made acutely aware of just how important to their survival the air mail subsidies were. The setback to profitability generated by the lack of passengers in 1929 and 1930, however, proved temporary, and its essential aberrational mark related to a rash of amalgamations and link-ups that occurred as weaker organizations sold out to or teamed up with the stronger ones.

Although the government was finally out of the transportation business when it offered mail contracts to BAT and NAT on the transcontinental, its actions remained a primary factor influencing the direction of airline growth. One of the most visionary spokesmen in government as the great airlines formed was Postmaster General Walter Folger Brown, a man as interested in America's passenger lines as in its air mail lines. In his overall plan, Brown sought to shape the destinies of some airlines while keeping in mind that only responsible bidders be granted air mail contracts if, and only if, they performed their service to the best advantage of the United States government. Brown, a man appointed by President Herbert Hoover, was placed in the position of postmaster general because his views on the future of America's air transport industry were as far reaching as Hoover's and his experience in transport affairs practical and to the point.

After diligent analysis of the transport structure, Brown realized that before anything could be done, new legislation was needed. The McNary-Watres Act followed, gaining approval of Congress on April 29, 1930. Among other things it specified that there would be no competitive bidding for routes, and that selection of carriers would be based upon the discretion of the

In 1926 Shirley J. Short logged 718 accident-free hours in the air, flying in all kinds of weather and half of the time at night. For this outstanding record, he received the Harmon Trophy—the first air mail pilot to achieve this honor. Lindbergh and Eielson, both former air mail pilots, won the same trophy in 1927 and 1928.

Opposite page: A successor to Praeger, Shaughnessy and Henderson was Assistant Postmaster General W. Irving Glover, who finally implemented day/night flights on the transcontinental. Glover studies a banner proposed for all U.S. air mail fields.

postmaster general. This point was disputed and finally removed, but the end result was about the same. Smaller companies were automatically excluded from the mail service because they could not maintain the expected criteria of having flown routes of at least 250 miles at night for at least six months on a daily basis. Armed with this bill, Walter F. Brown reorganized the airline map to best accommodate both the carrier and the government. Meetings held by Brown with the heads of the airlines during the period between May 15 and June 9, 1930, were later referred to as the "Spoils Conference."

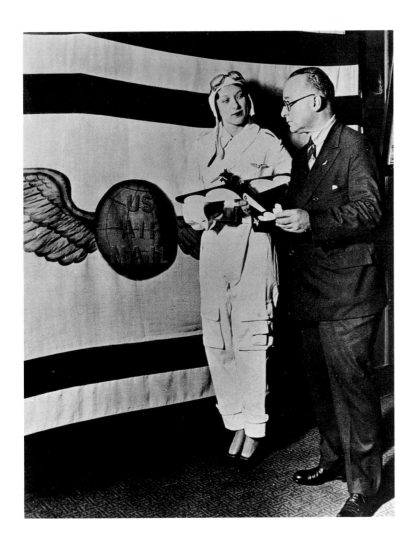

airline headed by financier C. T. Ludington, Lewis delved into the Post Office Department and airline records and soon came up with what he felt was a scandal. He fed the story to Hearst in January 1932.

By September 26, 1933, the Lewis story had its effect. A Special Committee on Investigation of the Air Mail and Ocean Mail Contracts was set up by the Senate, with Senator Hugo LaFayette Black of Alabama as chairman. A. G. Patterson was appointed special investigator. During these hearings, the Lewis documents pertaining to the spoils conferences were invoked and the jury was all too happy to find the Republican postmaster general guilty of collusion. Although found innocent and exonerated years later, Brown was deeply hurt that the strings he had pulled to make a stronger airline system and government were the same that virtually trapped him in 1934. William Boeing was so disgusted by the affair that he left the aviation business for good. The results of the Black Committee's investigation caused an irate Franklin D. Roosevelt to cancel precipitously all existing air mail contracts on February 9, 1934. By doing this, the selection of carriers would be based upon the discretion of the tenets of the Kelly Air Mail Act and its amendments were nullified. The president then turned to his Chief of the Army Air Service to carry the mail, with the well-known sad results.

Regardless of the number of committees, investigations, hearings, presidential directives, recriminations and regulations, the airline die was cast during Walter Folger Brown's incumbency. The years 1929 and 1930 witnessed the coalescence, at least in skeleton form, of the major domestic airline systems that would serve as mail carriers for the next half century. To be sure, the Roosevelt administration did decree that airlines were to be separated from aircraft manufacturers, and it announced various necessary stipulations designed to insure that fairness ruled over favoritism in the granting of air mail contracts. Nevertheless, the inflated number of participating bidders—forty-five—for the revamped contracts failed to alter greatly the basic structure that had manifested itself but a few short years earlier.

As the dust settled in 1934, United Air Lines, Inc. remained the largest airmail contractor. Three early CAM operators—Varney, Ford and Pacific Air Transport—eventually were incorporated into the United family.

Other major airlines that came into being in the 1929–30 period and survived the post-Brown upset of 1934 were Transcontinental and Western Air, Inc., known as Trans World Airlines since May of 1950; Eastern Air Transport, which came into being on January 17, 1930 under Clement M. Keys' North American Aviation group and was the predecessor company of Eastern Air Lines; and finally, American Airways, which was born early in 1930 as a result of three important mergers under a year-old

By the time Brown left office in November 1932, his dream of a cohesive air mail network was established, along with a new generation of commercial passenger airliners. America now led in aircraft technology and performance, and the aircraft were about to take to the skies.

When Roosevelt and the Democrats took office in March 1933, there was a minor investigation into the Post Office Department activities during Brown's regime, but this investigation took second place to a story by Hearst reporter Fulton Lewis. Upon hearing about the questionable loss of a contract by a small holding company known as the Aviation Corporation (AVCO) and which became American Airlines in 1934. Each of these airlines, products of old companies and new ones that evolved out of mergers, can ultimately trace its lineage back to one or more of the early air mail carriers on the first CAM routes.

As difficult as it is to unscramble the lines of connection between the plethora of small aviation companies and the larger holding companies from which the giants came, so it is difficult to follow the careers of many of the men whose energy, enterprise, and vision helped establish an aviation industry in the United States. Their names recur with frequency, but often in a strange context or an unexpected place as they moved from one employer to another, from one opportunity to the next. Yet Jack Frye and Howard Coffin, Harold Pitcairn and Cyrus R. Smith will be remembered for the tremendous impact of their work; with their colleagues, like Jack Franklin, Harris Hanshue, Sherman Fairchild, Jack Maddux, and Charles Lindbergh, these pioneers of commercial routes, these builders of the planes, these perpetrators of a great service industry will remain important names in the annals of air mail history.

During the early years of the contract air mail era, congressional committees paid impromptu visits to flying fields to inspect facilities and study operations. Garbed in ill-fitting coveralls, but with dignity preserved by omnipresent hats, this group of congressmen was engaged in such a fact-finding mission.

Pacific and Atlantic services

Once Juan Terry Trippe had inaugurated FAM 4 between Key West and Havana, the aircraft he used thereafter were the Fokker F-7 and F-10 tri-motors. As he expanded in the Caribbean, he realized that much of the route could be shortened if flights were made over water. Pan Am's chief engineer, André Priester, Dutch-born and formerly with KLM, saw the suitability of Igor Sikorsky's amphibian, the S-36, for this task. The S-36 was a 34-foot boat-shaped hull with a high upper wing and two engines suspended below it. The plane's tail surfaces were connected by twin booms converging from the trailing edge of the wing. The cabin area held eight passengers, the same as the Fokker F-7.

In 1928, a larger version of the S-36 was developed called the S-38. This amphibian had a 40-foot hull and held ten passengers. The two Pratt and Whitney Wasp engines of 400 hp were a definite improvement over their sluggish predecessors. Wheels were folded in beside the fuselage for landings on water. Charles A. Lindbergh, who became technical advisor to Pan Am in January 1929, made several survey flights in the Caribbean area in this type of plane. His first official flight for Pan Am inaugurated FAM 5 between Miami and Cristobal in the Canal Zone on February 4, 1929. He flew the 2,300-mile flight from Miami via Havana through Belize (British Honduras) to Managua and Panta Arenas (Costa Rica) and on to Cristobal. With him flew Pan Am's John Hambleton, and Henry L. Buskey, the radio operator and flight engineer.

In September 1929, Lindbergh and his co-pilot Basil Rowe flew from Havana in the S-38 along the eastern rim of the Caribbean through the Leeward and Windward Islands to the northern coast of South America. They landed at Paramaribo, (Dutch Guiana), which later became Pan Am's South American base. On this flight were Mr. and Mrs. Juan Trippe and Lindbergh's wife, Anne Morrow Lindbergh. These flights pioneered Pan American's future air mail routes.

Pressured by the necessity for faster air mail service, Trippe felt that if part of what had become known as the Lindbergh Circle was eliminated, a full day's flight time would be too. By flying directly from Puerto Cabejas in Nicaragua to Cristobal, over a thus far uncharted 1,294 miles of water, 200 miles would be saved. The inaugural flight took place on April 26, 1930 in an S-38 flying boat #NC142M carrying only mail. Pilots Lindbergh and Rowe left Miami at 3:29 P.M. with 249 pounds of mail, 520 gallons of gasoline, and radio operator Bert Denicke. Although many more survey flights were made throughout the Caribbean in Igor Sikorsky's "Ugly Duckling," it was not this small but faithful amphibian that was to hold the immortal Pan American designation of clipper. This was to come a little later. On December 20, 1929, Pan Am placed an order with Sikorsky for a four-engine aircraft able to carry forty passengers and a crew of six. Sikorsky, always a master at developing grand aircraft, larger than anything then in the air, employed some of the design features of the S-38 and developed the S-40.

Lindbergh flew the first S-40 on November 19, 1931, from Miami to the Canal Zone. Pan Am received three S-40s, then the largest civil aircraft in service, but by 1932 ordered two S-42s—a larger, more advanced amphibian. Although this twenty-ton aircraft only carried thirty-two passengers, it was faster, had greater range (750 miles greater), could carry more weight (8,060 pounds total) and was more comfortable than its antecedents. The S-42s, powered by four Pratt and Whitney Hornets, went into service on August 15, 1934, on the Miami to Rio de Janeiro route, after breaking several international records for flying boats in the fields of altitude, payload, and speed during the trials. With an aerial counterpart of the great nineteenth-century clipper ships in his possession at last, Juan Trippe turned with eagerness toward the waiting oceans.

Logic decreed that Trippe and Lindbergh would consider the Atlantic Ocean as a place to start. And indeed, Charles and Anne Lindbergh departed from Flushing Bay, New York on July 9, 1933, in their custom-built Lockheed Sirius for an Atlantic survey. They returned from the long flight of over 30,000 miles on December 19. Meanwhile, hedging his company against any problems with the Atlantic route, Juan Trippe had been busy laying steps for his secondary goal, a Pacific route to the Orient. In support of this effort, the Lindberghs in 1931 had made a survey flight in their Sirius from New York to China, flying through Nome, Alaska, the northwest part of Siberia, the Kurile Islands, and Japan. Unfortunately, this route had to be abandoned when Russia would not allow American aircraft to use any Soviet bases. Hardly disconcerted, Trippe reverted to an island-hopping route of United States owned territories. William Grooch, formerly New York, Rio, and Buenos Aires (NYRBA) Line's chief pilot, led a party of 118 workers to begin setting up landing bases on the islands of Hawaii, Midway, Wake and Guam, and at Manila in the Philippines.

For a number of reasons Juan Trippe's secondary goal gradually became his primary one. The essential reasons for this reordering—Atlantic priorities receding into the background until the late thirties—related to the lack of British cooperation in terms of North Atlantic landing rights and the burgeoning of world interest in Far Eastern commercial attractions in the pre-World War II era. In 1935, the United States simply could not afford to be three weeks away by ocean steamer from rich Asiatic markets. Thus it was that a 9,100 mile ocean highway from Alameda to Hong Kong became a reality even before the 3,400 mile airlane linking London with New York.

Pan Am, early in 1935, refitted one of its Sikorsky S-42s into a long range survey aircraft, giving it a range of 3,000 miles. On March 23 it flew in sweeping archs from Miami to the Virgin Islands and back nonstop, covering a distance of 2,500 miles. From here it was ferried to Pan Am's newly-formed Pacific Divisional Headquarters in Alameda on the edge of San Francisco Bay. On April 16 the S-42 *Pan American Clipper* began its first round-trip survey flight to Honolulu from Alameda with Captain Edwin C. Musick, Pan Am's chief pilot, in command. On June 12, 1935, with Musick again at the controls, the Honolulu–Midway sector witnessed a trial flight and this was followed on August 9 and October 5 by experimental flights to Midway–Wake and Wake–Guam respectively. Upon returning to San Francisco from Guam, Pan American Airways was assured of its transpacific (San Francisco to Manila) FAM 14, contract which had first been advertised in August of 1935. It had been clear from the outset that Pan Am would be the only company able to fulfill the contract.

While the world was on its way to becoming substantially smaller by virtue of Pan American's pioneer efforts, the challenges of transocean flight became infinitely clearer. It was natural that the airline would consider every available aircraft in order to utilize the very best plane. André Priester's watchword was safety. On its flight deck five men of a Pan American crew of

190

eight would know how to fly, navigate, and operate its radio as well as its engines. Mechanics had to be able to reach every foot of fuel line or make in-flight repairs on any of its power plants. When the airline let it be known in 1931 that its expansion path would require a long-range flying boat, the announced specifications were precise, demanding, and thorough.

Eventually only two companies submitted bids. Sikorsky came forward with its S-42, and the Glenn L. Martin Company of Baltimore responded with the details of their proposed M-130. In the end it became clear that the Martin flying boat incorporated the best features offered by the S-42 plus additional advantages, including a slightly greater cruising speed and an 800-mile greater range. Trippe ordered three M-130s from the Martin Company. NC14716, nicknamed Sweet Sixteen by Martin personnel, proved to be the first Martin delivered to Pan American in October 1935. Immediately christened *China Clipper*, this plane was destined to fly the historic first scheduled air mail flight across the Pacific on November 22, 1935.

Among the dignitaries gathered at Alameda for the inaugural flight to Manila were Juan Trippe and Postmaster General James A. Farley. The most widely broadcast aeronautical event (until America's Apollo 11 moon-landing reportage in 1969), the *China Clipper*'s departure was listened to by millions across the country. All heard the announcer say that "this vast Pacific

Souvenir mail was carried on Pan American's Pacific survey
flights to simulate load conditions and to provide publicity in
advance of mail route openings. The top cover, signed by Captain
Musick made the round-trip to Honolulu in April of 1935, while the
lower one went as far as Wake Island in the third survey flight.
Captain R.O.D. Sullivan flew and signed this cover for Juan Trippe.
The U.S. Clipper stamp, designed by Alvin R. Meissner, was
prepared for November inaugurals. Letter rates (per ½ ounce) were
25¢ to Hawaii, 50¢ to Guam and 75¢ to Manila.

Opposite: With Chief Pilot Edwin C. Musick at the controls, the
Sikorsky S-42 Pan American Clipper wings its way westward on
the first of several Pacific route survey flights. This April 16, 1935,
flight will go as far as Honolulu. The plane is seen over a great new
Golden Gate bridge, then under construction.

Ocean at our feet (has) stood as an unconquerable barrier between the east and the west. Now at long last, this barrier is to be
no more. On the wings of these sturdy Clipper Ships are pinned
the hopes of America's commerce for a rightful standing in the
teeming markets of the Orient. In no other section of the United
States is that feeling more keen than here on the Pacific coast, the
Orient's nearest neighbor.

"Along the catwalk, now, seven uniformed figures—in navy
blue, with white visored caps—Pan American's colors, are moving along the narrow catwalk to the front hatch of the giant
airliner. There is little excitement about them. They are the
flight officers of the *China Clipper*, the winged pioneers about to
set out on an ocean's conquest." Then the commentator announced the names of the crew one by one. First aboard was R.
O. D. Sullivan, first officer, the man who commanded the final
two S-42 survey flights to Wake and Guam. He was followed by
Fred Noonan, navigation officer; George King, an ocean pilot in
training; C. D. Wright and Victor Wright, first and second engineering officers (not related to each other); and by William
Jarboe, the radio officer. The last one aboard was Edwin C.
Musick, Pan American's chief pilot and captain of the *China
Clipper*.

"Seven men in the crew," said the radio announcer. "And
what a crew! Five of those seven are transport pilots. Three of

them registered aeronautical engineers. Three of them licensed radio officers. Two of them are Master Mariners, and two others have their navigator's papers. That will give you some idea of the preparation behind America's conquest of an ocean!"

Shortly before the *China Clipper*'s engines turned over, Juan Trippe was in radio contact with his flight crew:

"Stand by all stations," he requested. Then turning to a gentleman standing nearby, he said, "Postmaster General Farley, I have the honor to report, sir, that the transpacific airway is ready to inaugurate air mail service of the United States Post Office from the mainland across the Pacific to the Philippines, by way of Hawaii, Midway, Wake, and Guam Islands."

"Mr. Trippe," responded Farley, "it is an honor and a privilege for me, as Postmaster General of the United States of America, to hereby order the inauguration of the first scheduled service on Foreign Air Mail Route Number Fourteen at 3:28 P.M., Pacific Standard Time, on this day which will forever mark a new chapter in the glorious history of our nation...a new era in world transportation...a new and binding bond that will link, for the first time in history, the people of the east and the west."

President Juan Trippe then ordered, "Captain Musick...you have your sailing orders. Cast off and depart for Manila in accordance therewith."

When the *China Clipper* took off at 3:46 P.M. on November 22, she carried a total of 1,837 pounds of mail in 58 mail bags, 110,865 letters in all, of which 46,561 were to be left at Honolulu; 19,958 at Guam; and 44,346 letters at Manila. On the day of the inaugural flight, 206,414 copies of a brand new twenty-five-cent blue air mail were sold. Designed especially for use on the transpacific route, it bore the legend "November 1935," centered above a head-on depiction of the *China Clipper*. The government of the Philippines overprinted two stamps especially for the return mail flight. Both the Philippine and United States Post Offices authorized special cachets for this momentous occasion.

Luck and skill rode with the crew on this flight. The initial entry in the crew-maintained log seemed to set the tone for the entire journey to Manila: "The Pacific welcomed the first modern Clipper bound for the Orient with a blazing sunset. Day passes into night with unmatched swiftness over the ocean, and before a final flying check was made by all officers, we were swallowed by darkness. No stars were visible through the ceiling of clouds above. A solid floor of clouds two thousand feet below closed out the sea.... The radium-painted dials on the 197 flight and engine instruments glow eerily.... Through the portholes the blue flames off the outboard engines's exhaust flash out into pitch blackness." On November 29, after a safe and easy journey of 8,210 miles, accomplished in just under 60 hours of

192

Ceremonies preceding the China Clipper's departure for the Far East on November 22, 1935 were broadcast across the nation to a thrilled audience. Participating in the formal departure are Postmaster General James A. Farley and Juan Terry Trippe of Pan American. After 59 hours and 48 minutes of flying time, Captain Musick and First Officer Sullivan (on ramp beside plane) will set the big Martin M-130 down safely in Manila Bay.

actual flying time, Musick settled the *Clipper* gently on the waters of Manila Bay, bringing to an end an initial effort to complete air mail linkage of the entire world.

On the return flight, which arrived back in San Francisco on December 6, more than 79,000 letters were delivered to postal handlers at Alameda. Actually, a total of 1,789 pounds of mail were carried in 49 bags, but many of the letters were for Guam and Honolulu. While *China Clipper* (NC14716) was en route to the Orient, NC14715, the second Martin M-130, called *Philippine Clipper*, was delivered. The last Martin flying boat ordered, NC14714, the *Hawaii Clipper*, arrived on the coast on December 24, 1935, ready for service.

On October 21, 1936, using the *Hawaii Clipper*, Pan American began carrying passengers along with the mail on regularly scheduled flights to the Far East. At the end of a full year of flying on FAM 14, the Martin Clippers had flown 2,731,312 miles, carried 1,986 passengers and more than 500,000 pounds of cargo, a good portion of which was air mail. On April 21, 1937, the first extension of this route occurred when Pan Am carried mail on beyond Manila to Hong Kong and Macao, the first air mail connections between the United States and mainland China.

Coincidentally, on November 22, 1935, the same day that the Clippers initiated regular service to the Far East from San Francisco, the government of New Zealand approved the landing of Pan American flying boats at Auckland. After overseeing the welcome addition of passengers on the transpacific route in 1936, Captain Edwin C. Musick turned his attention to surveys of a possible route to New Zealand via Hawaii, Kingman Reef and Pago Pago, American Samoa. Musick completed a successful first survey flight over this projected route in April 1937, having flown a Sikorsky S-42B (registration NC16734) since the M-130s were still employed on FAM 14. Tragically, Musick and his entire crew were lost in the same S-42B, *Pan American Clipper II* renamed by then *Samoan Clipper*, on January 11 of the following year during a return flight to Auckland. The Clipper disappeared a short time after departing Pago Pago enroute to New Zealand. Several months later a second tragedy struck Pan American's Pacific forces when the *Hawaii Clipper* was lost without a trace while flying passengers and mail between Guam and Manila. Captain Leo Terlatzky, his crew, and passengers and mail were never heard from again. The high cost of building the FAM routes seemed reminiscent of earlier days on the CAMs.

With the tragic loss of Edwin Musick and two crews of its missing aircraft, Pan Am faced a depressing year. Also, with the small payload of the Martins, the maintenance costs of the islands, the crews for the planes on each island, and a fixed air

Postmaster General Farley handles a few of the total of 58 mail bags at Alameda, prior to the transpacific inaugural flight of 1935. Those mail bags contained over 110,000 letters, many sporting one or more of the new 25¢ airmails. An almost equal number of letters were transported across the Atlantic, when in 1939 Pan American also pioneered the first regular transatlantic service.

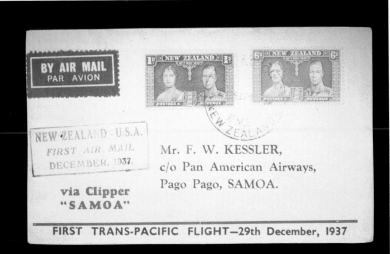

mail rate of $2.00 per mile, the airline was losing money. After Musick's disappearance at sea, the proposed mail flights to New Zealand were suspended and not resumed for almost two and a half years. After the Civil Aeronautics Act was passed in 1938, the mail rate was increased to $3.35 per mile, effective April 1, 1939. Then new survey flights to Auckland via Canton Island and Noumea were conducted in August and November of 1939. A route certificate was granted on June 7, 1940, and the first air mail flight to Auckland left San Francisco on July 12, 1940. The aircraft used was the *American Clipper* (NC18606), a new Boeing 314, which had twice the power of the M-130s and carried 74 passengers on short hops. Pan American had received its first Boeing on January 27, 1939. By July 12, 1940, the date of the New Zealand inaugural flight under the direction of Captain

John H. Tilton, the airline was granted FAM 19, a route which left San Francisco for Los Angeles, advancing to Honolulu, Canton Island, and Noumea, and finally Auckland. Almost 100,000 letters were aboard on the inaugural flight. After November 5, 1941, the route was shortened when the British consented to have Pan American land at Suva, Fiji. Within a month, the United States would be at war with Japan and not able to fly the route again for civilian purposes until February 21, 1947, when FAM 19 was extended well beyond Auckland to Sydney, Australia.

With the Pacific largely under the wings of his Clippers, Juan Trippe turned once again to the Atlantic. On February 22, 1937, the British government authorized Pan American clearance on a North Atlantic air service to London, but only in cooperation

194

An air mail network spans the Earth. Far left: *Two Pacific flight covers—the top one carried to Manila on the China Clipper's epic flight of November, 1935, displays the official FAM 14 cachet and Juan Trippe's signature. The lower one was carried on Captain Edwin Musick's final mail flight in the Samoan Clipper on New Year's Day, 1938. Near left: A pilot-signed cover from the first regular air mail between U.S.A. and Europe. Franked by a new U.S. 30¢ airmail intended for transatlantic use, the cover displays an official FAM 18 cachet. China National Aviation Corporation, formed in 1930 with U.S. backing, transported the lower first-flight cover in April, 1931. The Australian cover (below) represents a new over-water connection as does the 1947 Swiss airmail, valid only for a single flight.*

with Imperial Airlines. Pan Am also received operating rights from France on January 17, 1939, and in February the Portuguese opened up Lisbon and the Azores for the airline's operations. Mrs. Franklin D. Roosevelt christened Pan Am's first Boeing 314, the *Yankee Clipper* (NC18603) and on March 26, the four-engined flying boat made its first transatlantic flight. The actual certificate giving Pan Am permission to fly the North Atlantic route was issued by the Civil Aeronautics Authority on May 17, 1939. On May 20, the twelfth anniversary of Charles A. Lindbergh's solo transatlantic flight, *Yankee Clipper* flew America's—and the world's—first heavier-than-air regularly scheduled transatlantic air mail service. Commanding the Clipper was Captain A. E. LaPorte, who made the flight in less than 29 hours, with stops in the Azores and Lisbon. On the twenty-second, the *Yankee Clipper* landed in the Mediterranean near Marseilles, France. The total weight of the 112,574 first-flight covers carried was slightly under one ton.

The following month, on June 24, Captain Harold E. Gray opened the northern route, which hitherto had been closed by the British who had insisted upon reciprocal flights to America with Imperial Airways. Realizing that their Empire Flying Boats were no match for the long transatlantic route yet, the British nonetheless gave Pan American a warm welcome after the flight from America to Southhampton by way of Shediac, New Brunswick; Botwood, Newfoundland; and Foynes, Ireland. The amount of mail carried on this flight of the *Yankee Clipper* slightly outweighed LaPorte's earlier cargo as 121,380 letters and postcards were off-loaded in England.

The *Dixie Clipper* (NC18605), a second Boeing 314, was given the honor of being the first heavier-than-air craft to inaugurate passenger service between Europe and America. On June 28, 1939, Captain R. O. D. Sullivan, the late Edwin C. Musick's first officer in 1935 and now commander of the *Dixie Clipper*, opened up the first transatlantic passenger service when he flew twenty-two people to Europe via the southern route. On July 8, *Yankee Clipper* opened the northern route to passengers when it carried seventeen individuals at a fare of $375 one-way, $675 round-trip.

Unfortunately, the advent of World War II blocked any extension of the commercial trail-blazing of the advanced Boeing flying boats, and by the time commercial flights were resumed in 1946, long-range, land-based aircraft technology had evolved to the point of making obsolete the slower, water-dependent Clippers. Nevertheless, it was their effectiveness in the days of the magnificent and awesome flying boats that allowed Pan American Airways to move to the forefront of international carriers in twelve short years and to gain and enjoy its worldwide influence and prestige.

7

Toward
new horizons

Short-haul air mail In the late 1930's one memorable focus of the air mail enterprise in the U.S. related to the problem posed by smallness—the problem of "in between" cities or towns and the rural communities. Would not air mail benefit commerce in these areas as well? In 1938 only 210 cities of the more than 4,000 with a population of over 5,000 inhabitants were part of the commercial air network in the United States.

Therefore, in the spring of 1938 Congress, with President Roosevelt's full approval, authorized the creation of two experimental air mail routes to see what kind of daily air mail service could be offered to the smaller cities.

The brightest prospect centered upon a unique nonstop pick-up and delivery method dreamed up by Dr. Lytle S. Adams, a clever medical practitioner from Irwin, Pennsylvania.

More complex than it might seem on the surface, and twelve years in development, the *Adams air mail pick-up system* enabled a small airplane, flying close to the ground, to latch on to a mail bag suspended between two tall poles set 60 feet apart, picking it up without an interruption in the progess of the plane. In the instant before picking up the bag of outgoing mail, an incoming bag of mail was dropped from the gliding aircraft. An intricate set of pulleys and shock absorbers guided the pick-up mechanism. Great care was taken to build safety features into the system.

When bids were solicited for two experimental routes, only one company responded—All American Aviation, Inc. of Wilmington, Delaware—and the firm eventually received the contract. All American, headed by Richard C. duPont, named Dr. Lytle S. Adams a vice president. The company's first task was to sell various communities along the proposed routes on the idea of participating for a year at a cost to them of $450—about $150 for installation of the ground equipment and a $300 contribution to the salary of a ground attendant. After a community had agreed to cooperate, town officials and All American Aviation would search out the best drop-off and pick-up site at that location.

All American decided to use single-engine, gull-wing SR-10F Stinson *Reliants* on its two routes. Passenger seats had been removed from the planes, making space for specially-made mail containers. Each plane would be manned by a pilot and a winch operator and would trail a wooden pole with a grappling hook. This hook was attached to a cable for the pick-up and to a rope leading to the container of mail to be left behind.

When operations began on the two pick-up service routes in May of 1939, fifty-five communities between Huntingdon, West Virginia and Philadelphia, Pennsylvania, were included in the "Star Route" system. Pittsburgh was the terminus for each of the routes and the geographical center of the system. The route

197

running north and east from Pittsburgh to Philadelphia via Wilmington was designated Air Mail Route #1001. Route #1002 involved 28 pick-up points and ran generally in a south-westerly direction from Pittsburgh to Huntingdon.

Public interest in the experiment was high, and newspapers were filled with the details of inaugural flights on opening day, May 12th. About 100,000 pieces of mail—including many cacheted souvenir first-flight letters—were transported in the seven weeks required to bring all 55 towns into service on Routes 1001 and 1002. Until commercial feeder airlines were prepared to serve small cities in the United States, the All American Aviation mail pick-up system devised by the doctor-dentist from Pennsylvania continued to perform with distinction.

Another answer to the "short haul" need, as transport aviation's microcosmic origins were lost amidst the macrocosmic intricacies of a full-blown transportation network in the United States, involved commercial uses of *rotary-winged aircraft*. One pre-war venture in the Philadelphia area featured the autogiro; several post-war enterprises centered around the helicopter's short-haul capabilities. In each case, the transport of mail was the initial purpose. Unfortunately, since the planned routes traversed densely populated urban areas, noise and safety factors presented severe problems.

Pilot John M. Miller, limited to 150 pounds of mail per flight, made on July 6, 1939 three autogiro flights with inaugural covers such as this one. On this short-lived experimental route, Eastern Air Lines, Inc. contracted for five flights daily.

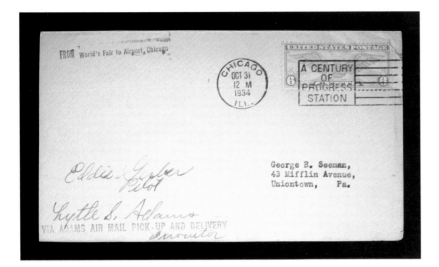

Before Adams' air mail pick-up and delivery system officially began service between Huntington, W.Va. and Philadelphia, it was demonstrated publicly on many occasions. This cover, signed by inventor Adams and pilot Gerber, was lifted in a Braniff Airways plane in 1934 from the Chicago World's Fair Lagoon and carried experimentally to the city's main airport.

This cover, signed by New York Postmaster Albert Goldman, was flown on the first day of a new 5¢ air mail rate October 1, 1946. As the cachet indicates, it was also serviced aboard a demonstration flight of a flying "mailcar" to test the feasibility of processing long-distance air mail in flight.

On July 6, 1939, Eastern Air Lines and Pilot John M. Miller inaugurated the world's first scheduled rotary-winged service of air mail, transferring mail in both directions between Philadelphia's main post office and the region's primary airport at Camden, New Jersey. On that day bold letters printed on the sides of the Kellett KD-1B autogiro called attention to this unique air-mail route. The effort survived for about a year, but failed to survive an accident which saw one autogiro plummet from the post-office roof to the street below.

Following World War II, similar ventures to carry mail by *helicopter* originated in the metropolitan centers of Los Angeles, Chicago and New York. Between July 1946 and May 1947, United Air Lines undertook a series of brief trials with the Sikorsky S-51 helicopter, intending to move mail on five separate routes extending outward from Midway Airport near Chicago and touching thirty-two suburban locations. However, this operation foundered for economic reasons and was abandoned.

In 1944, long before United began its demonstration flights, the Post Office Department was already considering Los Angeles as the site of an experimental helicopter air mail service. Los Angeles Airways (LAA) was founded on May 11, 1944 by a group of businessmen from Los Angeles. They applied for a temporary three-year experimental certificate to carry local mail and received it on May 22, 1947.

On October 1, 1947, Igor Sikorsky was on hand to witness the first regularly scheduled helicopter air mail service, which employed his S-51. With him was LAA's president Clarence M. Belinn, who devised a route shaped like four spokes emanating from the central hub of Los Angeles International Airport. These airlanes terminated at the downtown post office, San Fernando Valley, San Bernardino, and Newport Beach—all within a sixty-mile radius of the airport. By July 1948, LAA's helicopter service was carrying passengers on route extensions circling the Los Angeles point of origin.

When United abandoned helicopter service in Chicago in 1947, Helicopter Air Services (HAS) of Chicago took up the projected flights from August 20, 1949. HAS used six Bell 47D helicopters on their shuttle route between Midway Airport and the Chicago Post Office. Later that year, fifty-four post offices on three circular routes were being serviced within a fifty-mile radius of Chicago.

By 1952, the third helicopter operation was established in New York. On July 8th, New York Airways began an inter-airport service using Sikorsky S-55's. Besides carrying mail as the others did, NYA also carried passengers—to New Brunswick, Princeton and Trenton, New Jersey.

Adams air mail pick-up device

The Adams air mail pick-up system permitted between 1929 and 1939 All American Aviation to provide successful air mail service to various small cities in east-central United States. This method required one ground attendant in each city served. The attendant would place out-going mail in a shockproof container before attaching the container to a rope line for pick-up. The A.A.A. pilots, using Stinson SR-10F aircraft, were eventually able to perform the in-flight pick-ups and deliveries at a speed of 100 mph. Early-developed shock absorbing equipment was later replaced by an electrically operated winch device which absorbed the shock of attachment more efficiently.
A pick-up plane and ground-rig are preserved in the National Air and Space Museum.

Flying mail car

Following World War II the U.S. domestic air mail rate was reduced from 8¢ to 5¢. Desiring to publicize the new rate and anticipating heavy air mail volume, postal officials arranged to have TWA, American and United Airlines test the feasibility of sorting mail in flight. Accordingly, on Tuesday, October 1, 1946, the first day of the new rate, United made its test, using a converted army Fairchild "Packet" cargo plane on an all-mail flight from New York (La Guardia) to San Francisco. The Packet's huge cargo hold was transformed into a mail processing station and three P.O. superintendents were aboard to sort the mail. Powered by two Pratt & Whitney 2,100 hp engines, the all-mail plane could carry an 18,000 pound payload. TWA made its all-mail flights on September 25 and 26, using a converted DC-4 airliner.

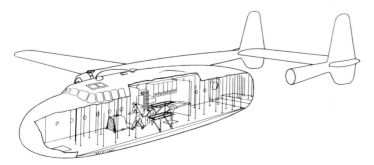

1939-1969

Global routes, giant loads At the other end of the spectrum from the short-range, rotary-wing aircraft were *the jets*—remarkable long-distance planes that were a spin-off of pre-World War II aeronautical technology. Surprisingly early, the first flight of a jet-propelled aircraft took place in Germany one of the Ernst Heinkel's He 178's took to the air on the 27th of August, 1939. Hardly anyone outside of Germany, however, knew of this flight until the war's end. Thus jet know-how seemed to emerge in 1945.

Actually, the origins of this new concept in speed had begun in Great Britain with the experiments of Sir (then Pilot Officer) Frank Whittle. In 1928 he recognized the limitations of the propeller-driven, piston-engined aircraft and began testing a reaction-propelled engine, which he patented in 1930. By April 1937 Whittle had completed the world's first turbojet, and the Air Ministry began to look more closely at the ideas of this young officer. They gave him a contract to develop a revolutionary new aircraft engine. In a cooperation between Whittle and the Gloster Aircraft Company, the Gloster E-28/39 experimental jet aircraft was built, and flown on May 15, 1941, almost two years after the Heinkel had flown in Germany.

During the war, other countries experimented with jet propulsion. In Italy, during 1939, Secondo Campini built a jet prototype under the auspices of the Caproni manufacturers. The Caproni-Campini CC.2 was tested by Mario de Bernardi (of early air-mail fame) on August 28, 1940, but proved to be ineffectual. Americans were working on a similar project in 1941, and through the Durand Committee contracts for the development of a jet-type engine were issued to Westinghouse, General Electric, Allis-Chalmers and Northrop.

Already looking to the future of aviation, Lord Brabazon, Great Britain's chairman of Aircraft Production, set up plans during 1942–43 for the post-war production of a jet-propelled, mail-carrying civil transport to cross the Atlantic Ocean. When the concept changed from that of a transport to a passenger carrier, experiments were made with the DH.106 prototype design in which four de Havilland Ghost turbo-jets were enclosed within the leading edges of the wings. This new swept-wing advancement was given the name *Comet* (reusing the name of the Mac Robertson race winner of 1934), and it made its first flight at speeds up to 490 mph, on July 27, 1949. British Overseas Airways Corporation (BOAC) placed an advance order for the *Comet* as early as October 1946 and on May 2, 1952, inaugurated the world's first scheduled jet passenger service, operating on routes throughout the Empire.

202

In September of 1950, Bill Allen, President of Boeing, and designer Maynard Pennell witnessed the power of the Comet at the Farnborough Air Show. They felt at that time they could

With the Douglas DC-7C and Lockheed L.1649A aircraft, Pan American and T.W.A. were able to join Scandinavian Airlines System and Canadian Pacific Airlines on the trans-polar route between Europe and California. This cover made the first Pan Am trans-polar flight from Paris in 1957.

Japan Air Lines, formed in 1951 and reorganized in 1953, overcame many post-war hurdles to advance to a high ranking position among international air carriers. As early as 1954, using converted DC-6As, J.A.L. established weekly service between Tokyo and San Francisco. This cover was carried on later J.A.L.'s Tokyo-Los Angeles inaugural flight.

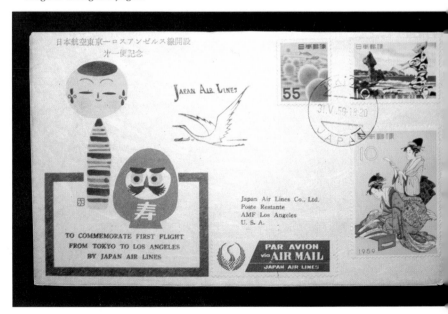

Pan American introduced the Boeing 707 on international runs in
October, 1958. Powered by four Pratt & Whitney JT3C-6 turbojet
engines, the revolutionary jets immediately slashed flying times
almost in half, cruising at 570 mph with a 46,153 lb. payload. Now
all-cargo "Jumbo" jets carry an astounding 100 tons.

build a competitive jet airliner, and on May 16, 1952 they
formally initiated the project. Allen believed that by using
newly developed Pratt & Whitney JT3 jet engines, and having
the support of a government subsidy, he could produce a jet
which could make a direct trans-Atlantic flight—something the
Comet could not then achieve. The new aircraft, designated the
Boeing 707, became America's first jet—capable of carrying 179
passengers at 600 miles per hour. The 707 was flown for the first
time on July 15, 1954, exactly two months after its rollout debut.

On October 13, 1955, Pan American Airways, still the world's
largest international airline, announced the purchase of twenty
Boeing 707's and twenty-five Douglas DC8's, the first jet-liner
developed by the merged McDonnell and Douglas Aircraft
Companies. While the jets were being readied, an intermediate
aircraft came to prominence—the turbo-prop. Turbo-prop
engines were a positive economical note for the air carriers,
since they were a step up in power from the piston engine and
obtained superior cruising speeds wherever employed. The
Vickers Viscount, Bristol's Britannia, Lockheed's Electra, and
the Russian Ilyushin IL-18 were among the turbo-prop airliners
that served the airlines well even after the long-range jets came
into use. All of these planes were designed as passenger transports with passenger comforts in mind, but they also flew the
mail and freight for a decade, beginning in the mid-nineteen-
fifties.

When a new Pratt & Whitney jet engine (the JT3C-6) was

completed and fitted to the Boeing 707-120, Juan Trippe and Pan
American were prepared to span the Atlantic. The inaugural
transatlantic jet service honors did not go to Pan American,
however. Fittingly, the de Havilland Comet 4 of BOAC achieved
that honor three weeks prior to Pan Am's flight of October 26,
1958. From the time in 1954 when the Comet 1 was taken from
the air after two fatal crashes until October 1958, when it
returned and achieved the first transatlantic jet flight, Russia's
Aeroflot Tu-104 was the only regularly scheduled jet transport
service operating anywhere in the world. A. N. Tupolev, like
Igor Sikorsky, was a believer in giant aircraft and this factor led
to the creation in December 1968 of the Russian Tu-144, the
world's first supersonic transport.

Pointing the way to the supersonic age were a string of short-
haul and medium-range jets produced by firms like British Aircraft, Boeing and McDonnell-Douglas, and the long-range
Jumbo or wide-body jets that came into being when Pan American placed an order in April 1966 for twenty-five aircraft "to
accommodate up to 450 passengers." The Jumbo jets were the
epitome of speed and comfort. They helped provide an answer
to the high operating costs the airlines faced in the early 1970's.
Boeing's 747 first flew shortly before man's first moon landing,
the maiden flight of the 747 taking place on February 19, 1969.
By January of 1970 the giant plane, with a range of 4,600 miles
and a maximum payload of 199,500 pounds, was ready to be
placed in service by Pan American.

1959

Faster than sound Today's generations have been raised in the aura of previously unimagined scientific exploration, science-fiction and space flight. Small wonder then that a popular, though necessarily small, area of specialization in aerophilately's broad province concerns *rocket mail*. Happily, this on-going story has been carefully recorded in the *Ellington-Zwisler Rocket Mail Catalogue*, a two-volume work published in the United States by the American Air Mail Society.

Though many nations have engaged in experimentation with rockets and rocket flight, most of the credit for the development of early rocket technology must be given to German engineers and mathematicians. How early their interest developed can be seen in the title of an article by Heinrich von Kleist, the editor of *Berliner Abendblätter*, that appeared on October 10, 1810—"Primary Thoughts About Mortar Mail." The military use as suggested in the von Kleist text involved propelling official messages from one artillery position to another through the use of hollow shells filled with letters and/or dispatches of a critical nature.

While America had its aerospace pioneer in Robert H. Goddard, who launched a ten-foot rocket as early as March 8, 1926, and who envisioned interplanetary travel by virtue of his tentative successes with liquid hydrogen and oxygen propellants,

most rocket development work took place in Austria and Germany. Beginning in 1931, Austrian rocketeer Friedrich Schmiedl sent hundreds of letters through the air in his solid-propellant rockets at the same time that Reinhold Tilling was firing off mail-carrying rockets in northern Germany. Gerhard Zucker, another pioneer, unsuccessfully attempted a rocket mail carry over a stretch of water between the islands of Harris and Scarp off Scotland's west coast in 1934.

When Dr. Willy Ley emigrated to America from Germany in 1935, his rocketry experiments continued. In February of the next year two small rocket planes were launched from Greenwood Lake, New York under his supervision. Neither was a complete success. One lost its wings in 15 seconds, and the other fell spinning to the ground after reaching 1,000 feet. Nevertheless, at least some of the 6,146 pieces of mail they carried landed across the state border in New Jersey, were retrieved, and were passed on to the U.S. Post Office there at Hewitt. Later the same year international rocket mail was tried for apparently the first time. A private venture in Texas sent a mail rocket over the Rio Grande from McAllen to the town of Reynosa, Mexico. Mexican officials stubbornly refused to release this mail for many years, being much aggrieved because the rocket struck a building on its descent to earth.

First supersonic transport to fly successfully, the Russian Tupolev TU-144 (left) became airborne on December 31, 1968, and was in cargo service between Moscow and Alma-Ata seven years later. Sporting the same "droop-snoot" front fuselage for landing and take-off, the more familiar British/French Concorde (above) inaugurated SST passenger service in January, 1976 between Paris and Rio de Janeiro. Cruising speeds of both craft exceed 1,450 mph.

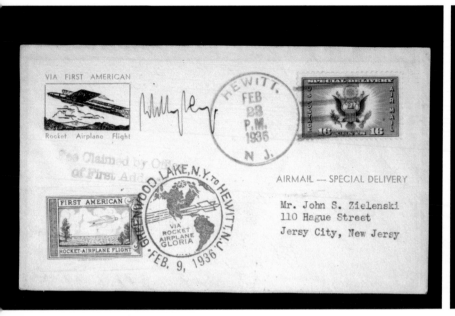

A specimen of the early rocket mail experimental flight of February 1936 at Greenwood Lake. This cover displays a printed cachet (upper left corner), a rocket label of private origin, a rubber-stamp cachet and Willy Ley's signature. Franking is provided by the U.S. Air Mail-Special Delivery issue of 1934.

The 40th anniversary of the world's first jet flight by a Heinkel He-178 is commemorated by this German cover from 1979. Featuring an artist's rendition of that historic achievement, the cover also reports a commemorative flight by German Air Force pilots.

After World War II, air intake rockets were made rather than the more expensive liquid-propelled or solid-fuel rockets. The United States' first official missile mail was carried on June 8, 1959. A Regulus I guided missile was launched from the submarine *Barbero*, off the Florida coast, to the Naval Auxiliary Air Station at Mayport. Twenty-one minutes after launching, at 9:31 a.m., Postmaster General Arthur E. Summerfield was holding delivered mail. The 3,000 letters with the "First Official Missile-Mail–U.S. Post Office Department" catchet were cancelled with the date and *U.S.S. Barbero* stamped onto each cover.

Today missile air mail service still seems unlikely to become an everyday occurance. The cost of manufacturing rockets has far outweighed the profit potential, and the rapid development of conventional air transport modes has made any advantage gained by missile mail altogether slight. Perhaps an era of orbiting space stations will bring missile mail to the fore in service of a united planetary civilization.

One of the most thoroughly documented events in all of aviation history has been the development, test program, and intro-

duction into commercial service of supersonic transport (SST) planes produced by Russia and by the cooperative effort of British and French companies that brought forth the Concorde. When Russia's Tu-144 inaugurated the world's first commercial supersonic service on December 26, 1975, and carried its first passengers over the same route between Moscow to Alma-Ata on November 1, 1977 (a journey of about 2,000 miles) the world was led into a new unity. Those inclined toward aerophilatelic pursuits were introduced to a dazzling new avenue of collecting down which their interests could entice them, for although very few countries have been involved in operating these swiftest of commercial carriers, there has been no dearth of SST philatelic offerings.

Enough material exists now for the classification and listing process to have begun in earnest. And what had been suspected all along now seems confirmed—very few SST covers have been flown as official mail. Overwhelmingly, the greatest amount of supersonic-related materials fall into the souvenir category—material flown to be sure, but carried aboard by a courier and flown as baggage rather than being flown and carried as part of

A cover that commemorates a first flight of the British Concorde from Singapore to London in December 1977. Like most Concorde covers, this one went non-postally by courier.

an officially authorized carry of mail. Even covers officially authorized by the airlines, and officially stamped before take-off, and officially dated upon arrival, still fall outside the category of "mail." Nevertheless, interesting collections are now being assembled, and the record of specific flights and significant milestones of the SST era is being preserved with bona fide air mail covers as well as with commercially prepared souvenir covers.

SST flights that have attracted great interest include the first official international flight with passengers (Paris to Rio de Janeiro on January 21st, 1976), the first flights to Washington and New York (May 24, 1976 and November 22, 1977 respectively), and the first international interchange flights (which saw Braniff International fly two Concordes, with the cooperation of British Airways and Air France, over domestic United States routes to Dallas-Fort Worth—January 12, 1979). Although no fewer than 150,000 covers were flown as official mail on the first commercial flight into Rio de Janeiro in January of 1976, it is generally the case that early Concorde material is already scarce and obtaining high prices in postal history auctions.

Middle value of a 3-stamp British series commemorating the Concorde's first flight at Toulouse, France March 1, 1969. Issued 3/3/'69, this stamp displays both French and British flags.

207

Mail in space

Philately is one hobby that serves as an effective mirror of mankind's story, even that part of history that has yet to be assimilated by a majority of people. Nowhere is this mirroring dimension more evident than in the topical area of *space*.

It is not that space collections are replete with covers that have left the gravitational pull of earth and flown on distant missions. The very opposite is true. Philatelic space collections, except in rare instances, contain no flown covers. Prevalent are unflown souvenir covers that act as reminders of particular events.

Flown space covers are symbolic evidences of a great leap in consciousness that was attendant with Armstrong and Aldrin's landing on the lunar surface in July of 1969. As such, these covers continue to confirm the cultural importance of philately. Recognition of philately's status is also part of the "official" record. Is it not significant that in many of the Apollo landing modules, where storage room and weight were understandably at a critical premium, a place was found for stamped envelopes and cancelling equipment? It was as though NASA administrators recognized that moon shots needed to be remembered not only as exploratory ventures, but also as trail-blazing stages of a new communications network that would someday transcend present limits.

Wherein the Apollo astronauts acted as the world's first space mailmen, the covers which they took with them into the cosmos must stand among the most interesting artifacts in all of postal history.

The noted Italian philatelist Alberto Bolaffi, Jr. has pointed to one additonal aspect of the space story. Recognizing the unparalleled endorsement that philately received when covers were permitted to be part of the astronaut's baggage, Bolaffi suggested that the hobby had turned "a new page in its history, the most fascinating not only for the event represented by the moon envelopes but because, for the first time, envelopes have transcended the nationalistic bounds of our albums and become symbols for collectors all over the world." Bolaffi believes that these very covers, which have been a low-profile part of the space program (except to collectors), will someday become the museum pieces that go on public view not because they have a greater value than moon rocks and official and scientific documentation of the space program, but because philatelic material provided the first available handle for many individuals the world over to incorporate the meaning of the moon trip into their lives.

The number of covers carried to and from the moon during the Apollo space program in the United States will probably remain forever uncertain. Only a few flown covers have reached collectors' hands, and careful documentation has been necessary to establish their authenticity.

Space covers, unlike other flown pieces, do not possess the usual postal markings. Departure and arrival markings and date stamps that help prove when, where and how a cover have traveled, cannot be easily obtained because of pre- and post-flight quarantine procedures. Therefore, a collector must rely on other evidence such as the cachet, an authorized signature, or perhaps an official statement certifying that the cover was indeed carried into space. It is known that some covers have been flown on the flights of Apollo 11, Apollo 14 and Apollo 15.

Neil Armstrong and Buzz Aldrin carried some philatelic items to the moon in 1969. After their lunar module, Eagle, had landed at *Tranquility Base*, the astronauts made a stamp impression from the master die of the United States 10¢ airmail commemorating their landing. In essence, they were "pulling" a proof from the die, but it could also be argued that they actually created the first lunar postage stamp. When they also cancelled an imperforate color die proof of the same stamp, affixed to a plain cover, they were possibly operating the first authorized outer-space post office. This cancelling operation took place on July 22nd, early in their return flight, and the cover became the property of the United States Postal Service, touring the country during USPS promotional exhibitions. The circular date stamp used by the Apollo 11 crew read "MOON LANDING—USA" with July 20, 1969 in the center.

It is fitting that in 1979 the U.S. Postal Service authorized the use of at least 16 special pictorial cancellations in various locations around the country to commemorate the tenth anniversary of the successful Apollo 11 mission. These cancellations were all different, and were initiated for the most part in conjunction with postage stamp exhibitions and shows.

The Apollo 14 mission took place between January 31st and February 9th, 1971. On the return from this mission the astronauts Alan B. Shepard and Edgar D. Mitchell were supposed to have had some flown covers cancelled in Houston, Texas near the Lunar Receiving Laboratory. One of these covers, auctioned off for more than $4,000 in 1977, displayed a cancellation date of February 26, 1971. Signed by one of the Apollo 14 astronauts, the cover also bore a rubber stamp cachet of private origin which read "DELAYED IN QUARANTINE AT/LUNAR RECEIVING LABORATORY/MSC HOUSTON, TEXAS." Since the cachet described was not official, the only verification of flight was the astronaut's signature. Most collectors, knowing that the astronauts graciously signed a good many commemorative covers for collectors, would insist, before paying $4,000 for a cover which may not have flown, upon further certification from the astronaut that he did carry this particular item with him to the moon. Until outer-space locations are equipped with authorized receipt stamps of some distinctive kind, the issue of what has flown or not flown may remain.

The Apollo 15 project, carried out by astronauts Scott, Irwin and Worden between July 26th and August 8th, 1971, actually included the postmarking of a cover on the moon before an international television audience. In conjunction with the issuance on August 2, 1971 of a se-tenant pair of 8¢ United States stamps at the Kennedy Space Center in Florida, astronaut David R. Scott hand-cancelled hand-perforated die proofs of the new stamps on a cover, making this the first cover to actually land on the moon. Other "moon" covers had remained in the command modules orbiting the moon, and the Apollo 11 moon walkers had carried only the master die of the 10¢ airmail to the lunar surface. The die proofs that Scott cancelled were representations of the regular U.S. stamp issue which saluted the completion of ten years of space exploration by the United States.

With fellow astronaut James B. Irwin picking up Col. Scott on the lunar TV camera, Scott began his postal exercise with the following commentary:

> "To show that our good postal service delivers any place in the universe, I have the pleasant task of cancelling here on the moon, the first stamp(s) of a new issue dedicated to commemorate United States achievements in space. And I'm sure a lot of people have seen pictures of the stamp(s). The first one here on an envelope, at the bottom it says 'United States in Space, a Decade of Achievement,' and I'm very proud to have the opportunity here to play postman. I'll just pull out a cancellation device and cancel this stamp. The date is August second, 1971, the first day of issue. What can be a better place to cancel a stamp than right here, the Hadley Rille."

The postmark which David R. Scott applied to his cover (plain except for the pair of stamps) reads "UNITED STATES/ON THE MOON" around the outer edge of the circle. The three-line date—"Aug 2 1971"—is in the center of the circle.

Collectors of space material have commemoratively documented every area of the space program—manned and unmanned launches, prime recovery ships, secondary recovery ships, space probes, tracking stations, the X-1 flights, the X-15 flights, Skylab, Apollo-Soyuz link-up, interplanetary explorations, hometowns of the astronauts, autographs, new equipment tests—but of all of the categories, that which is in greatest favor and shortest supply is the flown cover.

An aerophilatelist who has been associated with his hobby for fifty years has had the opportunity not only to capture a good share of aviation history in his collection, but to live through most of that history. In the area of Jackson, Michigan, lives such a collector, Forrest Cook. In the years since his retirement from business, Mr. Cook has retained an active interest in collecting

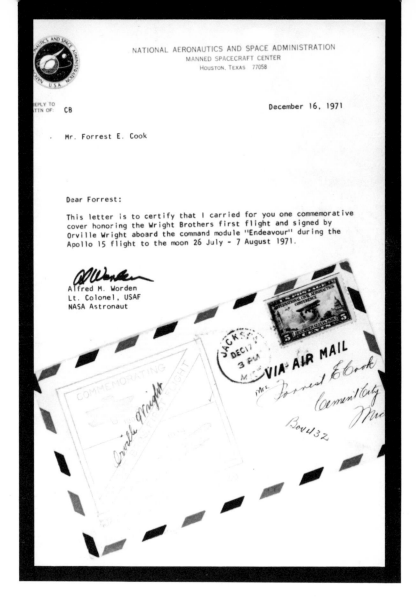

stamps, flown covers and pilot autographs. He has also, for very special reasons, maintained a keen interest in the unfolding story of man's venture into space.

Through his personal friendship with astronauts James A. McDivitt and Alfred M. Worden, Mr. Cook had the opportunity to meet a number of NASA astronauts and to travel to Florida to witness first-hand several of the launchings from Cape Kennedy.

Early in 1971, it was announced that Lt. Col. Alfred M. Worden had been assigned to the Apollo 15 mission crew. Forrest Cook sent to Worden a cover from his collection that Orville Wright had autographed for him years earlier, and asked the astronaut to carry it on his mission to the moon. Many months later Worden returned the Wright cover to Forrest Cook with an accompanying letter confirming that the letter had traveled through space to the moon. Since Col. Worden piloted the command module during the mission, the letter stayed with him in lunar orbit and never actually descended to the moon's surface.

A special Russian cover celebrates the first anniversary of man's entry into space. The Russian commemorative stamp of 1961 issue and both cachets (printed and rubber-stamped) honor Soviet Cosmonaut Yuri Gagarin, who made the epoch flight on April 12, 1961 and who signed this cover in 1962.

The gesture of a NASA astronaut and the imaginative impulse of a collector combined to undertake an unusual tribute to the world's first aeroplane pilot and to produce a unique space cover. Mr. Cook later had an opportunity to meet the rest of the Apollo 15 crew at the University of Michigan in November of 1971. In introducing the aerophilatelist to his fellow crew members, Col. Worden said, "This is Forrest Cook—we took his Orville Wright cover to the moon." The collector recalls having felt an overwhelming sense of gratitude that he could have experienced in one lifetime the thrill of corresponding with Orville Wright and the joy of meeting with men who had walked on the moon.

Philately has been called "the king of hobbies and the hobby of kings"—and certainly magnificent collections have been assembled by heads of state and other important individuals. Yet the hobby really belongs to the likes of Forrest Cook, to the many collectors who possess a heightened sense of history and who find pleasure in preserving and sharing this history with others.

Separate rates for domestic air mail were abandoned in the United States in October of 1975. To many Americans, and to most aerophilatelists, this event signaled the end of an era. Now, *all* first-class mail that travels much beyond the local region likely goes by air. The basic first class rate obtains the air mail privilege within the country; air mail stamps and air mail postal stationery items that can be purchased in all United States post offices are intended for foreign use.

It is probably fair to say that an initial and fascinating phase of the endeavor to efficiently move great numbers of written and printed communications and parcels by air—an undertaking that has spanned most of this century—is now over. Past development of the air mail enterprise has produced a series of exciting and colorful events in the history of human communications. There is much about this air mail process that deserves to be remembered, for the air mail enterprise itself is still very much alive around the world, expanding into a vast network of connections and linkages that staggers the mind.

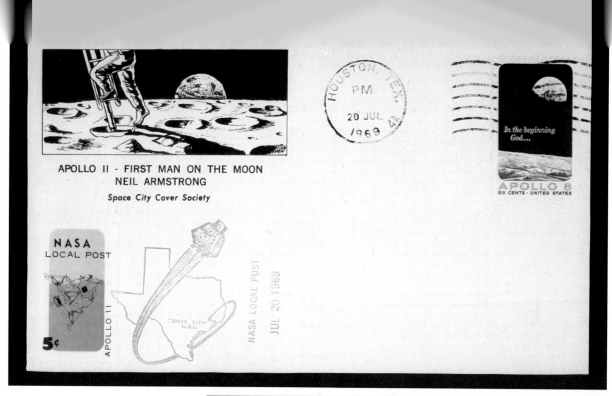

A date—July 20, 1969—will be remembered by future generations. Cancelled at Houston, Texas, on the day astronauts Armstrong and Aldrin first set foot on the moon, this cover also bears in the lower left hand corner a special cachet-cancel for the NASA local post franking.

The 10¢ airmails of 1969 were printed from a master die that was carried to the moon by Apollo 11 astronauts; 50% larger than previous U.S. commemoratives, the stamp occasioned a record 8,743,070 first day covers. A die-proof franked a letter carried and cancelled by Neil Armstrong and Edwin Aldrin, Jr. on their mission, setting a distance-traveled record for a piece of mail.

Issued simultaneously at Kennedy Space Center, Florida, Houston, Texas and Huntsville, Alabama on August 2, 1971, the U.S. "Decade in Space" pair of 8¢ stamps was printed se-tenant and helped commemorate the Apollo 15 moon exploration mission.

211

The real significance of our landing on the Moon was not the technological feat, not the opportunity to explore the lunar surface, nor even the drama nor the courage of the astronauts. It was that so much of Mankind was enabled for the first time to see, by television, our planet Earth. The real significance of our venture into space lay in the gigantic leap in consciousness that occurred as we saw where we are and who we are. The story of the airplane and air mail is the story of the beginnings of global communication, an earlier step in our awakening to each other. It is also part of the ever-old and ever-new story of men in process...of men finding out who they are by leaping into the unknown, by risking, trusting, adventuring...ultimately, an expression of life force.

Robert G. Blakesley
The Findhorn Community
Scotland

April 1979

ПО ВЪЗДУХА
PAR AVION

空 航
BY AIR MAIL

BY AIR MAIL
PER LUGPOS
PAR AVION

MED LUFTPOST
PAR AVION

PAR AVION
PER VLIEGTUIG

LUFTPOST
PAR AVION VIA AEREA

PAR AVION
LETECKY

AIR MAIL
PAR AVION

PAR AVION

PAR AVION

LOTNICZA
PAR AVION

ہوائی ڈاک
PAR AVION

PAR AVION
AERPHOST

PAR AVION
ΑΕΡΟΠΟΡΙΚΩΣ

Grateful acknowledgment is made to the following for permission to reprint some parts of their copyrighted material:

DOUBLEDAY PUBLISHING COMPANY, NEW YORK

C.R. Rosenberry: *Glenn Curtiss-Pioneer of Flight*; 1972

HUTCHINSON PUBLISHING GROUP, LTD., LONDON, ENGLAND

Walter Windham: *Waves, Wheels, Wings*; c. 1943

AMERICAN AIR MAIL SOCIETY, HIGHLAND PARK, ILLINOIS

Thomas J. O'Sullivan and Karl B. Weber:
*History of the United States Pioneer and Government
Operated Air Mail Service 1910-1928*; 1973

Max Kronstein: *Pioneer Airpost Flights of
the World 1830-1935*; 1973

American Air Mail Catalogue, 5th Edition-vol. 1; 1974

FOLLETT PUBLISHING COMPANY, CHICAGO, ILLINOIS

Benjamin B. Lipsner: *The Airmail-Jennies to Jets*; 1951

CUB FLIERS ENTERPRISES, INC., KANSAS CITY, KANSAS

Edith Dood Culver: *The Day the Airmail Began*; 1971

NATIONAL GEOGRAPHIC MAGAZINE, WASHINGTON, D.C.

J. Parker Van Zandt: *On the Trail of the Air Mail*;
vol. XLIX, no: 1

LINN'S STAMP NEWS, SIDNEY, OHIO

Fred Boughner: *Western Air Express carries first CAM*;
June 27, 1977 issue

Alberto Bolaffi: *Flown covers record space achievements*;
July 16, 1979 issue

CHARLES SCRIBNER'S SONS, PUBLISHERS, NEW YORK

Charles A. Lindbergh: *The Spirit of St. Louis*; copyright 1953
by Charles Scribner's Sons; copyright renewed.
Reprinted with the permission of Charles Scribner's Sons.

CHATTO & WINDUS, LTD., LONDON, ENGLAND

Claude Grahame-White: *Flying-An Epitome and a Forecast*; 1930

THE HAYNES PUBLISHING GROUP, SPARKFORD-YEOVIL, ENGLAND

Robin Higham: *Britain's Imperial Air Routes-1918 to 1939*;
published by G.T. Foulis & Company; 1960

Illustration credits

PHOTOS

All photos not listed are of unknown origin. The Author regrets that he was unable to locate
the sources of such pictures, which often seem to be copies of old originals.
Sincere apology is offered for any unintentional omission or mistake.

Photo Collection / Library of National Air and Space Museum,
Smithsonian Institution:

pp.: vi; 10; 11; 31; 32 top; 34 top; 40; 50; 51; 57 right; 60; 61; 62; 63; 66;
  67; 71; 72 bottom; 79; 82; 95 top; 97 bottom; 103; 105; 116;
  117 right; 120; 123; 126; 127; 128; 129; 130-131; 131; 132;
  133; 134; 139; 141; 143; 153; 154; 155; 157; 160 top;
  162; 182 top left; bottom; 187; 188; 190; 198; 200; 201.

Photo Collection of National Archives:

pp.: ii; xii; 87; 88; 89; 90-91; 91; 92; 94; 95 bottom; 100; 107;
  160 bottom; 163; 186.

Photo Collection / Library of United States Postal Service:

pp.: 3; 136; 137.

Tippecanoe Historical Association; Lafayette, Indiana:

pp.: 4; 7.

Ernst M. Cohn Collection / Photo by Adrien Boutrelle:

pp.: 11 right.

Curtiss Museum; Hammondsport, N.Y.:

pp.: 32 bottom; 33; 34-35.

Al Starkweather Collection:

pp.: 56 bottom.

Montana Historical Society; Helena, Montana:

pp.: 73 bottom.

Phil Silver Collection:

pp.: 97.

E. Hamilton Lee Collection:

pp.: 117.

United Airlines Archives:

pp.: 122; 150 top; 151.

Pan American World Airways:

pp.: 164; 182 top right; 192; 193; 203.

John W. Underwood Collection:

pp.: 166.

British Airways:

pp.: 173 bottom; 176; 196; 205.

Los Angeles Department of Airports:

pp.: 180.

Forrest E. Cook Collection:

pp.: 209.

STAMPS

U.S. stamps shown on page 24 are under c   ght and rep   ed in this book
through courtesy of the United States Pos   vice.

National Philatelic Collection, Smithsonian Institution;

pp.: xiv; 96; 167.

Erik Hildesheim Collection:

pp.: 13.

Walter H. Ponichtera Collection:

pp.: 128; 178.

Bibliography

1 BOOKS

AIR MAIL HISTORY

Culver, Edith Dodd. THE DAY THE AIR-MAIL BEGAN.
   Kansas City, Ka.: Cub Flyers Enterprises, Inc., 1975.

Kronstein, Dr. Max, Edited by *Eisendrath, Joseph L.*
   PIONEER AIRPOST FLIGHTS OF THE WORLD 1830-1935.
   American Air Mail Society, 1978.

Lipsner, Captain Benjamin B. as told to *Hilts, Leonard Finley.*
   THE AIRMAIL—JENNIES TO JETS.
   Chicago, Ill.: Wilcox & Follett Co., 1951.

Luning, Orjan. LUFTPOSTENSHISTORIA i NORDEN
   (THE HISTORY OF AIRMAIL IN SCANDINAVIA).
   Sveriges Filaterlist-Forbund, 1978.

Naudet, G. AVIATION VIGNETTES OF FRANCE TO 1940.

O'Sullivan, Thomas J. and *Weber, Karl B.,* Edited by *Eisendrath, Joseph L.* HISTORY OF THE UNITED STATES PIONEER AND GOVERNMENT-OPERATED AIR MAIL SERVICE 1910-1928.
   American Air Mail Society, 1973.

AVIATION HISTORY

Casey, Louis S. and *Batchelor, John.* THE ILLUSTRATED HISTORY OF SEAPLANES AND FLYING BOATS.
   New York: Exeter Books; London: Phoebus Publishing Co., 1980.

Davies, R.E.G. A HISTORY OF THE WORLD'S AIRLINES.
   London: Oxford University Press, 1964

THE FIRST AIR VOYAGE IN AMERICA *(in two parts).* By *Carroll Frey* and *Jean Pierre Blanchard* ("Journal of my Forty-Fifth Ascension" reprinted).
   Philadelphis: The Penn Mutual Life Insurance Co., 1943.

Gann, Ernest K. FLYING CIRCUS.
   New York: Macmillan Publishing Co., Inc. 1974.

Higham, Robin. BRITAIN'S IMPERIAL AIR ROUTES 1918-1939.
   London: G.T. Foulis, 1960.

Joblonski, Edward. MAN WITH WINGS.
   New York: Doubleday & Company, Inc., 1980.

Joblonski, Edward, SEA WINGS—The Romance of the Flying Boats.
   New York: Doubleday & Company, Inc., 1972.

Jackson, Robert. AIRSHIPS—A popular History of Dirigibles, Zeppelins, Blimps and Other Lighter-than-air Craft.
   Garden City, N.Y.: Doubleday & Company, Inc., 1973.

Lindbergh, Charles A. AUTOBIOGRAPHY OF VALUES
   (William Jovanovich, Editor)
   New York: Harcourt Brace Jovanovich, 1976.

Lindbergh, Charles A. THE SPIRIT OF ST. LOUIS.
   New York: Charles Scribner's Sons, 1953.

Monday, David, General Editor. THE INTERNATIONAL ENCYCLOPEDIA OF AVIATION.
   New York: Crown Publishing, 1977.

Munson, Kenneth. THE POCKET ENCYCLOPEDIA OF WORLD AIRCRAFT
   IN COLOR. A Series. Civil Airliners/since 1946, 1967; Pioneer Aircraft/1903-14, 1969; Flying Boats and Seaplanes/since 1910, 1971; Airliners Between the Wars/1919-39, 1972.
   New York: The Macmillan Company, 1972; Blandford Press, Ltd., 1967, 1969, 1971.

Roseberry, C.R. GLENN CURTISS: PIONEER OF FLIGHT.
   Garden City, N.Y.: Doubleday & Co., 1972.

Saint-Exupery, Antoine de, with a foreword by *Andre Gide.*
   NIGHT FLIGHT. A Signet Classic.
   New York: The New American Library, Inc. by arrangement with Harcourt, Brace & World, Inc., 1942.

Saint-Exupery, Antoine de. WIND, SAND AND STARS.
   New York: Reynal & Hitchcock, 14th printing, 1940.

Taylor, John W.R. HISTORY OF AVIATION—The Full Story of Flight
   New York: Crown Publishers, Inc., 1972.

Taylor, John W.R., Editor. THE LORE OF FLIGHT.
   (AB Nordbok, Gothenburg, Sweden-1974),
   New York: Crescent Books, 1978.

Villard, Henry Serrano. CONTACT—The Story of the Early Birds.
   New York: Bonanza Books (a Division of Crown Publishers), 1968.

Windham, Comdr. Sir Walter. WAVES ● WHEELS ● WINGS—AN AUTOBIOGRAPHY.
   London, England: Hutchinson & Co., Ltd., (circa 1942).

PHILATELIC REFERENCE

AMERICAN AIR MAIL CATALOGUE. Vol. 1. 1974; Vol. 2, 1977; Vol. 3, 1978.
   American Air Mail Society.

Cherubini, Cherubino and *Taragni, Sandro; Editore, G. Orlandini.*
   CATALOGO ITALIANO DELLA POSTA AEREA.
   Vol. 1 (1846-1930).
   Firenze, Italy: G. Orlandini, 1974.

THE ELLINGTON-ZWISLER ROCKET MAIL CATALOGUE. Vol. 1, 1904-1967.
   American Air Mail Society.

MICHEL KATALOGS. Deutschland, special, Katalog, 1981; Schweiz/Liechtenstein, special, Katalog, 1980; Osterreich, special, Katalog, 1980.
   Munchen, West Germany: Schwaneberger Verlag Gmb H.

SCOTT SPECIALIZED CATALOGUE OF UNITED STATES STAMPS 1981,   59th edition, New York:
   Scott Publishing Company.

THE WORLD AIRMAIL CATALOGUE 1966.
   Ridgefield, Ct.: Nicolas Sanabria Company, Inc., 1965.

POSTAL HISTORY

Scheele, Carl H. A SHORT HISTORY OF THE MAIL SERVICE.
   Washington, D.C.: Smithsonian Institution Press, 1970.

2 PUBLICATIONS

THE AIRPOST JOURNAL, published monthly without interruption since 1930 by the American Air Mail Society, affiliate 77 of the American Philatelic Society.

THE AERO PHILATELIST ANNALS, currently a publication of the American Air Mail Society, issued semi-annually in January and July as a supplement to THE AIRPOST JOURNAL. Formerly published by Aero Philatelists, Inc., New York.

LINN'S STAMP NEWS, a weekly newspaper with articles of interest to postage stamp and postal history collectors.
   A Divison of Amos Press, Inc. of Sidney, Ohio.

Philatelic reference

*Postage stamps and other adhesives are listed
in order of their appearance in this book.*

*The contemporary value shown in the fourth column
approximates 1981 catalog listings
for unused, very fine, unhinged stamps with full original gum.*

page	nation and postal value	year & type of issue	contemporary value–U.S. $	special remarks
xiv	Great Britain 1 penny	1840 regular	2,250.00	the world's first general issue postage stamp
xiv	U.S.A. 5 cents	1847 regular	4,500.00	first U.S. general issue —became invalid 1851
8	U.S.A. 7 cents	1959 air mail	.30	issued on 100th anniv. of John Wise mail carry
12	France 12 francs + 3 fr.	1955 semi-postal	6.50	issued on "Stamp Day", 1955 —surtax for Red Cross
12	France 95 centimes	1971 air mail	1.65	issued on 100th anniv. of famed "Balloon Poste" of 1870–71
13	U.S.A. 5 cents	1877 private issue	4,500.00	printed in tête-bêche strips of 20
16	France 15 francs	1957 commemorative	.50	salute to a swift flier & carrier of messages
20	Germany 40 pfennigs + 20 pf.	1978 semi-postal	.75	surtax for the benefit of youth
21	Germany 3 marks	1934 air mail	50.00	high value of a definitive air mail series
24	U.S.A. (2) 31 cents each	1978 air mail	1.20 (2)	overseas air mail rate— marking 75th anniv. of world's first airplane flight
25	U.S.A. 20 cents	1912 parcel post	185.00	world's first official stamp to picture an airplane
25	U.S.A. 2 cents	1928 commemorative	3.00	issued to salute international civil aviation conference, December 1928
25	Latvia 20 santims + 100 sant.	1932 semi-postal/ air mail	12.50	series honors aviation pioneers —surtax to aid wounded Latvian aviators
28	San Marino 10 lire	1962 commemorative	.10	historic aircraft series
28	Malagasy Repub. 5 francs	1967 commemorative	.15	one of a series recalling Madagascar's aviation history

28	France 2.25 francs	1934 air mail	22.50	commemorating Louis Blériot's flight of July 25, 1909
29	Latvia 25 santims + 125 sant.	1932 semi-postal/ air mail	12.50	series honoring aviation pioneers—surtax to aid wounded Latvian aviators
29	Monaco 1.50 francs	1933 air mail	20.50	Monaco's first airmail— a Blériot profile placed on a 1925 issue
38	France no value	1909 label	15–20.00	promotional label of the first major international aviation meet
38	San Marino 5 lire	1962 commemorative	.10	historic aircraft series
42	India 5 naye paise	1961 commemorative	.20	issued on 50th anniv. of world's 1st sanctioned air mail flight
43	India 1 rupee	1961 commemorative	2.00	of the series mentioned above
46	Great Britain no value	1913 label	30–40.00	used to seal tobacco samples delivered on 1913 flights— England
46	Great Britain (1 penny)	1923 essay	10–15.00	a British Post Office design never finalized
69	Australia 5 pence	1964 commemorative	.35	issued on 50th anniv. of first air mail flown in Australia
69	Germany (Berlin) .60 pfennigs	1962 commemorative	.55	marking 50th anniv. of first German air mail
69	South Africa 3 cents	1961 commemorative	.55	marking 50th anniv. of South Africa's first air mail
69	Japan 10 yen	1960 commemorative	.50	commemorating 50 years of aviation in Japan
69	France 1.50 francs	1978 air mail	.75	marking 65th anniv. of an early air mail flight
69	Germany 70 pfennigs + 35 pf.	1978 semi-postal	1.85	aviation series with surtax for benefit of youth
76	Switzerland 50 centimes	1913 semi-official air mail	75–100.00	4,500 used for a Bider national flugspende flight from Aarau on April 6, 1913

76	Switzerland no value	1913 label	20–25.00	marking Bider's historic alpine crossing to Milan in July 1913
76	Switzerland 40 centimes	1977 commemorative	.50	low value in a series of 4 stamps honoring Swiss aviation pioneers
77	Italy 25 centesimi	1917 air mail	8–9.00	world's first official air mail stamp—a provisional issue for temporary use on experimental route
77	Italy 40 lire	1967 commemorative	.15	celebrating 50th anniv. of first air mail stamp
81	Austria (3) 1.50 krone 2.50 krone 4 krone	1918 air mail	30–35.00 (3)	Austria's first air mail series—a provisional set of 3 used on military air courier service of 1918
81	Austria 5 schilling	1961 commemorative	1.40	issued to publicize a Vienna aerophilatelic exhibition, May 1961
96	U.S.A. 24 cents	1918 air mail (error)	140,000.00 (error variety)	world's first definitive airmail— 1st airmail to include an air- plane in its design—100 copies with inverted vignette found
101	U.S.A. 10 cents	1975 commemorative	.35	marks the bicentennial of U.S. postal service
113	Denmark (pair) 5 kroner	1919 semi-official air mail	30–40.00 ea.	3,200 printed—used on alternate route: Copenhagen to Aarhus on Sept. 11, 1919
113	Switzerland 10 centimes	1944 air mail	.15	low value of a 3-stamp series marking 25 years of Swiss air mail service
128	U.S.A. (3) 8 cents 16 cents 24 cents	1923 air mail	120.00 300.00 350.00	all 3 stamps issued to conform to rates on a U.S. trans- continental zone system
137	U.S.A. 7 cents	1959 air mail	.35	commemorating Alaskan statehood—Jan. 3, 1959
149	U.S.A. (3) 10 cents 15 cents 20 cents	1926 & 1927 air mail	8.50 8–10.00 35–40.00	issued to conform to rates established for first U.S. contract air mail routes—to be used for air mail only
167	Newfoundland 50 cents	1931 air mail	16.50	issued to meet rate set for letters to Canada & U.S.A.

167	Newfoundland 3 cents	1919 air mail	16,000.00	200 issued for mail carried on the unsuccessful Hawker-Grieve transatlantic flight attempt
170	Columbia no value	no issue date label	———	produced for mail carried by SCADTA airline—operated in Colombia between 1919–1939
170	France 30 centimes	1937 commemorative	.50	honors famed mail pilot lost at sea in December, 1936
170	France 20 francs	1970 air mail	9.00	commemorates two French air mail pioneers
170	France 1.50 francs	1936 air mail	12.50	marking Aeropostale's 100th South Atlantic crossing
174	Belgian Congo 2 francs	1920 air mail	1.25	part of first air mail issue for African continent
174	China 30 cents	1929 air mail	4.25	like first U.S. airmail, this issue pictures a Curtiss *Jenny*
178	U.S.A. 65 cents	1930 air mail	900– 1,200.00	post card rate—Lakehurst, N.J. to Friedrichshafen
178	Liechtenstein 80 rappen	1979 commemorative	1.00	Europa issue recalling first Graf Zeppelin flight to Liechtenstein in June, 1930
191	U.S.A. 25 cents	1935 air mail	5.50–7.50	for use on U.S. transpacific air mail
195	Switzerland 2.50 francs	1947 air mail	16.50	valid only for May 2, 1947 flight —mail carried on first service of Swiss Air to U.S.A.
207	Great Britain 9 pence	1969 commemorative	.25	marking maiden flight of *Concorde* prototype at Toulouse, France—March 1, 1969
211	U.S.A. 10 cents	1969 air mail	.40	celebrating mankind's first moon landing—July 20, 1969
211	U.S.A. (2) 8 cents each	1971 commemorative	.50 (2)	astronaut Scott announced release of this issue from the moon's surface—August 2, 1971

Index

223

■